NEW FORUM BOOKS   *Robert P. George, Series Editor*

A list of titles in the series
appears at the back of the book

PRAISE AND BLAME

✤

PRAISE AND BLAME

MORAL REALISM AND ITS APPLICATIONS

✣

Daniel N. Robinson

PRINCETON UNIVERSITY PRESS

PRINCETON AND OXFORD

COPYRIGHT © 2002 BY PRINCETON UNIVERSITY PRESS

PUBLISHED BY PRINCETON UNIVERSITY PRESS, 41 WILLIAM STREET,

PRINCETON, NEW JERSEY 08540

IN THE UNITED KINGDOM: PRINCETON UNIVERSITY PRESS,

3 MARKET PLACE, WOODSTOCK, OXFORDSHIRE OX20 1SY

LIBRARY OF CONGRESS CATALOGING-IN-PUBLICATION DATA

ROBINSON, DANIEL N., 1937–

PRAISE AND BLAME : MORAL REALISM AND ITS APPLICATIONS / DANIEL N. ROBINSON.

P.   CM.—(NEW FORUM BOOKS)

INCLUDES BIBLIOGRAPHICAL REFERENCES AND INDEX.

ISBN 0-691-05724-9 (ALK. PAPER)

1. MORAL REALISM. I. TITLE. II SERIES.

BJ1500.M67 R63 2002

170—DC21   2001051042

THIS BOOK HAS BEEN COMPOSED IN BERKELEY BOOK MODIFIED TYPEFACE

PRINTED ON ACID-FREE PAPER. ∞

WWW.PUPRESS.PRINCETON.EDU

PRINTED IN THE UNITED STATES OF AMERICA

1   3   5   7   9   10   8   6   4   2

For Ciny

✛ CONTENTS ✛

✤ ACKNOWLEDGMENTS ✤

I THANK Professor Robert George, the general editor of the series, for inviting me to contribute a volume. He has been unstinting in his encouragement and support. The original prospectus for the book was commented on at length and most usefully by Roger Crisp. His suggestions have been incorporated in the final version. The penultimate version of the book was closely considered by Edward Pols, his comments, too, strengthening the work.

Ten terms of lectures for Oxford's Sub-Faculty of Philosophy, spread over the recent decade, could only sharpen my understanding of the issues examined in this book. The atmosphere of the Philosophy Centre and the sheer intellectual integrity of those privileged to teach and to learn there have been a source of nurturance and inspiration. For the present volume, special thanks are owed to Roger Crisp, James Griffin, Richard Sorabji, Galen Strawson, and Richard Swinburne. My editors at Princeton, Chuck Myers and Sara Lerner, have been more than helpful at every stage of the project. Finally, to the sturdy legion of unnamed students, so patient as listeners, so generous as questioners, I say thank you—and thank you yet again.

PRAISE AND BLAME are central features of scripture, of ethics and moral philosophy, of ancient schools of rhetoric, of criminal and civil law, of the behavioral and social sciences. They are the tested tools of childrearing and interpersonal influence, staples in the busy world of advertising and the murky world of propaganda. They are the means by which attention is drawn to the hero and the villain, the saint and the sinner, the victor and the vanquished.

If praise and blame are ubiquitous, they are also subject to misleading and sometimes gross misapplication. The burglar who can open nearly any safe excites feelings of awe, easily mistaken for admiration. The great athlete, of prodigious power and agility, arouses sentiments of admiration, easily mistaken for estimations of *moral* worth. The eager and loving parents, whose children can do no wrong, lavish on the most mundane performance praise otherwise due to prodigies, or engage in relentless blaming, fearful that otherwise the children will develop weak character. At the level of common understanding, it is clear that praise and blame, both as nouns and as verbs, are subject to misuse, misapprehension, disproportionality, error, and confusion. As these very nouns—these very verbs—are the lingua franca of all moral appraisal, they provide ready access to the wider and ever more cluttered domain of morality.

This book is offered as a critical inquiry into the sources and uses of praise and blame. It offers as well a defense of a form of moral "realism" by which to determine the validity and aptness of those moral appraisals expressed as praise and blame. The target of criticism is, of course, moral "relativism," but these terms—realism and relativism—are laden with quirky and provincial connotations. Some defenders of moral realism are defending not the existence of actual moral entities or properties, but the prevalence of certain feelings or judgments that are in some sense "moral." On this account, what is real is the psychological state, not its content. The patient in Ward-C truly believes he is a unicorn. The psychological state of belief is taken to be real; the content of the belief, nonexistent.

Moral relativism has appeared variously, but always has this signal feature by which it can be recognized. To argue that the ultimate grounding of moral judgments is relative to any of the following is *not* to argue as a moral relativist: human tendencies, cultural values, contextual factors, historical forces, hereditary predispositions, and/or sentiment. Rather, the moral relativist is one who contends that the ultimate *validity* of moral judgments is determined by such factors. It may well be the case that, for many, a correct moral appraisal arises as a result of what has been learned from the wider culture, or imposed by the present context, or closely tied to a personal feeling or sentiment made ever sharper as a result of certain biological processes. The moral realist distinguishes between *how* a right answer is reached in the matter of moral assessments and what the right answer is; or, more modestly, that there *is* a right answer, and one that is independent of psychological, biological, and social contingencies. To say, then, that the target of criticism in this book is moral relativism is to say that moral questions are questions about reality, and, as such, are subject to correct answers.

It is in the nature of the subject itself that an author's realistic aspiration is, as it were, to fail well. Most learned opinion on the matter of morality agrees that it is inextricably bound up with the needs, habits, dispositions, and eccentricities of human nature, shaped by the shifting challenges and opportunities afforded by the environments in which that nature finds itself. Protean though that nature is, there is a strong genetic component so widely distributed as to create the appearance of moral absolutes. Behind the scenes, however, it is evolutionary pressure that has pruned and shaped the genome in such a way as to yield creatures with strong and common tendencies even under the widest range of cultural and local influences. The story thus told is coherent, the database broad and thick. It would be rash to think that a radically different theory would succeed in replacing this now nearly official version.

There are, however, good reasons to doubt the adequacy of the currently dominant view. These reasons are reviewed in chapter 1, in which the general claims and counterclaims of the relativist and realist are examined. What this examination leads to is the recognition that, at the end of the day, the controversy turns on the nature and limits of "determinism." Moral realism, in this light, is counterintuitive, just in case one continues to subscribe to versions of the "unity of sciences" thesis affirmed by scientists since the time of Newton. In chapter 2 the major historical figures in the free will—determinism debate are discussed, less as an exercise in intellectual history than as a reflection on the current value of what the better minds of history had to say on the subject. The determinism that would tell against moral realism is one that reduces moral properties to human properties, and especially to those on which emotion and motivation are assumed to depend. The weaknesses of determinism are then revealed through a closer inspection of the sorts of motivational and emotional theories (erroneously) supposed to be operative. Objective moral worth is understood as falling beyond the ambit of "constitutive" factors such as one's physical features or hereditary endowment.

Chapter 3 then addresses the interesting challenges to moral realism arising from what is taken to be good or bad "moral luck." Important distinctions must be made between event-luck and nurturance-luck. The graphic and instructive scenarios composed by Thomas Nagel and Bernard Williams, among others, are considered and found to be wanting as accounts of genuinely *moral* significance.

In chapter 4 the claims of moral realism are challenged by the implications thought to arise from certain psychological states and processes: unconscious motivation, retardation, severe psychological disturbances. If fitness for moral assessment presupposes intentions and desires, then how can one be blamed or praised for undertakings prompted by motives of which the actor is totally oblivious? Here, again, the challenge to moral realism is more apparent than real. As with moral and constitutive luck, psychological disturbances or peculiarities challenge moral realism only when the relativism-realism question is begged rather than addressed. The version of moral realism defended is one that is, or at least is free to be, neutral on the question of whether anyone actually comprehends the moral properties that inhere in persons and events. Accordingly, just in case any number of conditions are morally incapacitating, these morally real properties are unaffected, even if undetected. To argue against this by insisting that there cannot be such properties, except insofar as they are known, is merely to assert a version of the very relativistic thesis under consideration.

Finally, there is a chapter on punishment and forgiveness, concluding with a brief disquisition on saints and heroes, those whose own moral properties (i.e., character) and comprehension of the moral properties of others rise sharply above the prevailing standards. Moral realism entails morally right answers. It entails, too, morally defensible modes of punishment and forgiveness. Chapter 5 considers this in relation to states' powers of punishment and forgiveness.

Five chapters and some one hundred thousand words cannot do justice to all the factors that enter into this subject. One of the chief motives for writing the book will be satisfied if readers are encouraged to reconsider prevailing conceptions of morality, prevailing commitments to reductionistic modes of inquiry, prevailing tendencies to conflate the "natural" with the "physical." There is nothing unnatural about moral properties, though there is nothing physical about them either. Just in case they are, indeed, natural—but not physical—they call for a natural mode of comprehension, but not one that is reducible to empirical forms of verification. But here I anticipate myself. . . .

1.

DEFINING THE SUBJECT

The final sentence, it is probable, which pronounces
characters and actions amiable or odious, praise-worthy or blameable;
that which stamps on them the mark of honour or infamy,
approbation or censure; that which renders morality an active
principle and constitutes virtue our happiness and vice our
misery; it is probable, I say, that this final sentence depends on
some internal sense or feeling, which nature has made
universal in the whole species. —DAVID HUME, *An Enquiry
Concerning the Principles of Morals, Section 1*

Why has Thou made me thus? —ROMANS 9:20

The Greatest Horseman

There is a scene in Book XXII of the *Iliad*, much discussed by those seeking to comprehend the complex meritocracy of the Homeric world. The epic is nearly concluded. Troy has been defeated and many of the Achaians have already set sail for their homeward journeys. Patroclus has been honored, his bones cremated by his dear lamenting friend. Now is the time for celebration and the holding of games. A great chariot race is staged and concludes with honors and prizes. At this point, however, the modern reader is perplexed to discover that these are not to be awarded simply on the basis of how the contestants actually finished in the race. Rather, seemingly irrelevant factors lead to contentious exchanges.

It was Diomedes who finished in first place, followed next by Antilochos, then by Menelaos, the henchman Meriones, and finally by Eumelos. Presumably, that should have settled the matter. Instead, the results lead to discord and debate. Achilles, judging Eumelos to be "the best man," insists that he therefore be given the top prize, and that Diomedes then receive second honors. Menelaos, edged out by the younger and more impetuous Antilochos, contends that he was defeated by guile, and demands that Antilochos's prize be withdrawn. What does Antilochos say? Without hesitation and in full agreement, he surrenders his prize because Menelaos is, as he says, "the greater" and therefore should go before him in such matters.

If modern sensibilities are amused by the spectacle, it may be the result of taking for granted suppositions that actually call for closer examination. How, after all, should a prize be awarded after a horse race? Should it go to the best horseman, the best person, or the one who actually finishes first?

Suppose one contestant draws a horse patently superior to all the rest, such that victory is a certainty. Or suppose the winner wins by luck or by deceit, or by drugging the competing horses, or by bribing competitors, or by threatening them with violence. Indeed suppose, as was the case in Troy, the gods take sides to the advantage of one charioteer and at the expense of others? Was it not Apollo who pulled the whip from the hand of Diomedes, and was it not wrathful Athene who, in response, returned it to Diomedes and then broke the axle of Eumelos's chariot? Indeed, in any contest of any kind whatever, who can say where true merit and worthiness end, and where luck, fortune, accident, the gods, and myriad uncontrollable contingencies decisively intervene? Had modern geneticists been present at Troy on the day of that epic race, they might have added yet another complication to the arguments offered for and against the several contestants. They might have informed Achilles that the sense in which Eumelos is "the best man" depends upon attributes for which Eumelos himself deserves no credit at all. To be the best charioteer requires skill, no doubt, but also the physical strength, endurance, family background, and general resources needed for any skill to reach the level of its full potential. And, of course, even under the most favorable conditions, this level of skill will count for nothing should the unseen stone in the road flatten a tire, or if the snake in the grass should cause the horses to bridle. Who can choose with finality those actions and persons warranting praise and blame or, in the words of Scripture, who has the unrestricted right and authority to throw the first stone?

The nature and purposes of praise and blame are at the center of moral judgment, legal sanctions, and social practices and, as such, illuminate otherwise overlooked aspects of all three. The aim of this first chapter is to reach a more precise understanding of the sources and the essential character of praise and blame. At the most molar level, it is important to establish whether so vast a subject is but a topic within an enlarged cultural anthropology or descriptive social psychology. If these are the proper disciplines, then moral philosophy and jurisprudence would call for the same classification. Attributing blame and rendering praise, it may be declared, is a form of giving vent to sentiments of aversion or pleasure. There is nothing of an objective nature in this, for to pay with praise and blame is to use a personal currency whose value can rise no higher than what is ordained by the prevailing and typically local customs.

Against this are arguments to the effect that moral terms have objective standing and reach something actually (objectively) at work in the world. On this understanding, of which the present volume is offered as a defense, praise and blame are topics within a systematic moral science, its practical application appearing in such disciplines as law and rhetoric. Moral science may be served by the social sciences but not exhaustively defined or explained by them. Rather, the moral realm derives its content from modes of knowing that are in a sense intuitive but no more "subjective" for that reason. This intuitively reached knowledge is then absorbed into essentially rational modes of argument for the purpose of solving moral problems and providing moral direction. The relevant psychological characteristics warranting inclusion within a developed moral science are just those rational/intuitive powers, cognitive powers, by which proportionality, aptness, equity, guilt and innocence, and myriad comparable judgments are made in every culture, from the remote past to the current day.

The subject is, alas, vast and vexed. One moves toward it tentatively.

Praise and Blame: Legitimacy, Authority, and Consensus

The vignette from the *Iliad* prompts the question: should praise be reserved to persons or to outcomes? Should the object or target be those somehow known to be worthy, or, instead, should praise and blame be assigned to anyone who has satisfied a valued objective, no matter who performed the act, no matter what the impelling motive was? Put another way, can bad men do good things? Do good consequences arising from malign motives deserve to be praised? Even within an utterly utilitarian ethical framework, is it only the successful maximizing of utility or is it the *desire* to do so that should earn praise?

To ask whether an evil person can do good would seem to beg a larger question. Without a defensible theory of good and evil—a theory that dictates how praise and blame are to be distributed—it is unclear just how it is possible for the "good" or "bad" person to be identified. Presumably, one who does good would seem to satisfy at least the commonsense criterion for being a good person, but there are many instances of unintended good, as well as bad, consequences arising from noble intentions. A loud sneeze awakens a neighbor whose alarm clock failed. Thanks to the sneeze, the neighbor reaches the airport and retrieves the packaged kidney scheduled for implantation. The sneeze, however, occurred because of an allergic reaction to pollen which entered the house owing to a window left open by a thief in the night. No thief, no open window. No open window, no allergic response. No response, no sneeze. No sneeze, no kidney transplant. Thus, no unlawful intruder and uncle Toby dies. There are many such instances of good consequences at the end of a chain that include links that are morally jejune, tainted, even felonious, or just plainly fortuitous.

In referring to questions about the manner in which praise and blame are to be distributed, still another dilemma arises, this one pertaining to "collective guilt." To what extent are bystanders blameworthy when, though taking no part in causing harm, they do nothing to prevent it? Are they as blameworthy as the perpetrator and, if not, what principle might be invoked by which to assess the degree of mitigation? To what extent can moral responsibility be *shared* and, if shared, is it thereby reduced in proportion to the number of persons sharing it? There are sound reasons for insisting that the fault of others does nothing to diminish one's own.[1] The driver of the getaway car may face the same legal penalties as those who committed robbery and assault, though the driver was nowhere near the scene of the crime. This, too, calls for critical analysis.

What do we seek to achieve or assert or affirm through praise and blame? Apart from material rewards and punishments, which could be rendered in the form of monetary emoluments and penalties, praise and blame seem to have, but not symmetrically, special places set aside for special kinds of actions. Though those who commit crimes are blamed, those who do not are not praised. Furthermore, to pay someone not to commit a violent crime would seem odd, and especially so as a form of "reward" or praise. It would be comparably peculiar to reward one for doing what everyone routinely does. Praise and blame are not reducible to material costs and penalties and are often blatantly out of place in the circumstance. Most would judge it to be insulting to offer a high salary to Mother Teresa, even on the assumption that this might encourage others to perform the saintly work for which she was known.

It seems, then, that praise and blame, to the extent that they are in some sense akin to rewards and punishments, are rewards and punishments of an unusual type. This alone indicates that they are intended to function in a way not fully embraced by standard forms of reward and punishment. Consider one of the expected consequences of blame. When validly directed at a person, blame is expected to cause feelings of guilt, remorse, and shame. Conversely, when wrongly leveled it may often cause anger, indignation, and the impulse toward reprisal. For praise and blame to achieve desired ends, there would seem to be at least four conditions that must be met, each different from those adequate to the purposes of ordinary rewards and punishments. First, the ascriptions must be *correct*. Heaping praise for heroism on the wrong person or blame for malfeasance on the innocent increases neither self-worth in the one nor shame in the other. Accordingly, a straightforward behavioristic analysis of the efficacy of praise and blame inevitably leaves out too much, for neither praise nor blame can function per se unless their ascription is apt.

Furthermore, the praising and blaming of actions or events must match up with something relevant about the recipients and *acknowledged* as such by them. A cash prize given to the thousandth person entering the new supermarket is surely rewarding, but winning it is not laudatory. Increasing the rate of taxation of those with the highest earnings is a species of penalty, but not a condemnation. Again, the connotations of "praise" and "blame" are not fully paralleled by rewards and penalties. Nor are they simple performatives. When one says, "I promise," the utterance constitutes the actual performance. But when one says, "I praise," the utterance is subject to any number of tests and criteria having to do with the standing of the speaker, the aims and conduct of the intended beneficiary, as well as the social and cultural values that qualify both the intentions and the respective standing of speaker and target.

Additionally, for praise or blame to be accepted as such, the source must be recognized as authoritative and not merely in possession of power or material resources. Not only must the dispensers of praise and blame have standing, but the standing must be relevant to the context. Praise for achievements in physics proffered by the coach of the winning football match would be no cause for pride. Indeed, in certain contexts, the character of the dispenser of blame could raise blame itself to the level of an honor while sinking praise to that of censure. Whether in the form of utterances or of palpable objects (statues, certificates, gold stars) praise and blame presume standing and authority on the part of the source. It is not the utterance or the object that carries the moral content, but the office that bestows it. This will be considered at greater length in chapter 2 in connection with rhetoric as a source of action.

Tied to these conditions is another: the efficacy and legitimacy of praise or blame depend upon *shared moral understandings*, absent which the utterances and objects are unintelligible. It is owing to this feature that persons generally regarded as possessing utterly unique moral qualities often and honestly wonder what all the fuss is about! By ordinary standards, relinquishing one's material possessions to devote oneself totally to those in need is taken to be supererogatory. It is doubtful in the extreme, however, that Mother Teresa, for example, regarded her actions as in any sense above and beyond the call of duty. Quite the contrary. It is part of the makeup of saints and heroes that they find nothing exceptional in their own undertakings. If they are at one extreme point on the continuum of moral sensibility, those referred to as sociopaths would be at the other end; those who do not grasp what all the fuss is about when apprehended for repeated and unrepentant criminal conduct. To the ordinary observer, saintly or heroic self-sacrifice, like habitual criminality, are often inexplicable. The average person cannot readily imagine living either form of life, but has sufficient empathic resources to admire the one and condemn the other.

What some have concluded from this is that morality is but a species of consensus, formed within a given culture to satisfy the terms of life adopted by the members of that culture. Just in case, for whatever reason, one proves to be refractory in adhering to the local standards, one can expect to suffer the wages of sin. The aggressive, hostile, physically assaultive person who, in time of war, is turned loose on the enemy, returns from battle to receive honor and decorations. The same person, similarly disposed and active within the local community is apprehended by the police and subsequently deprived of liberty. Praise and blame, then, seem so fully dependent on context and on the shifting desiderata of majorities as to have no stable content at all. A personality that expresses itself in aggressive and hostile fashion may be little more than a genetic outcome and is thus not a question of vice or virtue but of luck, in this case "constitutive luck" (chapter 2). Whether these foreordained expressions of personality result in honor or incarceration is, on this theory, less a question of vice or virtue than of luck, in this case the "moral luck" of finding oneself in one culture rather than another or with one set of parents rather than another, and so forth (chapter 3).

Praise and blame are surely tied to the customs and beliefs of those who have the required standing to proffer or receive them; to personal characteristics that depend to some uncertain degree on constitutive and cultural factors; to the vagaries of context and the sudden demands of the hour. At first blush, then, we seem to be steeped in sociological and psychological considerations that some would take as exhausting the sources and actual content of moral ascriptions. "Standing," after all, is something conferred, and based on attributes regarded differently within different cultures and epochs. The standing of the shaman and witch doctor may oscillate between unchallenged authority and laughable quackery as one moves just a few degrees in latitude and longitude. Even within a given culture, one's own standing can change markedly from neighborhood to neighborhood, from one church to another, from one playground or classroom or union hall to another. With each of these variants, praise and blame will take on a different character, will engage a different set of perceptions, will result in different patterns of accommodation and adjustment.

This is not the end of the difficulty, for still unanswered are questions concerning moral standing and not simply "standing." Noted above is the requirement of a shared moral understanding, but what needs to be filled out is just what makes an understanding "moral," as well as the degree to which it must be shared for there to be a recognizable moral community. Tied to all this are enduring questions regarding the alleged subjectivity and relativity of morals, the allegedly unbreachable chasm between *is* and *ought*, and various perplexities nested within these. If praise and blame are to be understood as moral resources, then just what can be claimed for judgments of that sort remains to be settled. When one is praised or blamed, and thus assigned a moral property, is there anything whatever of an "objective" nature in the assignation? To define the subject, then, the first step calls for an examination of moral ascriptions and judgments at large. Is there anything in external reality to which such ascriptions refer, or are they little more than terms tied to tastes and sentiments?

Against Moral Realism

Not much research is needed to establish the wide variations across cultures in what are taken to be praiseworthy and blameworthy activities. The basis of status and celebrity reveals nearly wanton diversity from place to place, era to era. In the matter of praise and blame, for example, there are rather striking consistencies observed in a wide variety of contexts; consistencies treated under the heading, "the fundamental attribution error."[2] Where untoward outcomes are judged to have been avoidable, observers are quite strongly inclined to discover causality in the moral defects of the actor, though not in themselves. Thus, *you* slip on the wet floor because of clumsiness, *I* because the floor is wet, and the like.

"Blaming the victim" is habitual, even when rationalized in other terms. Rationalization itself often finds praise and blame allotted for little purpose beyond the need to render the affairs of the world more intelligible. How right it is that the impoverished family won the lottery. And is it not a kind of cosmic justice that lands the millionaire in prison for his greedy stock manipulations? There is a form of emotional gratification that attends the apparent labor of the Fates. Not only do the local practices of a given community but also the ticks of time bring alterations, some of them truly major, in the attributes held in highest esteem or greatest contempt. The present age admires the winning jockey and gives trophies for horsemanship, but it is obvious that much more was at stake in the Mycenaean age of Homer. In light of this, one might go so far as to insist that the targets of praise and blame have actually been the targets of good and bad luck, for what is likely to elicit moral judgments depends on passing fashions and the parade of cultures. As previously noted, understood in these terms praise and blame are instruments for preserving the customary practices on which the local community or tribe or an entire nation depends for its identity and continuity. The arriving stranger may cross the border with a radically different moral calculus, but its application, far from establishing an objective measure of what is found in the new land, can do no more than underscore the root fact of the subjectivity and relativity of morals.

These apparent inadequacies of and challenges to theories of moral realism and the supposed objectivity of morals have been advanced in every age of sustained moral discourse, from remote antiquity to the present. Bernard Williams has pointedly contrasted ethics and science in terms of the power of the latter to address questions that converge on ultimately settled answers. To explain the success of this convergence Williams attributes to scientific answers their representation of "how things are," whereas in ethics "there is no such coherent hope."[3]

Whatever that calculus by which to gauge worthiness for praise or blame, it would seem to have little in common with the tried and true methods of science. Moral standards seems hopelessly internalized, even when constructed and maintained by the community. Indeed, "community standards" is a term referring only to those evaluative precepts that have been internalized by most if not all the members of the community. It is this feature of moral ascriptions that has encouraged many to remove them from that very reality with which scientific inquiry is concerned, the reality that addresses "how things are." Arthur Fine puts it succinctly (here, as elsewhere in this study, italicized words in quoted materials appear thus in the original unless otherwise specified):

> For realism, science is *about* something; something *out there*, "external" and (largely) independent of us. The traditional conjunction of externality and independence leads to the realist picture of an objective, external world; what I shall call the *World*. According to realism, science is about <u>that</u>. Being about the *World* is what gives significance to science.[4]

Moral Science and Natural Science: The House Divided

A persistent critique of moral theories finds them based not on fact but rather on custom and, as such, not accounts of the world as it is but a collection of artifacts designed to preserve a kind of local order. On this account, persons, too, are socially constructed by the forces of acculturation at work from birth and throughout the course of a lifetime. These forces supply values, dispositions, basic understandings, goals, and core principles. It is, of course, unarguable that social influences are formidable in the life of persons, especially in the early years of life, but there remains the question of just how determinative they are—the question of whether, in the process, the person is passively constructed or instead is, from the first, an active, selective participant.

There are moderate and quite radical forms of *social constructionism*. The most radical forms could not possibly be evaluated in terms acceptable to their adherents, for the analytical tools of challenge and criticism would be dismissed as coming from the very stores in which protected forms of thought and judgment have been preserved by the dominant culture. Such radical versions raise and have raised comparable objections to defenses of scientific objectivity. The claims of the moral realist, in the circumstance, would hardly be taken seriously.

Before such radical proposals could seem to be worthy of consideration, there had to be something of a rupture within the once unified (if bickering) community of searchers after truth; a rejection of the once widely shared "common notions" and fundamental precepts; a division of all that is thinkable into the mutually exclusive domains of fact and value.

The argument found its voice earlier in the Enlightenment, many concluding that there was a clear separation to be honored between psychological and moral modes of understanding and explanation. For all the energy and analytical rigor Hume spent in defending the distinction, however, he was still committed to the development of a moral science, one based on the general features of human life wherever it is found, on the needs, desires and habits broadly, if not universally, distributed in human communities. That is, Hume could maintain that "is" and "ought" can never be substituted for each other, that the two are drawn from utterly distinct ontological domains, and still aim to develop a moral *science* based on a universalistic anthropology.

All this is to say that the moral and scientific controversies abounding in Enlightenment circles were nonetheless beholden to those "methods of Bacon and Newton," referred to like a mantra. These methods and the perspective reinforced by them comprised the stock notions of the Enlightenment. A far more fundamental division was to occur in the following century, however, and with it the long fruitful if hostile exchanges between the two schools of natural philosophy suddenly went silent. One consequence of the suspension of serious debate is the hardened confidence each side has in its central precepts. Contemporary opposition to moral realism and to the mere possibility of moral objectivity comes from quarters as divergent and independent as sociology and neurophysiology that have little else in common. The winner-take-all attitude of the protagonists is won at the cost of the mutually refining functions of critical inquiry. Examples abound. In *The Fragmentation of Reason*, Stephen Stitch defends a radical reductionistic scheme that would embrace all rational inquiry and understanding. To speak of knowledge as a justified true belief now requires translation into statements about processes and states in the brain, "mapped by an interpretation function."[5]

A theory of this sort is intended to replace views judged to be outworn, superstitious, bankrupt. At the other end of the theoretical continuum, Kenneth Gergen defends what he has called "social epistemology." He rejects out of hand all claims of objectivity, and denies that there can be any systematic inquiry that is ultimate, whatever the subject matter.[6] Those persuaded by Stitch's reductionist account (of which there are numerous variants) must judge the culture of science to be little more than certain habitual modes of information processing, subject to the contingent nature of brain function. Defenders of strong versions of the sociology of science regard the culture of science as just one among a wide range of cultures, none having trumping powers over the rest. It is worth repeating that these views, though controversial, have a long pedigree dating at least to the ancient Atomists and Skeptics. What is different now is neither the content of the theories nor the extremes to which they are stretched, but rather that, to a worrisome degree, the major contestants write as if the argument was over, the other side having nothing to say that is worth hearing. Owing to their practical and theoretical achievements, the developed sciences were for some time insulated from the more radical critiques, the easiest targets typically drawn from moral philosophy. But that, too, has changed. To the confident dismissal of "value" as little more than prejudice posing as principle has been added the classification of science as just another cultural "artifact," no more rational or protected than the rest. How did all this come about?

The Age of Newton—the era that included Francis Bacon, Newton, Galileo, Boyle, and Descartes—was the pillar that would support the entire Enlightenment project of reform and revolution. If the savants of the eighteenth century seem too confident under contemporary lights, it is partly because that very illumination includes rays and hues refracted by the late eighteenth- and early nineteenth-century disciples of romanticism.

In 1810 the first edition of Goethe's *Theory of Colours* appeared.[7] It is a detailed treatise of various color perceptions, in health and disease and under a very wide range of natural viewing conditions. Taken in its wholeness, the *Theory of Colours* is a rich documentation of the thesis that color phenomena must be understood subjectively, not objectively, and that the entire matter had been put on the wrong track by Newton. "The theory of colours," says Goethe,

> has suffered much, and its progress has been incalculably retarded by having been mixed up with optics generally, a science which cannot dispense with mathematics; whereas the theory of colours, in strictness, may be investigated quite independently of optics.[8]

Rejecting the analytical, reductive strategy of the received Newtonian science, Goethe warns his readers that

> the worst that can happen to physical science as well as to many other kinds of knowledge is, that men should treat a secondary phenomenon as a primordial one. . . . Hence arises an endless confusion, a mere verbiage, a constant endeavour to seek and to find subterfuges whenever truth presents itself and threatens to be overpowering.[9]

The object of criticism is again Newtonian science (though, it may be noted, not Newton's own!), and the Enlightenment conviction that complex phenomena are fully understandable through a process of reductive, abstract analysis and simplistic research.

The influence of Goethe's thinking on Hegel is a worthy chapter in intellectual history but also beyond the scope of the present chapter. Nor was Goethe's a lonely voice in a wilderness. In his *Critique of Pure Reason* Kant set logical and conceptual limits on what is knowable, and advanced a formidable argument to the effect that all epistemic claims are located within the fixed categories of quantity, quality, modality, and relation. So, too, is all experience grounded in the "pure intuitions" of time and space. Accordingly, what can be known or experienced is tied to the very modes and forms of thought and perception. There is no point outside these frameworks from which one might attain a critical perspective. In a word, the knowable is bounded, not limitless, and the modes of knowing cannot find validation outside the range of their own limited forms.

The German *Kritik* is, of course, not a "criticism" of pure (*reinen*) reason (*vernunft*) but a systematic account of the necessary preconditions permitting anything to be known through experience. The preconditions are the a priori constraints, the a priori filters, as it were, through which the knowable must pass if it is to be known. Kant's, then, was not a veiled skepticism but an analysis of the structure of knowledge and, therefore, the limits of reason's reach. His division of reality into "phenomena" and "noumena"—reality as perceived and reality as it is *in itself*—constituted no denial of the latter; only a recognition of the percipient's dependence on the limited processes and apparatus of perception. In discovering the limits of experience and rational understanding, Kant perhaps unwittingly extended an invitation to those who would advance still other, and allegedly less limited, modes of knowing. For the romantic idealists, to comprehend that which transcends the sensual is to have intuitive and aesthetic powers not respected in some philosopher's dull chapters on logic and epistemology.

Neither Goethe nor Kant nor Hegel was a relativist. None was hostile to science, though each found in the received sciences of the time a narrow one-sidedness, a complacency arising from the very commitment to simplification and reductionism. By the middle of the nineteenth century, the tensions were palpable. The world of systematic thinking was dividing itself into increasingly hard-line and defensive scientism and hard-line, aggressive Hegelianism. In an address delivered at Heidelberg in the Fall of 1862, Hermann von Helmholtz considered the essentially complete divorce that had taken place between science and philosophy. Searching for a brief way to convey the complication of causes, he pointed to the works of Hegel and declared, "His system of nature seemed, at least to natural philosophers, absolutely crazy. Of all the distinguished scientific men who were his contemporaries, not one was to stand up for his ideas."[10]

Hegel's followers were devoted to a grand system able to overcome the limitations of conventional science. The latter would then be subsumed under this more general system, one able to explain the rational character of the world as given. The general system was to be ultimate in that it would ground all knowledge. Hegel had dubbed this "phenomenology," a detailed science of the mind's own rational operations and transforming powers. Through this science it becomes possible to move from the mere causes of phenomena to the rational principles they express and realize. Conventional science can do no more—can attempt no more—than uncover assortments of otherwise unconnected descriptions and coincidences. Faced with this sort of criticism, Helmholtz noted, scientists "went so far as to condemn philosophy altogether." Prophetically, Helmholtz then concluded this part of his lecture with reservations regarding science's agenda for moral issues:

> We see, then, that in proportion as the experimental investigation of facts has recovered its importance in the moral sciences, the opposition between them and the physical sciences has become less and less marked. Yet we must not forget that, though this opposition was brought out in unnecessarily exaggerated form by the Hegelian philosophy, it has its foundations in the very nature of things, and must, sooner or later, make itself felt.[11]

The so-called "romantic revolution," the Kantian appraisal of the nature and limits of the knowable, the progress of Hegelian philosophy—these were the chief influences at work as the nineteenth century tested the optimistic promises of the Enlightenment. Though with various and numerous shadings, two distinct perspectives were developed and defended by the leaders of thought. In the patrimony of Hegel any number of sobering treatises rejected the ultimacy of science and even its relevance to an understanding of social, historical, and moral dimensions of life. In the patrimony of the Enlightenment, a confident positivism answered these claims and kept alive the optimistic conviction that disinterested, systematic, scientific research would answer the ageless questions—or show them to be nothing but verbal quibbles.

Against this background, it is less startling to confront, say, Paul Feyerabend's *Against Method*, which dismisses science's claimed allegiance to disinterested, rational inquiry. Rather, one must recognize the essentially rhetorical function of "science" in preserving a particular set of cultural values.[12] Against all of this are recent defenders of a realist metaphysics able to afford safe epistemological moorings. Susan Haack's *Manifesto of a Passionate Moderate* is, indeed, a passionate defense of Enlightenment values, including the deference owed to authentic scientific undertakings. Those who must be answered, she says, are the

> radical sociologists, radical feminists, radical Afro-centrists, and radical followers of (by now somewhat dated) Paris fashions in rhetoric and semiology (who) have turned their attention to science. Now it is commonplace to hear that science is largely or even wholly a matter of social interests, negotiation, myth-making. . . . 'objectivity' and 'rationality' are nothing but ideological constructs.[13]

If the developed sciences require so spirited a defense, one wonders whether it is even plausible to consider moral issues as in any sense distinguishable from "social interests, negotiation, myth-making," their allegedly objective and rational character in fact being nothing but veiled "ideological constructs." We see, then, that the case against moral realism boils down to the claim that moral entities, owing to their utter dependence on the internalized values and sentiments of persons essentially "constructed" by way of genetic and cultural resources, are not external and independent in the required sense. They are not in the *world*. Even to assemble an evaluative inventory of actions and meanings requires a method by which to equate the inevitably different forms of action and of utterance. Thus, one cannot classify an action as a "theft" or an actor as a "thief" except by way of a necessarily flexible algorithm. Indeed, in the end, there are no "purely descriptive" inquiries in any field of scholarship, let alone one as charged with interpretive energy and diversity as the subject of morals.

With pure description off the table, what remains can only be an essentially psychological approach to the subject, in contrast to abstract philosophical approaches. The latter sooner or later must make contact with the actual moral work of the world, however this is to be identified and defined, and thus may be properly guided by that work at the outset. One might say that the criticism of moral realism here is an exhortation to moralists that they be realistic.

Defending the epistemological standing of the natural sciences, however, is typically a prelude to defending this same standing when it comes to claims originating outside the sphere of settled scientific fact and theory. If, as it were, the last word on ontological and epistemological matters must be drawn from the accepted vocabulary of the natural sciences, then a defense of moral realism is essentially ruled out ab initio. The vocabulary of the natural sciences produces accounts of causal determination, physical processes, energy exchanges, and the like. The realms of aesthetics, politics, and morality are then located within a promissory framework of projects to be completed when the foundational sciences are up to the task. Presumably it would be some rich combination of evolutionary biology and cognitive neuroscience that would take on the burden: if not they, then no one.

If there is a generally accepted body of reservations voiced in opposition, it comes from the *social* sciences, from cultural anthropology and more philosophically informed versions of social psychology. The reservations, sometimes expressed in a form dismissive of even the certainties of the physical sciences, are predicated on what are taken to be the fundamental differences between physical events and social practices. The latter, as irreducibly cultural, enter into the very "construction" of persons such that social beings are unimaginable in their absence.

As major sections of the next two chapters examine deterministic challenges to libertarian or absolutist or "incompatibilist" theories of moral freedom, it is sufficient here to sketch these two different forms of determinism, one "hard" and the other in some way less hard and perhaps more porous. The sketches include an estimation of the extent to which a realist theory of morality is put at risk by them.

Moral Science and Natural Science (Again)

The methods and findings of the natural sciences are so considerable and broadly applicable as to raise serious questions about the reality of anything alleged to fall beyond their reach. Though serious, these questions either miss the intended mark or prove to be less questions than the begging of same. "Natural sciences" covers a remarkably wide range. Across this range the thick book of facts often conceals philosophically arguable assumptions. Moreover, not every fact as such finds a perfectly proportioned niche within the framework of scientific understanding. Not every fact bears directly, or even by implication, on the large and indubitable affairs of life. There may be some sense in which the regular motion of large bodies (e.g., planets, neighbors, and the Clapham omnibus) "supervene" on the uncertainty relations at the level of particle physics, but there is neither a reason nor a means by which to include the former in intelligible and coherent accounts of the latter.

In yet another way, the very framing of the issue as one pitting facts against values—one pitting natural science against moral science—begs the central question: whether the last word on all matters of real, abiding significance is to be supplied by the natural sciences; put in other terms, whether the natural sciences, as now understood, possess not only the best, but, indeed the only, means by which to embrace the full range of facts, events, and phenomena constitutive of reality. There is something entirely evasive about dismissing as "values" whatever fails to fit readily into the received ontology of the natural sciences. Thus classified, "values" is a category that soon comes to include nearly all that matters, and thus the natural sciences are left with what nearly doesn't matter at all; namely, with dead matter.

Lest the inventory be thus depleted, defenders of the ultimacy of scientific authority adopt reductionistic modes of inquiry and explanation such that the once refractory facts, events, and phenomena are now accessible to scientific treatment. In a most discerning critique of what he calls *the received scientific doctrine of causality*, Edward Pols summarizes the ruling dogma:

> The procedures of science are capable of discovering the causes of things and thus of providing the only adequate explanation of things. . . . Causality has no telic feature, although human beings tend to attribute teleology . . . to nature. . . . Agency as such, whether divine or human, forms no part of a scientific causal explanation."[14]

According to the received doctrine, then, the perception of color ceases to be a matter of aesthetics, for it is now understood as depending on coding mechanisms within the lateral geniculate nucleus and cerebral cortex. Anger, mediated as it is at the level of the limbic system, can be initiated and terminated by stereotaxically positioned electrodes. The measured successes at this level then support a widespread confidence that this same reductive strategy will, in the end, absorb whatever is, indeed, real, the balance confidently classified as a species of "noise" in the system.

This perspective has strong and worthy support within philosophy of science, strong and worthy opposition within philosophy at large. It is not necessary here to rehearse William Dray's critique of Carl Hempel's project, for anticipations of this important debate were fully expressed in the so-called romantic rebellion late in the Enlightenment.[15] What makes certain properties of reality interesting often includes elements that, if "reduced," are no longer explicable in terms that match up with reality itself. What makes the Battle of Waterloo a *battle* is not recoverable from even the most detailed account of the physiology and biochemistry of the participants. As Dray made clear, significant historical events are sui generis, not suited to modes of explanation based on a repeated-measures paradigm, and utterly lost once reduced to a collection of corpuscular interactions. The Battle of Waterloo is no less "real" for being incompatible with reductionistic analyses or covering-law modes of explanation. The incompatibility is not a sign of ambiguous ontological standing but of the variegated nature of the reality with which the human understanding must contend. The tools forged by the human imagination include those of science itself, but there is no user's manual able to declare in advance just which tool is not only the right but also only one for the multitude of problems arising from the complexities of real life as really lived. Accordingly, it is less hubristic than absurd to dismiss as somehow unreal the entire class of facts, events, and phenomena transparently inaccessible to reductionistic forms of analysis and explanation.

As will be discussed in the next section and elsewhere in this volume, the contents of moral science have been accepted by influential theorists as factual—even subject to a systematic treatment culminating in a bona fide "moral science"—but nonetheless to be understood as the merely contingent features of human psychology. The entire school of moral sentimentalists would defend this perspective. Thus construed, moral discourse can and should be converted into a descriptive psychology, making it possible to "explain" morality in nonmoral terms. Each factual "is" in this descriptive science is then shielded from any corresponding moral "ought" which, after all, cannot be connected to any describable feature of the perceptible world.

There is much to recommend in this move, but also much to criticize. If descriptive psychology is to be the guide, it becomes relevant that persons have no difficulty at all distinguishing between their sentiments on the one hand and their judgments as to whether a course of action is right or wrong in moral terms. That is, the actual persons who comprise the subject matter of this descriptive psychology do not reach or defend their judgments on the alleged affective basis, even in childhood! As John Darley and Thomas Shultz conclude, after a critical appraisal of scores of studies:

The learning of moral judgment begins early in life and is of great consequence to the child. Given this early appearance and importance, we
doubt that the understanding of the moral and intentional world depends on the comprehension of many aspects of the physical world. . . .
As we read the evidence, children make good, early progress in understanding both the moral and physical domains and do not often (as
many have suggested) confuse the two.[16]

The process of moral judgment is not one of conflating external facts and
internal feelings, nor is it one by which one attempts to rationalize a sentiment by incorporating it into a rule-structure. Moral judgment proceeds
from the assumption that actions of certain kind are *generic*, and are drawn
from genres that are readily classified according to the principles they instantiate. Competence in making such judgments is not easily acquired, may
be retarded by any number of factors, and, as a skill of sorts, benefits from
practice, good examples, instruction, motivation and perhaps some degree
of natural talent. The same is true of keyboard virtuosi who would find it
entirely unhelpful to be told that they need not worry, for all keyboard music
calls for no more than, and can be reduced to combinations of, only eighty-
eight keys.

Whether and to what extent the claims of a moral science match up with
what has become settled (inevitably pro tempore) within the scientific community sets challenges that work in both directions. Where the fit is poor,
it may signal the incomplete progress of science, the questionable content
of the moral claims, or both, or some other limitation only to be recognized
by later and wiser students.

Moral Science and Social Science (Again)

If moral realism is sound, there must be moral beings instantiating it. Moral
beings, at least as traditionally understood, are those with requisite powers
of self-control, judgment, and motivation to frame a course of action based
on sound moral precepts and then act accordingly. Merely doing the right
thing, however, does not certify the actor as a moral being, for one might
be made to do so by hypnotic suggestion, under duress, through inadvertence, or as a result of being a manufactured device designed to behave in a
certain way.

The source, nature, and standing of "moral beings" have been subjected
to ever more detailed investigations of culture. A growing body of thought
and theory stands behind the proposition that such beings are constructed,
as it were, from resources afforded by evolution, by local history, by the
vagaries of context. As genuinely cultural creations, moral beings and the
lives they live are beyond the resources of the purely natural sciences, for

such beings are "situated" in spaces that are irrelevantly geographic. They are situated within a complex matrix of discourses, values, patterns of affiliation, rules of membership, and the like Charles Taylor puts it this way:

> To know who I am is a species of knowing where I stand. My identity is defined by the commitments and identifications which provide the frame or horizon within which I can try to determine from case to case what is good, or valuable, or what ought to be done, or what I endorse or oppose.[17]

In a most interesting and suggestive account along these same lines, Ciaran Benson has written that "our system of core beliefs is the central nervous system of our identity."[18]

The conclusion reached by many in the vanguard of an otherwise liberated and enriched social psychology is that morality as such is a vital, cohesive and defining feature of real life; a source of one's identity, one's authentic *selfhood*; perhaps the pivotal chapter in that narrative one constructs (even daily) to know just who one is. For, to know who I am, as Charles Taylor says, is to know *where I stand*. Needless to say, however, this same conclusion must be at the expense of any version of moral realism that opposes the relativity of moral imperatives. Moral science now as social science emerges as an anthropological subject, enriched by evolutionary and genetic science, discourse analysis, autobiography, and rule-governed social practices.

What appears to be ruled out in such accounts are transcultural rules themselves, the very rules that the moral realist takes to be essentially non-contextual. One who insists that the rule "Killing the innocent is wrong on Tuesdays," contains two words too many need not be ignorant or intolerant of cultural diversity. But for the moral realist there is a limit to respect and tolerance, and that limit is reached when foundational moral tenets are violated.

The longer argument for moral realism is offered later in this chapter and again in following chapters. By way of introduction, however, it is useful to be reminded that a diversity of practices cannot of itself validate moral relativism. That there may be widespread differences in what various communities know or fail to know about the laws and principles of science may be an interesting study within cultural anthropology but surely has no bearing on the validity of the laws and principles themselves. By the same token, if every living person were to awaken on the morrow fully committed to precisely the same moral maxims, the ontological standing of those maxims would not thereby be established. In a word, whether there is a realm of reality constituted of moral entities is not a plebiscitary question. Real moral entities, just in case they turn out to be *persons*, but identifiable according to action-guiding principles of the right sort, would fill a defined moral space that is otherwise empty. But just in case an argument leading to this conclusion is defensible, neither the number of residents inside or outside that space nor the acknowledgment of those outside that space would have any bearing on the success of the argument itself.

It is tempting to translate this line of reasoning into the worst excesses of a complacent colonialism that would regard cultural nuances as evidence of incomplete human development; the once stridently affirmed "white man's burden." As with many depreciatory temptations, this one, too, should be strenuously resisted. A consistent theory of moral realism may result in the judgment that, at any given time in world history, there are no identifiable occupants in the defined moral space! More likely is the judgment that most candidate moral entities move often, and often uncertainly, across physical, social, and moral domains, frequently sacrificing one in the interest of gaining entry to one of the others; that most candidate moral entities might tend to confuse one domain with another. Two physically similar houses might find the new resident confusing a neighboring house for what is his *home*, here physical reality being taken as social reality. So, too, might the merely social domain of enjoyable affiliation come to be regarded as the moral domain of principled affiliation. Such confusions and conflations do not erase the conceptual and, it will be argued, the ontological distinctions between the physical, the social (cultural), and the moral.

With these sketches and sketchy defenses in place, we are able to return to the sentimentalist theory of morals, which would give morality real standing but only owing to certain contingent features of human nature. Just in case moral terms and categories are accompanied by, or responsive to, characteristic sentiments, the question will persist as to what it is about certain facts, events, and phenomena that so reliably results in their elicitation of "moral" feelings.

The Naturalization of Morality: Right and Wrong as Sentiments

The objections that must be overcome in any defense of moral realism were established authoritatively by David Hume, whose influence is unabated after two centuries. Hume understood morality as an essentially psychological phenomenon, grounded in sympathetic dispositions at once natural but shaped further and conditioned by associational processes. What is virtuous or vicious in an action is not something in the action itself but in the percipient's reaction to it. Moral content, properly understood, is not "out there" but internal and fully dependent on the sentiments of the witness.

> Vice and virtue, therefore, may be compar'd to sounds, colours, heat and cold, which, according to modern philosophy, are not qualities in objects, but perceptions in the mind: And this discovery in morals, like

that other in physics, is to be regarded as a considerable advancement of the speculative sciences; tho', like that too, it has little or no influence on practice.[19]

For Hume, there are widespread, even universal human tendencies to react to events in characteristic emotional ways. The grounding of these tendencies, however, is hedonic in that the moral judgments finally reached are tied to pleasure and pain. As "our own sensations determine the vice and virtue of any quality," different lives carry radically different experiences and thereby generate a diversity of sentimental attachments and associations.[20] How, then, is it possible for a shared moral outlook ever to arise? Hume answers:

> Every quality of the mind is denominated virtuous, which gives pleasure by the mere survey; as every quality, which produces pain, is call'd vicious. . . . Every particular person's pleasure and interest being different, 'tis impossible men cou'd ever agree in their sentiments and judgments, unless they chose some common point of view, from which they might survey their object, and which might cause it to appear the same to all of them.[21]

This common point of view on Hume's account turns out to be the *character* of the person whose actions are surveyed, as well as the character of those with whom that person associates. That is, by a process of association and generalization, the sentiments of sympathy are conditioned in such a way as to be attached to those thus judged "virtuous" or "vicious." Clearly, the moral ascriptions that arise from processes of this kind may be rationalized but are not themselves derived from reason. There can be no moral science as such, for the content is not in the "world" but in the person, in the passions.

There is value in considering at least part of the pedigree that includes Hume's theory. The period denominated "the Age of Newton" was one in which religious sensibilities were put on notice by the extraordinary achievements in natural science. Yet, even before Newton made a name for himself, there were religious philosophers striving to render the eternal truths compatible with the daily discoveries. Newton's Cambridge hosted the Cambridge Platonists, two of whose leading lights were Henry More and Ralph Cudworth. Although the latter's treatises on morality and free will did not reach a wider audience until the 1730s, they were composed and distributed nearly a century earlier. Given Cudworth's standing, these unpublished manuscripts, as well as his lectures and sermons, surely influenced the better minds of the period. Once published, Cudworth's work directly influenced Shaftesbury and Hume, to name only two of the British "sentimentalists," as well as Joseph Butler, whose *The Analogy of Religion* moved away from the deism of the scientist and toward an experience-based vindication of Christianity.[22] Butler's *Analogy* is considered in the next chapter.

In *A Treatise of Freewill*, Cudworth (1617–1688) opposes the materialism of Hobbes and a rapidly evolving deterministic Zeitgeist.[23] Against mechanism Cudworth opposes life and organicity. It is "necessary nature," he says, that "must be the beginner and spring of all action."[24] What nature itself expresses is that first principle of action—*to protos kinoun*—that "can be no other than a constant, restless, uninterrupted desire, or love of good as such, and happiness."[25]

It is by nature that man is equipped with "internal sense and common notions" and these are "confirmed by the Scriptures."[26] The springs of action are at once judgments and desires, complementing each other, rather than a "blind will" somehow directing the understanding. The will is not blind, though the summons of vulgar desire causes it to be distracted. The composite man, with powers of volition, thought, perception, and action, is the unit of moral regard, able to control himself and direct his actions toward what the soul senses:

> The soul of man hath in it . . . a certain vaticination, presage, scent, and odour of one *summum bonum*, one supreme highest good transcending all others, without which, they will be all ineffectual as to complete happiness, and signify nothing.[27]

Cudworth exemplifies those in the new age of science striving for a *pax philosophica* capable of distinguishing between matter and mechanism on the one hand, and spirit and moral liberty on the other. The essential instrument illuminating the differences is a sound "psychology" (Cudworth's prescient word), faithful to what each person finds when consulting one's most abiding longings. As noted, it is this attention to the evidence of direct personal experience that Butler will emphasize as an alternative to purely rational or analytical approaches to the great questions.

Long before the Darwinian revolution, then, the instructed mind understood that scriptural literalism was on a collision course with science, one in which the greater damage would be sustained by the faith and the faithful. The compromise struck between the claims of revealed truth and the truths revealed by science came to be that vaunted deism of the Enlightenment, but the foundations had long settled. They had been thickly laid in the century beginning about 1630, not only through such movements as Cambridge Platonism but by Newton himself and his scientific contemporaries. Locke's *The Reasonableness of Christianity* is perhaps the work most cited now, yet there were works of comparable and even greater influence. Shaftesbury's *Characteristics* (1711) was behind only Locke's *Second Treatise* on the list of the most frequently reprinted volumes in the eighteenth century.[28]

The fourth treatise within this multivolume collection is *An Inquiry Concerning Virtue or Merit*, which opens with the bold observation that many religious enthusiasts are patently lacking in virtue, whereas there are rank atheists of transparently good character. The point that Shaftesbury will develop is that virtue and, more generally, the moral dimensions of character are distinguishable from allegiance to doctrinal teachings or, more generally, to sectarian enthusiasms. The moral dimensions of character are found within the person, partly as a result of native endowments, partly as a measure of social and cultural influences. Beyond these,

> if there be any thing which teaches men either Treachery, Ingratitude, or Cruelty, by divine Warrant; or under colour and pretence of any present or future Good to Mankind; if there be any thing which teaches Men to persecute their Friends thro' love; or torment Captives of War in sport; or to offer human Sacrifice; or to torment, macerate, or mangle themselves, in a religious Zeal, before their God; or to commit any sort of Barbarity, or Brutality, as amiable or becoming: be it Custom which gives Applause, or Religion which gives a Sanction; this is not, nor ever can be *Virtue* of any kind, or in any sense.[29]

Shaftesbury goes on in the very next lines to insist that, apart from law, custom, fashion and religion, there are "the *eternal Measures*, and immutable independent Nature or *Worth* and VIRTUE".

To works such as Shaftesbury's *Characteristics* should be added his *The Freeholder's Political Catechism*, not to mention seminal treatises by John Toland, Matthew Tindal, Anthony Collins, Bolingbroke—the list is long and must include centrally Samuel Clarke's *Boyle Lectures*. Published as *A Demonstration of the Being and Attributes of God* (1705) and *A Discourse Concerning the Unchangeable Obligations of Natural Religion, and the Truth and Certainty of the Christian Religion* (1706) Clarke's lectures were probably even more influential than Locke's and surely aided in the construction of a religion of nature on the foundations of "natural religion." His incisive critique of determinism is considered in the next chapter.[30]

The common theme in these productions is naturalism itself; the reasonable assumption that the Author of Nature, expressing a visible *plan* in His works, is neither shaman nor mystic nor, in the vulgar sense, a miracle worker. Rather, the creation itself is the authoritative book. To consult its pages with an unprejudiced eye is find as much of the divinity as human powers can reach. Reason itself is limited. To compensate for its limitations, providence has seen fit to equip us with intuitive modes of knowing and with sentiments and native dispositions capable of directing our actions toward morally worthy and decent ends. Persons of sound judgment and an uncorrupted nature will agree fully enough on what is worthy and decent. It is in the court of common sensibility and common sentiment that actions are to be judged, and human nature itself has all the standing needed if the rulings are to be just.

Much of the naturalization of morality had already taken place years and even decades before Hume's first publications on the matter; publications that cited approvingly Locke and Lord Shaftesbury. Nor was Hume alone in raising the most pointed questions about traditional and conventional notions of morality. A summary of debates within the Enlightenment regarding the "right" and "wrong" of morals is given in the next chapter. Here we need only draw attention to what Hume found in the writings of Locke, Shaftesbury, Mandeville, and the rest: a commitment to unprejudiced observation of one's own mental and emotional life, one's natural sentiments as the means by which to understand the nature of all morality. The resulting introspective "data" would then be productive of general principles not unlike those unearthed by the inquiring scientific mind and surely could be incorporated ultimately into a systematic moral science. This, however, would be a science based on the contingent facts of human nature, which, had they been different, could well have yielded a radically different set of moral absolutes.

Sentimentalism—An Update (Ayer and Mackie)

This tradition, now more or less stripped of its once immensely important introspective methodology, is alive and prosperous in contemporary moral thought. It is as evident in Peter Strawson's theory of "reactive attitudes" (vide infra and again in chapter 2) as it is in neurobiological and evolutionary theories of emotion and motivation. The reasonable approach, on all of these accounts, is the scientific approach, and science begins with an impartial description of what is really there, or so the advocates have held. An authoritative recent version, calling for some amplification, is provided by A. J. Ayer:

> In so far as statements of value are significant, they are ordinary "scientific" statements; and . . . in so far as they are not scientific, they are not in the literal sense significant, but are simply expressions of emotion which can be neither true nor false.[31]

Ayer identified four types of propositions supporting four different systems of ethics. There are propositions that consider the definition of ethical terms; others describing what Ayer calls "moral experience"; still others that are no more than exhortations; and then those that seek to reach ethical judgments. Philosophy's task, as Ayer sees it, is confined to the first class of propositions; the second class is reserved to a scientific psychology. For Ayer, the exhortatory in ethics is nothing but a species of command, whereas the evaluative has no scientific or philosophical content at all. He concludes, "A strictly philosophical treatise on ethics should therefore make no ethical pronouncements." All the evaluative terms are to be "reduced" to descriptive terms, the result being not valid ethical judgments but topics for scientific (psychological) study. Not only is moral objectivity ruled out, but subjectivism, as such, fares no better, for personal sentiments cannot confer reality on morals as such. Nor does utilitarianism pass muster for Ayer, since there is no logical justification for treating expressions of the sort, "x is pleasant" or "x makes me happy" as equivalent to expressions of the sort "x is good."

In a way that would have won Hume's endorsement, Ayer contends that statements declaring that "stealing is wrong" add nothing not already included in the meaning of "stealing." What is added by including "is wrong" is not even or invariably a sign of the speaker's "moral sentiments." It is more akin to a cry of pain. In all, then, ethical philosophy consists simply in saying that

> ethical concepts are pseudo-concepts and therefore unanalysable. The further task of describing the different feelings that the different ethical terms are used to express, and the different reactions that they customarily provoke, is a task for the psychologist. There cannot be such a thing as ethical science, if by ethical science one means the elaboration of a "true" system of morals.[32]

In a related but different manner, J. L. Mackie would continue the attack on moral objectivism. The core question for Mackie has to do with what sorts of entities or items fill up the actual contents of the world. To answer this question within the context of morals, it would be sufficient for the antirealist to show that all values and moral ascriptions simply "are not part of the fabric of the world."[33] What Mackie's denial amounts to is the proposition that moral items or entities are not a "natural kind" and so their ontology is not to be found in the natural world as given.

Against Ayer's project, however, Mackie insists that the task of philosophy here cannot be limited to linguistic analysis. If there is a point to determining just what goodness is, it will never do to limit inquiry to "finding out what the word 'good' means, or what it is conventionally used to say or do."[34] The central task is not that of a linguistic but of an ontological analysis; to discover just what (if anything) moral ascriptions match up with in the real world. Mackie's approach here takes its lead from the notion of secondary qualities as advanced by Locke and Boyle in the seventeenth century. Granting that there are no blue or yellow photons as such, nonetheless certain dominant wavelengths reliably excite the sensations of blue or yellow. The secondary qualities of color are functionally tied to the (real) physical properties (primary qualities) of electromagnetic radiation. None of this could be established by a form of inquiry limited to how the terms "blue" and "yellow" are conventionally used.

What is clear to Mackie is that moral judgments are made by those who take them to be "objective." The task of philosophy is to determine whether this is sound or in error. At the level of linguistic analysis, what is readily discovered is that moral judgments already include an objectivist presumption and in this, according to Mackie, moral judgments are simply based on a mistake. In the Lockean language of primary and secondary qualities, Mackie would contend that the error is one of regarding a secondary quality (e.g., "blue") as if it were a primary quality, one that is independent of perceptual processes. It is akin to concluding, from the joint proposition that the light is corpuscular and is blue, that the corpuscles (photons) must be blue. Seeing through this error leads one to recognize that there are no moral facts as such, for morals do not figure among the furnishings of the world, even if certain objective events give rise to widespread perceptual or emotional responses of a "moral" sort.

Thus does Mackie frame his famous "argument from queerness": If there were real moral entities they could be known "only by some special faculty of moral perception or intuition utterly different from our ordinary ways of knowing everything else."[35] Intuitionism of this sort, he insists, is out of favor and implausible. Comparably implausible is the notion that such strange entities, found nowhere else in the universe, nevertheless are action-guiding and motivating; further, that they make direct contact of some sort with the natural occurrences that engage them. Assuming there is, for example, something morally wrong with cruelty, there would have to be a means by which empirical events (in this case, actions) are immediately recognized as "cruel" by our (alleged and required) intuitive powers. The cruelty would have to inhere objectively in the act and be *seen* as such. Clearly (on Mackie's understanding) there are no objectively "cruel" properties as such, so "cruelty" at most is in the eyes of beholders in much the same way that "blue" is.

None of this, in and of itself, would rule out widespread agreement on matters of moral consequence. All normally sighted persons, after all, will see "blue" under conditions that can be objectively specified. But what they see is different from what there is. In reality there are photons of a given wavelength and frequency capable of exciting the sensation of "blue." The sensation, however, is the result of specialized cellular and biochemical features of the primate visual system. The same electromagnetic radiation results in radically different sensations in different contexts, in conditions of disease, in species with different retinal pigments, and so forth.

In a similar vein, critics have used Occam's razor to strip away what they take to be the unwarranted assumptions of the moral realist. Richard Double is representative of a whole school of critics:

> *Theoretical postulations, in ethics as with ontology, in general, are justifiable only if: (a) The postulated entities fit into an otherwise acceptable theory of what exists in an understandable way (the conformity condition), and, (b) the data that we use to justify the postulation cannot be explained equally well without making the postulation (the simplicity condition).*[36]

Double concludes that moral realism fails to satisfy both conditions and, therefore, fails as a theoretical postulation.

An especially telling critique of moral realism has been developed over the years by Gilbert Harman, much of it a refinement and elaboration of an argument he set forth in *The Nature of Morality*.[37] It may be summarized as follows:

a. Moral statements are not entailed by descriptive statements of fact.

b. The only evidence for the truth of any moral statement would be in the form of inferences from true descriptive statements of fact, this being the very nature of evidence.

c. The only other basis on which to establish the truth of moral statements is intuitive and reached non-inferentially.

d. Owing to (a–c), factual evidence cannot establish either the truth of moral statements or the validity of non-inferential intuitive moral claims.

In a lengthy, if otherwise instructive, analysis of this argument, Judith Jarvis Thomson suggests counters based on the motivational power of certain beliefs, such that a moral statement of the form "x is kind to y" leads ultimately to some joyous bell-ringing celebration or announcement of x's moral standing. Harman's replies make clear that nothing essential to the adequacy of his aforementioned propositions is defeated by these counters.[38]

We see, then, that the case against moral realism is venerable, powerful, various. Can anything be said in its favor?

For Moral Realism

The defense of moral realism has both critical and constructive components. First, the limitations and defects of moral subjectivism must be examined, after which the facts and arguments that seem to tell in favor of moral realism may then be considered.

Perhaps it is best to begin with Double's useful denomination of the conditions that must be satisfied by theoretical postulates in ethics and ontology. Neither conformity nor simplicity is a univocal concept. Moreover, it is unclear just how a developed set of moral precepts could or should fit into an otherwise acceptable theory of what exists without begging the question. The moral realist affirms the existence of moral entities, taking them to be different from merely physical entities. The difference is essential, so the two cannot be expected to "fit into" the same ontological framework. No one seriously proposes eliminating the domain of physically real entities on the grounds that they fail to reflect moral properties.

"Simplicity," which is inevitably protean when invoked as a standard of explanation or, for that matter, of taste, might usefully be contrasted with "complexity" as understood in systems theory. The complexity of a system is expressed by the number of sentences required to account fully for the operation and performance of the system. On this understanding, any moral postulation achieving simplicity would be suspect on its face. To this point, then, the moral realist is able to defend the theory against criticisms based on positivistic assumptions expressly ruled out by the very nature of moral reality.

Beyond this, moral realists understand praise and blame as the means by which to evaluate persons and collectives objectively, and not as the privileged possessions of a local enclave. On this understanding, an account of what is valued and condemned leads not to a chapter in comparative anthropology but, as it were, to a diagnosis of moral health. The task is daunting, orderliness elusive, success partial at best. If there is to be a defense of moral realism it must be able to set aside skeptical arguments to the contrary where these rely not only on emotivist, subjectivist, and psychosocial alternatives, but also on the sort of conceptual challenge so skillfully developed by Harman and others. The last of these should be considered first, for if moral realism is ruled out conceptually, there would be little point in seeking its defense at some other level.

Is it the case that moral statements or claims are not entailed by descriptive statements of fact? This is a question riddled with subtle and protean terms. It might be understood as arising from the stock assertion of the moral skeptic; that is, *there are no moral facts as such*. If, indeed, there simply are no moral facts, then clearly no descriptive statement of fact can include a moral fact among its entailments. It might also be understood in a more subtle way: *How could evidence at the level of direct perception entail what cannot be known at that level or even reached by inference from one level to another?* In this form, the question would appear to ground a skepticism far too broad to be credible, and surely no more destructive of moral claims than of any number of nonmoral but objective facts of daily life. To wit: *How could evidence, in the form of factual description, entail that the musculoskeletal events displayed by the nine bodies distributed on the grassy field constitute the game of baseball?* And, of course, the answer is not that the musculoskeletal events *entail* the game of baseball but just constitute it. Given physical properties, the moral realist need not find an entailment-rule by which to reach moral properties. The moral realist need only argue that, comprehended properly, some occurrences are by their nature *moral*, though in some other sense also embodied.

If the question actually is predicated on the assumption that there are no moral facts as such, one must ask whether that assumption is broad enough to support skeptical conclusions regarding architecture (there are not Gothic cathedrals *as such*), national borders (there is no France *as such*), and so on. The arguments for moral realism are under no special burden in the matter of noninferential truth claims. In countless instances, an actuarial account of all that is directly perceived at the level of descriptive fact will fail to turn up what any competent observer would notice immediately: games, battles, strategies, possessions, gifts. If the skeptic's thesis is that no truth about wrapping paper and ribbons warrants the conclusion that a gift has been prepared, then we have one more instance of armchair skepticism. Once out and about, under the light of the heavens and immersed in the toss and tumble of the world, the skeptic abandons the major premise and records sincere gratitude for so lovely a *present*.

Turning to the allegedly sentimental grounding of morals, it is clear at the outset that persons making moral judgments understand themselves to be expressing something different from personal aversions, pleasures, or whims. There will be disagreement as to whether what is being affirmed is valid beyond the boundaries of their own culture or religious beliefs, but there will be widespread agreement that "good" and "evil," "right" and "wrong," "Well done!" and "Shame!" register something weightier than merely personal penchants. The limitations, and what is finally the sheer peculiarity, of sentimentalist theories of morality were put in sharp focus by G. E. Moore. The question Moore poses is whether the reference of all moral or ethical ascriptions "is simply and solely . . . a certain feeling." If this were the case, Moore concludes, it would follow that, "all the ideas with which Moral Philosophy is concerned are merely psychological ideas.[39] In addressing the question, Moore finds, at least tentatively, that the sentimentalist thesis is opaque, both as a moral psychology and as a philosophical doctrine. What troubled Moore can be instructively recast in the following way:

1. When I judge an action or event to be morally wrong, I am judging it to be the sort of action or event that tends to excite within me feelings of, say, indignation.

2. When I judge one action or event to be clearly more wrongful than another, I am actually basing the judgment on my estimation of which would create a greater indignation were both to occur at the same time.

3. When *you* make the judgments given in (1) and (2), then you are estimating how the action or event would tend to excite feelings in *you*.

4. As neither of us has any means by which to know such tendencies in the other, there is simply no basis on which either of us can make sense of how the other is using words such as "wrong." Moral terms as such could not rise higher in their import than a kind of noise.

5. It follows, then, that between two such persons "there is absolutely no such thing as a difference of opinion on moral questions."[40]

The problem for the moral sentimentalist does not end here, for if the thesis is not about the relationship between moral judgments and the feelings of the particular judge, then what relationship does it address? Moore regards as simply implausible the view that moral judgments can be based on guesses as to how someone else might feel when facing an action or event of a certain kind. And it goes beyond implausibility to suppose that, in the given circumstance, one can estimate the feelings excited in "all mankind." There is probably nothing in the realm of the possible that would engender precisely the same sentiment in the entire human race. Nor is there any evidence to suggest that, in making moral appraisals, persons engage in some form of actuarial exercise to calculate the fraction or percent of the human community likely to be excited to levels of indignation by an action or event. This is all sufficient for Moore to conclude that, whatever the reference of moral terms, it is not merely a psychological state or idea.

The persistence of sentimentalism within the body of moral thought requires additional comment here, partly by way of rehearsal, partly by way of amplification. For better or for worse, it is an undeniable fact of psychological life that one's emotional reaction to wrongdoing is of a decidedly different character when one is the target rather than an uninvolved witness. The witness to historical events of a malevolent nature is able to condemn without sharing the actual feelings of those who were victimized. Nor would the estimation of wrongdoing be affected in any way at all were it proven that the victims—owing to treatment by drugs or surgery or hypnosis—did not mind what was being done to them. There are, it might be supposed, relatively few persons who feel the loss of a murdered child as acutely as do the parents, but the judgment that a terrible wrong has been committed is no less certain for that. To explain the judgment on the basis of "empathy" is to introduce varieties of cognitive and conceptual resources well beyond the range of mere feelings. Sharing another's grief is at once to project oneself into the life of the other; to comprehend the other's scale of needs and values; and to shadow the aspirations and imagine the memories by which the grief is deepened and uniquely personalized. Even when the assumptions of the moral sentimentalist are warranted, therefore, it is obvious that the part taken by sentiment qua sentiment is more as corollary than as cause. In a word, there is nothing at the level of psychology or of conceptual analysis capable of sustaining the main arguments of the moral sentimentalist.

Moral Ascriptions (Praise and Blame) as Conventional and Discursive

Where ordinary opinions settle for the conclusion that praise and blame are just a species of reward and punishment, philosophical thought has been more subtle. It has focused on the discursive-linguistic resources by which a moral world may be brought about. On this understanding, praise and blame are essentially *rhetorical* devices, used to establish and maintain social structures of value to the discursive community. This, too, is a defensible but problematic thesis. It relies on a conventionalist theory of meaning, which itself is deeply problematical, despite an illustrious cast of defenders. To understand the deficiencies of this theory is to see further into the limitations of relativistic theories of morals.

Both Locke and Hume thought it obvious that the meaning of terms is established by social agreement or compact, as if that settled the question. As Thomas Reid observed, however, agreements and compacts require a language for their own production. Were there no means by which to signal approval and rejection, comprehension and confusion, and the like, there could be no "conventional" understanding at all. Rather, there must be some originating and entirely natural powers, widely shared and in place without benefit of learning or practice, by which to make public certain aims, feelings, desires, understandings. As Reid would argue, only if there is some natural language by which to signal agreement can there be the establishment of conventional meanings of signs and symbols in the first instance.[41]

Reid's "natural language" takes the form of postural and expressive signs of approval, agreement, fear, aversion, pleasure; the full panoply of sentiments and concepts by which compacts can be formed, meanings settled, rudimentary social interactions effected. This natural language is as much a fact of nature as is binocular vision or finger-thumb oppression. The latter is possible only as a result of the contingent fact that some creatures have fingers and thumbs. The contingent nature of digitation, however, is at no cost to finger-thumb oppression being an "objective" fact in the world. If postural and expressive actions are the comparably species-wide means by which cooperative and agonistic transactions are brought about, then they, too, are as facts of the natural world as "objective" as is the Krebs cycle or photosynthesis. It is useful to note in this connection that the efficacy of the very terms of a natural language would be rendered utterly meaningless by any sort of reductionistic analysis. It is the ensemble of postural, facial, and gestural actions that conveys the desire for assistance. Thus it would be idle to ask what sort of "sense organ" is responding to or recording the actor's plea for help. There is nothing in the transaction that is at all "queer," though there is also nothing that is essentially "sensory" or particular.

In the same vein, it is not in virtue of a judgment being shared "conventionally" that it lapses into the "subjective" mode. The term "subjective" may be applied to opinions or perceptions that are merely *personal*, but not to those shared by nearly every member of the species. It is easy to be misunderstood on this point, for it is always tempting to beg this sort of question by assuming that the only "natural kinds" are unitary objects, inevitably and exhaustively defined in physical terms.

Whether or not a complete description of the natural world can be rendered in exclusively physical terms is a metaphysical question of great subtlety. Common throughout the animal kingdom, at least as early in the phylogenetic series as the flatworm, is one or another sort of "dwelling." For some species the dwelling is within its own shell; others actually build such places. Although all such structures are physically describable, it is questionable whether even an exhaustive physical account conveys what it is that makes a physical entity a "dwelling." Even if such an account were produced, it is unquestionable but that it would fail to convey all that is readily conveyed by the notion of a "dwelling." Thus, although dwellings are utterly natural facts, they are not readily reducible to a congeries of fixed physical attributes. Presumably, such entities could be recognized as dwellings only by creatures who have—dwellings! Yet it would be odd to insist that, because of this, the concept of a dwelling is purely "subjective."

In this connection it is useful to consider again Mackie's "queerness" argument. John McDowell has expressed serious reservations about Mackie's position, again on the basis of the distinction between primary and secondary qualities.[42] Consider the sensation reliably associated with the word "blue." Here is a color-name assigned by normal percipients when short-wavelength radiation is incident on retinas with receptors of a certain type and at a certain level of adaptation. As a given percipient's "own" experience, blue may be said to enter into the subject's awareness ("subjectively"), yet this has no bearing whatever on the objective relationship between wavelength and sensory outcomes as mediated by the pigment chemistry of cone receptors.

It is, of course, unwarranted to conclude from the fact that something is the subject of experience that this "something" is subjective. Most of the facts, events and measurements integral to the developed sciences are "subjects of experience" but no less real for that. And, as noted, a large number of facts in the natural world of living, breeding, competing, cohabiting species are not only subjects of experience but intelligible only to creatures possessing kindred inclinations and adaptations.

In defense of Mackie's thesis it might be granted that "queerness" pertains not to every or any subject of experience but rather only to those subjects of experience denominated "good" or "bad" in the moral sense. Granting that there is a something generative of these assessments, just what this something is surely is not "in" the act itself. Relying again, as Hume himself did, on the concept of secondary qualities, the critic might insist that a given wavelength of incident light is generative of "blue," but that the photons themselves are colorless. "Blue" is thus understood not to be in the world but in the experience, and one is thus driven back to the question of natural kinds. What sort of entity would morals have to be to qualify as a *natural kind* of thing?

Whether moral entities ("good," "bad," and so forth) are real in the sense of being instances of natural kinds depends on what one requires of such kinds, and on this issue there is no settled position. Are species distinct and thus instances of a specific natural kind? What criteria are taken to be dispository in matters of this sort? Alexander Bird highlights the difficulty:

> When one visits a greengrocer, in the section devoted to fruit one will find, among other things, apples, strawberries, blackcurrants, rhubarb, and plums, while the vegetable display will present one with potatoes, cabbages, carrots, tomatoes, peppers and peas. If one were to ask a botanist to classify these items we will find rhubarb removed from the list of fruit and tomatoes and peppers added. . . . Following this line . . . one might conclude that there really is no absolute sense in which there is a natural classification of things into kinds.[43]

What is indubitable is that there are apples, rhubarb, and so on, which is to say that these names refer to entities that are reliable subjects of experience. They are no less reliable (and *real*) as subjects of experience for being difficult to classify in an undeviatingly consistent way. At a commonsense level, one would say that the term "apple" ranges over a variety of items with a set of attributes understood to be required if the term is to be applied correctly. Apples have a "nominal essence" that includes their shape and color, their taste and size, and the like. Actions and events routinely described as morally "good" or "bad" also have common properties and are classified, if not as consistently as apples are, with sufficient intersubjective reliability to qualify as having a nominal essence.

This is not to say that for anything to qualify as really existing it must have an abiding and universally recognized nominal essence. Consider only Saul Kripke's tiger critique: To say that the tiger has a nominal essence that includes "large, quadrupedal, carnivorous, black and yellow cat populous in India"—and that this qualifies tigers as a natural kind—is to fall prey to epistemic credulity. After all, those who were the first to see such creatures may have had defective vision, or may have seen only the few tigers who actually eat meat, or may even have failed to see a fifth leg on half of the specimens. The point, of course, is that descriptions, no matter how consistent, are fallible accounts of *what is there* and cannot, therefore, be the last word on the nominal essence of a thing.[44] By the same token, the very complexity of moral events lends them to a wider range of descriptions, each perhaps focused more on one cluster of features than on another. As descriptive consistency does not guarantee a correct essentialist account, neither does descriptive inconsistency rule out the possibility that the described entities are natural and *real*.

It is not only philosophers who have considered the reference of evaluative descriptions. It was a matter of great interest to psychologists in the Gestalt tradition. If the core precept of Gestalt psychology is confined to a sentence, it is *the whole is different from the sum of its parts*. Events perceived as having or embodying values offer suggestive examples of Gestalt principles of perception. A passage from Wolfgang Köhler is instructive here:

Value may reside in the most varied classes of things. A dress may look elegant or sloppy, a face hard or weak, a street cheerful or dismal, and in a tune there may be morose unrest or quiet power. I admit, one's own self is among the entities in which values may reside. Such is the case when we feel fit or, at another time, moody. But the thesis that it is always valuation as an act which imbues its object with value as a pseudo attribute is perhaps nowhere more artificial than precisely in this instance. Here the self would have to equip itself with value attributes such as fitness or utter fatigue. The idea seems slightly fantastic. And if in this instance a thing per se manages to have value characteristics, why should we deny this possibility where other percepts are concerned?[45]

It is, indeed, fantastic to assume that a percipient possesses a set of attributes such as, say, "fatigue," then deploys these (even inaccurately) as a way of describing some otherwise incompletely comprehended event, such as one's fatigue. Rather, the ascriptions reach something resident in the "thing per se," as Köhler says, as that something is registered in the process of perception itself. The clam withdrawing into its shell in response to a threat in the external environment is using the shell as a protective dwelling, which it is, and this property, the property of *being-a-dwelling* is as much in the shell as is calcium.

Objectivity and Intersubjectivity

Persons differ in their estimations of the morally good and bad and the degree of each. Such disagreements are routinely noted in attempts to establish the subjectivity of moral evaluations. Persons also differ in assigning names of colors, some of the differences based on the physical features of their different and nurturing environments. The Eskimo has many more words for snow than does the resident of equatorial regions and may also be more sensitive to the texture and color shadings of snowy scenes. It is a teasing question as to whether any two persons see the same "blue."

Though a teasing question, it is not without rigorous modes of address. Experimental psychologists settle questions of this sort according to the following general strategy: Find the range of stimulus variations over which both percipients assign the same term (e.g., "blue"), and that is the index of sameness of perception.[46] In this same connection, and still inspired by Mackie's critique or moral objectivity, suppose one were to ask whether "musical harmony" is part of the fabric of the world. The question would not be settled by the fact that harmony in music (as with "moral" for the moral realist) is rule-governed and thus permits assessments of success and failure, right and wrong. Chess, too, is rule-governed and certain moves can thus be classified as impermissible, though no one would claim that the game of chess is part of the very fabric of the world. But chess, as such, matches up with nothing that is already and incontestably part of the fabric of the world whereas music does; namely, vibratory phenomena falling within the range of human auditory perception. Music, then, is an instance of sound, and sound arises from the compression and rarefaction of molecules that are certainly part of the fabric of the physical world.

This much accepted, the question now can be rephrased: What is the ontological standing of those acoustical properties by which a given sample of sound is classified as "musical" and "harmonious"? One reply would have it that nothing more than the tastes or predilections of the listener need be consulted, thus reducing "harmonious music" to an utterly subjective phenomenon. A more rigorous reply would note the fact that some persons are tone-deaf but that their auditory pathology should not be confused with a general failure to classify instances of "harmonious music." Such persons may not hear the harmonies but could learn the theory of harmony and then test a given ensemble of acoustic frequencies against the theoretical requirements. There are mathematical criteria by which "harmonies" are understood, as well as the actual receptivity to such harmonies of specific auditory mechanisms, both peripherally and within the central nervous system. The finding, therefore, that there are widespread variations in musical genre and "music appreciation" would not, in and of itself, defeat the realist's claims. Just in case the Eskimo language contains many more words for "snow" than does that of the Kalihari bushman, "whiteness" is still part of the fabric of the world.

To consider the realist's claims in this context is to revive Thomas Reid's subtle and powerful rejoinders to those he attached to the "ideal" theory. What Reid found in Hume was a theory both ancient and common; a theory that denies the percipient access to things in the world, confining the contents of consciousness to some sort of "representation" of them. What can be known, then, are not the items and events in the world, but only ideas in the mind. Aristotle, Descartes, Locke, Malebranche, Hume—a veritable legion of philosophers accepted this thesis in one or another form and thus gave impetus to all varieties of skepticism.

Reid's defense of direct realism is now well rehearsed. It is a common sense defense, naturalistic and even Darwinian in its rationale. The lowly caterpillar crawls across a thousand leaves until it finds one right for its diet, an achievement that would be impossible were such a creature hostage to the allegedly "mental" nature of all perception and comprehension. Speaking of defenders of the ideal theory, Reid notes that.

> they made the secondary qualities mere sensations, and the primary ones resemblances of our sensations. They maintained, that colour, sound, and heat, are not anything in bodies, but sensations of the

mind. . . . Their paradoxes were only an abuse of words. For when they maintain, as an important modern discovery, that there is no heat in the fire, they mean no more than that the fire does not feel heat, which every one knew before.[47]

No one sees the discharges of optic nerve fibers. One sees what is *out there*. Perception is of events and things, not of "representations." How, after all, would the mind form an image of an odor? To repeat, from the fact that an event is the subject of experience, it does not follow that its standing is subjective. To the extent that the experience includes attributes not readily reduced to physical features it does not follow that the attributes are unnatural or "queer." And from the fact that there are widespread variations in the manner in which such events are classified and evaluated, it does not follow that the events themselves are unnatural or queer.

Widespread variations in the evaluation of actions and events are often invoked to defend relativistic alternatives to moral realism. The thesis, often explicit, is that variations in moral ascriptions applied to the same phenomenon leave no doubt as to the relativity of moral values. But further reflection shows this also to be either irrelevant or compatible with an (empirically supported) alternative explanation. It may be dismissed as irrelevant on the grounds that the failure of one, another, or *every* community to recognize the objective truth of a systematic science cannot possibly constitute a challenge to the objectivity of the claims of that science. Were there communities, none of whose members had depth perception and thus all of whom denied the objective validity of spherical geometry, their denials would play no part in an attempt to establish the validity of the axioms of this geometry.

The alternative explanation begins with the recognition that it may not be the *values* that vary from culture to culture but the *meaning* of the action or event being evaluated. To show no more than that two groups evaluate the "same" event differently requires a method and measurement capable of rendering the event itself the same for the two groups. Obviously, snow removal will be evaluated differently by one attempting to get out of the driveway on the day of the storm and one who operates a ski resort. This is an example of the well-known and uncontested dependence of valuations on context. But room for unwarranted and misleading conflations is great here. That snow is to be removed is an objective fact of the world. That this pleases the commuter and worries the ski resort operator is something else. The misleading conflation is one that takes their different reactions as raising doubts about the objective nature of the event in question.

Karl Dunker, another member of the Gestalt school of psychology, conducted experiments on this matter years ago. In an illustrative experiment Dunker found (unsurprisingly) that attitudes toward moneylending depend on whether the practice is perceived as a form of exploitation or a desire to assist.[48] This and related judgments clearly color and shape how a mere fact, such as the fact of lending "for a consideration," is incorporated into one's perceptual framework. Failing to probe more basic values, one is likely to conclude that it is attitudes toward usury that vary, rather than how the overall transaction, its purposes and affordances, are understood. What varies, of course, are attitudes toward actions judged as affirming, and attitudes toward actions judged as rejecting a settled moral precept. As it happens, the judgment that moneylending is a good practice owing to the assistance it gives to the borrower, and a bad practice owing to the usurious exploitation of the poor, is a judgment based on the same moral precepts. This is all too weighty to hang on the thin threads of a few psychology experiments. It is abundantly clear, with and without such research, that evaluations of events are subject to how the events are perceived in the first instance. To insist, therefore, that differences in the evaluations record differences in basic values is, in the circumstance, merely argumentative.

The Fabric of the World (Again)

Those attaching themselves to the empiricist school of realism cannot have it both ways. They cannot at once insist that all candidates for inclusion in "the fabric of the world" be reliably efficacious at the level of sensation and, at the same time, rule out a priori any number of experiences widely reported, reliably elicited, stubborn in their persistence. On the old, if troubled, Lockean notion of secondary qualities there are attributes of real things reflected in the manner in which they are perceived. Whatever stands behind "blue" or "harmonious" is really there, even if "blue" and "harmonious" require special apparatus, culturally modified, if they are to be sensed. The moral realist may contend without embarrassment that the moral sense of right and wrong is, too, generated by facts forming the fabric of the sensible world and experienced by creatures having adequate means by which to recognize these facts.

It should be noted, however, that the very concept of primary and secondary qualities was troubled from the first. George Berkeley was among the first to develop a systematic critique of the distinction, concluding that everything Locke would have as a primary quality was as much a subject of experience as were the secondary qualities. Stretching Locke's empiricism to what he took to be the limits of its tether, Berkeley concluded that all that is, to use Mackie's graphic expression, part of "the fabric of the world" is so in virtue of being perceived. *Esse est percipi.* A more plausible alternative rejects the notion of "qualities" altogether and contends that what is seen (heard, etc.) is just what is *there.*

Specifically rejected is that representational theory (as much Descartes's as Locke's) according to which we have knowledge only of our own representations of the external world rather than of that world directly. Indeed, the senses are prey to illusions but if there were not veridical perceptions there could be no category of the illusory. Reid again is the textbook realist, his criticisms of the representational ("ideal") theory now widely cited. The lynchpin of his argument is the demonstrable fact that the visually perceived world of figures has as its content the tangible properties of these figures and not the properties of their retinal projections. That is, the right-angle triangle drawn on the page is seen as rectilinear (it is seen as it would be felt) and not as the spherical triangle projected onto the retinal surface. For present purposes, this realist position translates directly into matters of value. That natural language that includes facial expression, posture, and vocal intonations is a language conveying states, dispositions, intentions, and feelings that are really there—really part of the fabric of the world. If it is a leap from this to the proposition that "cruelty" is *in the act* in just this way, it is at least not a heedless one. Just in case moral ascriptions are nonetheless taken to be in some sense akin to naming colors or identifying harmony, they still are not on that account subjective, let alone queer, and they may well on that account express an entirely natural connection. To test this further, two principal objections must be met; that identified as "the naturalistic fallacy," and the second arising from contemporary notions of objectivity itself.

Objectivity and the Naturalistic Fallacy

It may be argued that even a "natural connection," such as that between wavelength and sensed color or between an act and one's moral aversion to it, establishes no more than a matter of fact incapable of sustaining moral conclusions. Dubbed "the naturalistic fallacy" by G. E. Moore, the famous nondeducibility of "ought from is" was influentially anticipated by David Hume:

> In every system of morality . . . the author proceeds for some time in the ordinary way of reasoning . . . when, of a sudden . . . instead of the usual copulations of propositions, *is* and *is not*, I meet with no proposition that is not connected with an *ought* or an *ought not*.[49]

There have been numerous criticisms and defenses of the alleged naturalistic fallacy. Presumably, taking an oath is a fact that establishes an obligation and this has exemplified for some the possibility of deriving "ought" from "is." This line of defense, though suggestive, is different from what I would propose in the present context. Rather, I would ask directly the basis on which to reject the reality of moral "oughts" once it is granted that they arise from the stable dispositions and sentiments widespread in human communities. What is it that such dispositions and sentiments are lacking such that they fail to "objectify" moral obligations?

I recur yet again to the "secondary qualities," to "blue" and to "harmonious music." To insist that blue is not in the physical stimulus is to have some sort of theory that settles what is (naturally?) "in" a physical object. Surely any adequate theory by which to determine what is "in" an object must include any property that renders the object causally efficacious in its relationship with other objects and events. On this account, it would be a patently incomplete account of what is "in" electromagnetic radiation with a wavelength of 390 nanometers to leave out the property of causing the sensation blue in normal percipients. The same would be the case in any complete account of patterns of vibrations generating a major chord.

There appear to be aspects of the world that excite sentiments of approval and revulsion, these fully noted by Hume as he attempted to translate moral terms into psychological states. But one cannot eat one's cake and have it, too. If the ultimate authority on all matters of fact is that of experience, the widespread experiences of approval and revulsion—expressed also in the language of moral praise and blame—must be said to provide the very same grounding for moral ascriptions as is available for blue or harmonious music. What is relative in such a scheme is the relationship between events external to the percipient and the species-determined registration and interpretation of such events; that is, the causal consequences as determined by this relationship. Thus did Thomas Aquinas note, rather in passing, that, were our natures different, our duties would be different. But our natures are what they are, what they *really* are. The cognitive and conceptual resources available to us by which every other aspect of reality is established are available as well to establish the reality of moral events and items. This should be uncontroversial once "concept" is assigned a stable meaning. Laurence Bonjour has done as much when he concludes that, to have a concept such as "redness" is, among other considerations, to be able think about and represent a particular thing or kind of thing,

> where the item in question is usually represented as a feature or aspect of the objective world, of *an sich* reality. Thus, if I have the concept of red, I have therewith the ability to think of things as red, to reflect on the property redness, and normally at least to recognize things as red. There is nothing wrong with saying that my rational insight or justified belief that, for example, nothing can be red all over and green all over at the same time pertains to my concept of red (or redness), but this means merely, I suggest, that it pertains to the putatively objective property that I represent, not that it pertains to some distinct subjective entity, whose nature and metaphysical status would be extremely puzzling.[50]

Deriving "ought" from a complex pattern of events is no more puzzling, let alone fallacious, than to derive "blue" from wavelengths, just in case the two kinds of events are comparably common in human experience owing to their being tied to features of the natural world. In a word, the sense in which moral qualia are queer is no different from the sense in which all qualia are queer. Put another way, moral qualia are not to be denied the status of natural kinds on the grounds that they are qualia, for all natural kinds enter their taxonomic slots as a result of, alas, qualia.

The antirealist rejoinder is not that moral judgments fail to refer to a metaphysically puzzlingly subjective thing, but that what they refer to just is subjective; that is, feelings. And feelings are no more than feelings, no matter how natural or uniform or general in their distribution. Of contemporary writers on the subject, none has done more to "naturalize" the emotions and sentiments than has Peter Strawson in his essay "Freedom and resentment," where he develops the concept of "reactive attitudes."[51] The thesis will be considered again in chapter 3. Here it is useful to consider his thesis that there are utterly natural dispositions and emotions captured by such terms as "gratitude," "indignation," "resentment," "guilt," and that these are so integrally related to social and interpersonal life that such life would be inconceivable in their absence. In any direct combat, therefore, between determinism and the presumption of moral responsibility, the victory of the latter is ensured by the most fundamental pragmatic considerations. The reactive attitudes, at once natural and pervasive, give a protected status to the very terms of moral discourse, thus insulating it against the claims of science. If Strawson does not go as far as Hume in declaring the hegemonic status of passion in relation to the assertions of reason, he goes far enough to preserve the essentially social function of moral ascriptions.

One might agree with all of this and, turning the tables, go on to insist that this establishes the utterly subjective nature of morals. What is implicit in this rejoinder is a kinship between physical entities and objectivity, and between perception and subjectivity. Common though this implication is, it seems to be a distortion of the manner in which objectivity actually arises and is recognized in the realms of perception and judgment.

The widespread view is that genuinely scientific aspirations must incorporate and display "objectivity," and that this is achieved through a steadfast commitment to what is typically dubbed "value-neutrality." On this understanding, an enterprise is "scientific" to the extent that its claims and essential character are in no way obeisant to such (culturally based, fictitious, subjective, affective, sentimental . . .) "values" that are the stock-in-trade of morality. A value-neutral enterprise, so the account goes, places no special premium on one set of epistemic claims over another, for to assign standing is already to have adopted an axiology. Such an enterprise arises within, and claims fidelity to, no identifiable and merely "local" culture, for to have such a pedigree or allegiance is at once to embrace and to preserve a settled system of values; indeed, it is to be disposed to acquire and transmit ideas, practices, possessions in such a way as to honor and fortify the generative and nurturing culture.

This, however, has never been a valid characterization of science, nor could it have been. Rather, the emergence of what we might call the "culture of science" is dated from the birth of philosophy itself, when thinkers began to distinguish between facts and beliefs, knowledge and opinion, the enduring and the evanescent; when they were willing—often under pain of censure and even death—to draw a line between the received values and certainties of cohorts or kings, and the real certainties revealed through an unprejudiced and daring inquiry into the very nature of things. By whatever name, such an orientation and commitment cannot be understood in totally nonmoral terms.

What may be called the moral disposition of objectivity is not foundational for any and every mode of inquiry. There are many contexts in which hunches, guesses, hopefulness, unreflecting faith, coin tossing, and unbridled whim might well dispose someone to take a position, even a firm position, on something being so. Thoughtful persons cast votes, offer up prayers, buy lottery tickets, find perfection in their children, and something of their own identity in the local football team. None of this can be predicated on the moral requirement of indifference or judicious disinterest, which is precisely what "objectivity" entails. Indeed, the scientific community, which is in this capacity drawn from the moral community in just the way jurors are so chosen, is credible insofar as it is able to suspend just those dispositions that yield faith, hope, blind affection, party loyalty.

To hear parents blame teachers for the lackluster performance of their children is to be inclined to lower one's gaze in sympathetic embarrassment. One is far less inclined to censure the parents than to understand their controlling passions and motives. Yet to discover that a scientist has recast the data in order to render the findings more compatible with a favored hypothesis is to be shocked and to regard oneself not only as cheated but even imperiled. The offense now is on a par with forms of treason, for the deception is recognized as potentially harmful to all. As the parents are judged in sympathetic terms, the scientist is judged in moral terms; and this is as it should be.

This special status of the scientific enterprise is based less on cost-benefit calculations—by which it is not inevitably vindicated—than on the light it actually sheds on, yes, undisciplined subjectivity. The status of science is a reflection of a powerful, if often repressed, motive in human affairs, the motive to self-perfection: the motive a rational being has to become ever more rational, ever less vulnerable to the gothic productions of the unlit mind. If the scientific project serves a given culture it is not for that reason a mere expression of the values of the given culture. In this we discover what one might call a "culture of science" as a distinct historical undertaking, not unlike the "culture of law." The moral relativist's most important contribution is the reminder that attempts at "objectivity" are not routinely an unequivocal success. There is nothing, however, in the developed arguments of the relativist to establish the inevitability of failure, and the culture of science is but one source of modest optimism. This optimism is tested in a later chapter.

Cognitivism and "What Moves Us"

Moral theories are intended to explain what seems to be an otherwise eerie state of affairs; that is, the power of a moral judgment or belief to induce a course of action that may be complex, of long duration, sometimes at the personal expense of the actor. How, after all, can a mere state of mind generate such consequences? The difficulty faced by cognitivists is that they require of moral judgments and beliefs a rational character that is separated in fact and in principle from appetites and desires, but this very separation seems to strip them of what a genuinely motivating state of affairs possesses. The noncognitivist, on the other hand, requires of any motivating belief or judgment that it include the ingredient of desire or "conative" state, such that there is an impulse or commitment to act on the judgment or belief, this being the manner in which rhetorical exhortations are effective. In itself this is a thesis warranting careful examination. It is taken up in the next chapter in connection with just what it is in rhetoric that is capable of initiating and guiding action.

The cognitivist may and the noncognitivist must adopt an "internalist" thesis that locates the cause of actions in states within the actor that, by their very nature, are not "moral" states at all. Rather, they are emotional states of pleasure or dread or desire or revulsion. The cognitivist can accept this, while insisting that rational criteria and standards of evaluation must first qualify the objects of such emotions. This still would not establish an authentic moral realism, for the rational criteria may nonetheless be explained in terms of the nonmoral values, needs, and circumstances of the authorizing community. A defense of moral realism must therefore go beyond a defense of cognitivism. It must offer a compelling argument to the effect that one's powers of rational comprehension are able to identify the real moral content of actual or potential events.

Typically, there is a further cognitivist constraint on internalism, in that the internalist must offer a plausible account of the entirely practical, coherent, and predictable relationship between desires of a certain sort and the actions arising from them. As Michael Stocker has observed, there are clinical and quasi-clinical conditions (depression, apathy, weakness of the will) that seem to disrupt the relationship between moral judgments and beliefs and the actions that would ordinarily arise from them.[52] In response to this, the only option available to the internalist is to require that the connection between motives and actions is the basis on which to accept actors as, to use Michael Smith's term, "practically rational agents."[53]

One begins to sense a makeshift psychology at the bottom of all this, and one that William James might have absorbed into his notion of *the psychologist's fallacy*. The very nature of any systematic analysis of action is likely to find the analyst breaking the event into separate components—antecedent conditions, past "reinforcement history," current states of need or desire, behavioral options, the given course of behavior. But the leap from the unavoidable steps in a formal analysis to the conclusion that the action itself necessarily followed the same steps is at once daring and deceiving. If it is disconcerting to think that a judgment is able to induce a complex sequence of actions, it is no less so to think that the same is achieved by neuronal excitation, oxidation rates in the gastric epithelium, or patterns of activation in the extrapyramidal pathways.

Actions that warrant moral appraisal are more akin to playing a sonata than to striking a note. And, though, in a certain sense, the best explanation of a note being struck might be in terms of events at a given neuromuscular junction, that same explanation would be queer if offered as an account of a concert performance. That is, the best explanation of Emil Gilels's rendition of Beethoven's "Emperor" concerto is one that will include biographical, contextual, and even political factors unique to that performance and that performer; factors largely isolated from the particulars of neuromuscular "efficient causes." Whatever it is that qualifies an action as "moral," it is surely not merely the means by which it was produced. A lethal assault on the innocent is of the same moral quality whether the offending weapon is poison, gunshots, a sword, or a hired assassin.

Needless to say, actions presuppose actors and actors can achieve ends only by doing *something*. To suppose, however, that the right moral theory has some special obligation to identify the particular mechanical or biochemical mode of activation is a supposition that would reach comic proportions in any other sphere of significant human endeavor. The best accounts of the architect's plans, the university's curriculum, Fall fashions, and peace initiatives in the Middle East are not "internalist" or "externalist," but rather commonsense accounts, based on a folk psychology, the validity of which must be granted if the notion of an "account" is to be intelligible.

Must one have the desire to do good in order to do it? The question is miscast. Rather, it is understood that no one has "done good" in the world except in so far as this was the desire. To be sure, good ends can result from malign intentions or even by chance. In that case, the persons involved are judged respectively as either malign or as bystanders. We say of the first that they were "foiled," and of the second that they were just at the right place at the right time. But judgment, except in the formal contexts of philosophical analysis, scarcely ever partitions the actor into a cognizer, an emoter, an evaluator, a perceiver. We judge the *person*, recognizing (on the basis of our own moral experiences) that actions proceed from complex and often competing tendencies. Alfred Mele notes that the *self* of self-control is not properly identified with reason. It is, rather, to be identified with the *person*, broadly conceived. Even when one's passions and emotions run counter to one's better judgment, they are not plausibly seen as alien forces.[54]

How does rhetoric move us? It certainly does not move us as a mechanical device moves an object. Rather, we move ourselves in such contexts, typically as a result of a rational appraisal of options in light of our own powers, needs, sentiments, and duties. Aristotle knew how idle it was to ask which "part" of the soul is responsible for a significant undertaking, and he satisfied himself with the conclusion that it is the person who does these things. There is, indeed, something odd about a belief causing an action. Beliefs don't cause actions; rather, actors act, typically on the basis of beliefs as to the likely efficacy of their actions. There are, too, occasions calling for the futile gesture, this performed in full recognition that the action will not change the course of events but will stand itself as a rhetorical statement.

There is much more to be said on this point in the two succeeding chapters. Here it is sufficient to extricate moral phenomena from an explanatory thicket in which no robust form of human activity could find a place. If radical reductionistic analyses are transparently defective in explaining complex social, institutional, aesthetic, and historical phenomena, there is little cause for alarm in discovering that moral phenomena are comparably ill-suited. There is even less cause for alarm just in case moral beings themselves resist such modes of analysis.

A holistic perspective is inescapable in such matters, but one to be built on the discoveries, and not just the failures, of more granular approaches. Considerable progress has been won by patient inquiry into aspects of moral life that remain problematical chiefly because of enduring conceptual and linguistic ambiguities. If there is a moral dimension of events, it is one that must be extricated from the subtleties of discourse, but also from the narrow and artificial straits of semantics. It is simply counterintuitive to suggest that those moral issues that have stood as the defining marks of entire lifetimes—even entire epochs—have been rooted in nothing more substantial than the parts of speech!

Moral Realism: Praise and Blame Understood

Praise and blame are the instruments as well as the record of moral appraisal and thus, like the law itself, especially vivid expressions of deeper and often impenetrably complex moral theories. It would not be an exaggeration to suggest that much of both criminal and civil law serves as the institutionalized form of praise and blame. So, too, are those features of early education that are aimed at character, those features of our interpersonal relationships that would be considered "improving," those self-critical episodes that generate new resolutions, even entirely new ways of living.

Both as an instrument and as a record, the activity and content of praise and blame have been subjected to assessments leading to divergent conclusions. The primary objectives of this book are to test the major conclusions and, subsequently, to defend one against the rest. The objective is that of marking out the true contours of praise and blame, the conditions of their valid application, their proper location within a conceptual space that is distinguishable from the world of personal preferences and social practices. To accomplish this, it is necessary to consider with respectful care theories that have located morality precisely within the world of personal preferences, the world of sentiment and desire. Thus far I have noted only a few of the more influential theorists (Hume, Ayer, Mackie) opposed to moral realism and their attachment to one or another conventionalist or psychological alternative. In response to them I have sketched in bare outline a defense of moral realism. To this point, the defense has been limited to showing that moral properties are neither queer nor ineffable, and that they are surely not merely conventional in any transparent sense of the term.

I have added to this a gloss on the social constructionist account, itself a conventionalist theory of morals according to which morality is but the triumph of one set of values over others in the serious matter of preserving social cohesion. Thus understood praise and blame express our deeper (perhaps "natural") sentiments, provide a means by which to control others, and prevail upon us to comport ourselves in ways pleasing to the community in which one seeks to gain or preserve membership. Theories of this sort, as we have seen, explain praise and blame not as ascriptions correctly or wrongly assigned to the real moral properties of actions, but as consequences of a certain type of natural constitution, shaped by local customs and values. Specifically rejected is the very notion of "real moral properties," as well as the suggestion that local customs and values are subject to valid external moral appraisals. Also rejected is that version of libertarianism that renders the actor subject to praise and blame owing to powers of autonomy, rational deliberation, and self-determination. What libertarianism fails to acknowledge, critics insist, is that those actions that generally call for moral appraisal are so inextricably bound up with matters of luck, of chance and contingency, of personal biogenetic and biographical influences as to render the actions in question either inevitable or inexplicable.

Sentimentalism, social constructionism, conventionalism, subjectivism, emotivism—these are the worthy alternatives to a theory of moral realism that includes objective standards for the assignment of praise and blame. In succeeding chapters, variants of each of these alternatives are considered in greater depth and with attention to relevant historical foundations. The alternative theories are various but do have in common grave reservations about the very concept of moral freedom in the most robust (libertarian) sense. They are, then, deterministic and no less so when developed as one or another version of compatibilism. On various grounds, these theories, which might be referred to generically as "nonrealist" theories, are found to be deficient, the very deficiencies pointing toward what is most defensible in theories of moral realism and libertarianism.

The conclusions sketched in this chapter become more defined in succeeding chapters. They yield a theory of moral realism that includes these main points: first, that praise and blame are rhetorical actions. Often but not always verbal, they function in ways at once evaluative and educative, juridical, and motivational. The proper target, subject, or object toward which they are rightly applied is an assumed or inferred "real moral property" of actors, actions, and events. Typically, the real moral property of the actor is "character," as this term encompasses those volitional, evaluative, deliberative, and affective powers and dispositions generative of aims and actions. The manifestations of these powers and dispositions are public and give the powers and dispositions themselves the status of a natural kind. In this, there is a similarity between, on the one hand, the relationship between natural and artificial languages and, on the other, the relationship between the behavioral expression of these dispositions and the moral ascriptions developed and refined within the culture.

In speaking of powers and dispositions it is useful to recall the distinction G. E. Moore makes between "rules of duty" and "ideal rules."[55] Moore draws attention to a commandment of the form. "Do not steal" and contrasts it with one such as, "Do not covet." The difference is fundamental in that the former reaches actual actions over which one may be expected to have full control, whereas the latter refers to feelings and desires that may often fall beyond the range of personal control. To forbear from *taking* what belongs to another is to exercise a power that is different from what would be needed in the case of not *desiring* what belongs to another. Throughout the present work the term "character" should be understood as referring to those dispositions that incline one toward obedience to "ideal rules," where complete success is achieved rarely, if at all. One committed to obedience at this level would be expected to follow "rules of duty" more or less in passing, for these impose far looser constraints on conduct than those set by ideal rules. Commitment to the latter reflects a perfectionist disposition that is just the enlargement and refinement of those moral properties that comprise character as such.

The functions served by moral appraisal (praise and blame) require special standing on the part of those engaged in it, and suitable powers on the part of those fit to be thus evaluated. The practical function of praise and blame is *moral judgment and improvement*, understood as the enlargement of one's actual powers of self-improvement, as well as the moral improvement of the community. As moral properties themselves are real properties, the function of praise and blame is to alter that actual state of affairs obtaining in the world and in the actor. It is to restore or improve the *health* of persons otherwise competent to live a moral form of life. What is relative within the entire process is so with respect to the defining nature of rational beings for whom the flourishing life has a point that is itself ineliminably moral.

A theory of moral realism, if consistent, is ontologically radical. It requires of any complete account of the contents of reality entities that are inescapably and irreducibly moral. As these cannot be reduced to, for example, human sentiments or cultural habits, they must be assumed to have ontological standing independent of any and all merely biosocial aspects of this or any other world. Thus, if moral properties are *in the world* it is not because we, too, are in that world, although we, too, are in that world.

What, then, is the relationship between real moral entities and entities such as ourselves? The question is too broad as stated. Clearly, "entities such as ourselves" may call for either an essentialist account or a descriptive anthropological account. The category "entities such as ourselves" on one of these accounts will indifferently include infants, the brain-dead, the profoundly retarded—whole clusters of beings utterly uncomprehending of moral properties. It may also include those of such defective character as to render them inaccessible to such properties, though otherwise cognitively competent. It may include still other enclaves of those who, owing to limited resources, have not cultivated the powers of comprehension by which moral properties come to be known. Analogically speaking, this state of ignorance is akin to the enclave of accomplished physicists who lived before the discovery of subatomic particles. The (anthropological) fact that no scientist was then aware of subatomic particles had no bearing whatever on the ontological standing of muons. The (anthropological) fact that some number of persons cannot discover the moral properties inhering in persons, actions, and events has no bearing on the praise and blame correctly applied to these persons, actions, and events.

Centrally, praise and blame are properly applied on the basis of real, natural properties, though never *merely* physical (behavioral) properties as such. Rather, real moral properties are *known*, not *sensed*, just as the properties constitutive of dwellings, battles, and parades are known rather than sensed. Just as objects are perceived as being blue because, among other considerations, they *are* blue, so events and actions are known to be morally weighted because they include knowable and known moral properties giving them this weight. Moreover, as the moral ascriptions assigned to such events and actions arise from cognitive and epistemic processes, they are corrigible and thus fundamentally different from sentiments, sensations, and emotions. Contrary to Hume's proposed sequencing, the thesis defended here requires a rational appraisal of events and actions if they are to generate or sustain sentiments of any sort. Passion therefore is (as it ought to be) in the service of reason, at least if the "passion" in question is of any moral consequence. That the thesis defended in this book is, in the current parlance, "cognitivist" should be by now obvious.

Ruled out by a theory of moral realism is that *causal* account of praise and blame by which moral appraisals are thought to be (somehow) produced in those making the judgment or rendered efficacious in controlling others. One is not "caused" to praise in any sense akin to being "caused" to be thirsty or tired. Neither does praise (or blame) cause its target to do something in the way that coercion or low blood pressure or hypnosis might cause one to drop a glass. In the face of such declamations as "Well done!" or "Shame on you!", the response of the recipient is not based on the acoustic achievements of the speaker but on the rich congeries of factors previously discussed. Finally, one is not correctly praised or blamed "luckily" for, as noted in chapter 3, it is one of the aims of praise and blame to extract from the target-actions and events precisely those ingredients falling beyond the agent's powers of control or even contemplation, and reserving moral appraisal to what remains.

As will be developed in succeeding chapters, the very intelligibility of praise and blame arises from introspectively known powers of action and restraint, these subject to projection onto creatures of the same or similar type. Properly understood the objects of praise and blame are actions and events that alter by design the real value inhering in persons and things. Broad cultural variations in the targets of praise and blame signal variations in the comprehension of the meaning of actions and events rather than in the core precepts of morally competent beings. The comprehension of moral properties requires robust epistemic resources. There is no reason to expect uniformity of achievement. Similarly, there is also no a priori basis on which to foreclose the possibility of the enlargement of moral knowledge. Rather, it is to be expected that the comprehension of the moral realm will be progressive just in case it is subjected to the same disciplined, critical scrutiny that has guided progress in the other departments of knowledge. Indeed, an implicit defense of moral realism is that it provides the best explanation of moral progress itself.

2.

CONSTITUTIVE LUCK: ON BEING DETERMINED

Hermodorus the Poet made certaine verses in honour of
Antigonus, in which he called him the sonne of Phoebus; to whom
he replied; *My friend, He that emptieth my close-stoole knoweth
well, there is no such matter.* His is but a man at all assaies:
And if of himselfe he be a man ill borne, the Empire of the
whole world cannot restore him. —MICHEL DE MONTAIGNE'S
ESSAYES, bk. I, chap. XLII

"Man has free choice, or otherwise counsels, exhortations,
commands, prohibitions, rewards and punishments would be in
vain". —THOMAS AQUINAS, *SUMMA THEOLOGIAE*, Q. 83 Art.1

Einstein and Helen of Troy

Moral ascriptions are not rigidly tied to consequences. Rather, they typically
carry with them the assignment of responsibility such that nonmoral ascriptions are employed where no responsible agent can be identified. Outcomes
might be regarded as "tragic" or "fortunate," "pleasing" or "disgusting,"
without the added moral weight of responsibility. But to judge the actions
leading to such outcomes as "laudable" or "condemnable" is to assign responsibility. This very assignation entails an appraisal of the actor's competence, the actor's overall psychological makeup. Ceteris paribus, an action
is laudable when it expresses laudable aims competently realized in the face
of opposing forces or competing impulses to which many or even most other
persons would yield.

Except in adjudicative or other formal contexts where experts are assumed to be needed, such psychological appraisals are at once self-referen-
tial and conventional: *How would I act in the circumstance? How do most
persons act in such circumstances?* As will be discussed below, moral consensus is routinely invoked in attempts to justify or simply explain the judgments reached in appraising the actions of others. Are the actions in question
exceptional (i.e., uncommon)? Are they of a sort one would regard as personally daunting? The magnitude of praise or blame is then scaled according
to the rarity of the performance and the judged counterforces thought to
operate in such settings. The standards generally applied are both cognitive
and affective: It is assumed that most persons have the ability to comprehend
the nature and demands of the challenge they face, and that most persons,
confronting such challenges, will respond in a predictably emotional manner. The child on the verge of being run down by a speeding vehicle is thus

known to be imperiled, and the peril itself triggers the emotions of fear, alarm, excitement.

Failure to behave according to the moral consensus invites blame only in those cases in which the necessary and general level of competence is thought or shown to be present. Being ignorant of what is expected of one in such instances fails as an excuse. Lloyd Fields records the widely adopted attitude when he writes that

> a person's acceptance of certain moral principles is a constituent of his character. So a person who accepts morally bad moral principles has, to that extent, a defect of character. It is a sufficient condition of an agent's being morally responsible for his action that his action be indicative of a defect of character. Thus, a person who acts in accordance with morally bad moral principles shows a defect of character and is therefore morally responsible for what he has done.[1]

Clearly, one of the most common themes in the literature of saintly and heroic deeds, this covering a great span of time and welter of cultures, is this feature of overcoming. Not only are external obstacles considered in this light but, perhaps more significantly, the internal states and conditions that must be overcome if one is to rise to otherwise unexpected levels of achievement. This is as much the case when persons of very limited ability turn in performances above the average level as when persons of great ability accomplish even more than one might have predicted. In his own trenchant analysis, Richard Swinburne has summarized what seems to be the standard view of the relationship between the will and our judgment of moral worthiness:

> The most praise belongs to the action (or inaction) for which most effort was needed to overcome contrary desire; the most blame belongs to the action (or inaction) which could have been avoided with little effort. It follows also that an agent is not praiseworthy for doing a supererogatory good action unless he was subject to some contrary desire.[2]

But the standard view spawns a paradox. If, indeed, it is the strength of a competing desire that is the measure of the praise or blame owed to an action, then one who very greatly desires to do evil—but stops short—is more praiseworthy than one who harbors no such desire at all. Moreover, if the desire is both intense and would lead to a monstrously malevolent act, the person who forbears from gratifying this desire would, on the standard view, qualify for very special praise. The standard view, we see, when stretched to the end of its conceptual tether, installs the worst of persons as the best of persons, and this can't be.

What, after all, is the standard view seeking to capture about moral life? For the person whose desires are so muted and trite, there is nothing to overcome, and on one understanding of a moral life, such a person is simply not living it. Such a life is lacking in precisely those tensions, conflicts, and competing desires that give moral life its cast and color. On yet another understanding, however, richly indebted to Aristotle, the whole point of cultivating the virtues and putting them into daily practice is to transform oneself into a person for whom virtue has become "second nature." The very habit of virtue now relieves one of the burden of competing desires.

There is a locus between desires so grotesque as to leave no room for praise, even when the agent finally refuses to act on them, and desires so minimal as to spare the agent all forms of moral conflict. It is one of the tasks of a developed moral theory to locate that point or place, and the task of a developed psychological theory to identify the basis on which the agent becomes able to do the same.

In such matters it is always tempting to rely on what is sometimes called the common moral sense or sentiment. Turning again to Swinburne's *Responsibility and Atonement*, we find an argument for consensus in matters of this sort. On Swinburne's account, what makes actions good or bad is the possession of a certain universal property, as he calls it, "which has some connection with what many others of us recognize as making actions importantly worth doing or not doing."[3] Sound as far as it goes, such reliance can also yield profoundly counterintuitive outcomes, just in case the consensus is formed by morally wayward or defective majorities. Moreover, on those moral issues where there is the widest agreement within a given community, the issues themselves tend to be less than grave. It is where there are competing and fundamental interests *of consequence* that agreement fails to be widespread and in such circumstances the consensus is either ill-defined or shifting. Again, finding the moral space between controlled but grotesque desires and something akin to apathy is a task requiring resources that may include, but surely must go beyond, the collected moral sense of a given enclave, no matter how populous.

In the matter of common perceptions and sentiments, there is one context in which general dispositions and the actions tied to them would seem to defy the central canons of morality. Research leaves no doubt but that favors attach to physically attractive persons, and costs are endured by those perceived to be lacking in such purely "constitutive" endowments. Those who depart significantly from the average type within a given culture receive benefits when the departure is in the direction judged to be "attractive" and suffer disadvantages when their differences are perceived as undesirable. According to one celebrated theory, the Trojan War never would have taken place were the nose of Helen of Troy just a bit longer. If war itself needs a moral justification, something other than a face should be needed to launch a thousand ships!

Clearly, no one is praiseworthy merely because the genetic lottery churned out a physiognomy and body-type that others at a given time and within a given culture regard as beautiful; and no one is blameworthy for physical deformities or features others find ugly. Although there is ready agreement on such obvious points, the evidence still leaves no doubt but that the world at large favors the one class and puts the other at a disadvantage, undeservedly in both instances. It would be eccentric in light of this to go full circle and attempt to redeem the practice on the grounds that the practices are widespread! Here the well-known barrier between "is" and "ought" really should be impenetrable. There are good reasons for investigating the basis of such practices, while recognizing that resulting explanations would not of themselves constitute justifications.

It may be, for example, that the physically attractive excite pleasurable sensations that then must be interpreted or rationalized by the percipient. The result might be a species of cognitive consistency. Thus: Would I be so pleasantly disposed by someone who was not an exceptional person? Would I enjoy such sensations "merely" on the basis of rank appearances? Hume argued that there was a kinship between the moral sense and the aesthetic sense, both of them based on the feelings of pleasure they excite, and this very feeling itself bound up with considerations of usefulness. As he says, the pleasure "is owing to the beauty, which we find in every thing that is useful."[4] Current reliance on evolutionary biology for explanations of these tendencies is largely a refinement of Hume's "utility theory" of the sentiments. But credible or not, such explanations scarcely *justify* the practice of conferring moral superiority on the basis of physical attributes.

Favoring and disfavoring different physical types might well arise, as Hume thought, from the elicit movement of aesthetic judgments into the moral space in which praise and blame are properly located. There is widespread agreement within but not across cultures on those forms of art, music, and architecture that instantiate beauty and forms that fall far short of the ideal. If Mozart's compositions are "good" because they are beautiful, there may well develop the tendency to regard what is beautiful as therefore "good," the latter term now carrying moral and not merely aesthetic weight. So perhaps the advantages enjoyed by those perceived as being beautiful are the result of a conflation of the aesthetic and the moral, and the conflation of both with the useful. It is the task of a developed moral theory to go beyond such tendencies and test their coherence.

If praise and blame are misplaced when attached to physical phenotypes, they are no less misdirected when assigned to those judged to be intellectually superior or inferior. Most would assume that Einstein had a far better brain than the standard issue. On the assumption that his brain made his discoveries possible, why would we heap praise on Einstein himself? Why heap praise on a genius he had nothing to do with *personally*? Similarly, to act bravely in fearful situations presupposes a developed capacity for fear. Absent fear, there is no bravery as such. Absent conscience, there is no *mens rea*. Just in case one's motivational, emotional, and cognitive resources are largely set by the combination of genetic endowment, acculturation, and the powers and dispositions more or less cemented by these two influences, it would seem that nothing one does is validly subject to praise or blame. As Montaigne declared, one who is ill-born cannot be restored even by "the whole empire of the world." In this connection, Voltaire, who had read his Montaigne, thought it absurd to believe that all of the heavens should be causally governed by fixed laws and that a little creature, five feet tall, could act solely according to his own caprice.

The aim of this chapter is first to establish that such conclusions arise from a deterministic psychology capable, if accepted, of absorbing the entire sphere of moral thought; and, second, to argue that such a psychology deserves less fidelity than it has enjoyed. If, on the understanding to be developed and defended in this chapter, praise and blame are misplaced when attached either to physical or to intellectual phenotypes, then they are comparably misplaced when assigned on the basis of motivational and emotional resources that are no more than endowed or conditioned features of one's general physiology.

Who Needs Virtue? Challenges to Socrates

As with so much in moral philosophy, the various positions one might take on these matters were sketched, when they were not fully developed, in Plato's dialogues. Perhaps most germane to the issue at hand are the passages in *Republic* where Plato's brothers, Glaucon and Adeimantus, along with Thrasymachus, reduce justice and morality to a set of conventions.[5] Those with the best physical and psychological constitutions have no need of such conventions for, at base, all that is entailed by so-called justice is the right to be left alone, to pursue what pleases one, in response to one's own desires and motives. As the very best persons could not be obstructed by the weaker, they have no need of the protections afforded by such conventions. What moves persons finally is their appetitive motivation (*epithumia*) and the desire for more and more of whatever pleases (*pleonexia*). This version of the social contract is presented by Glaucon as the best course for the ordinary person who surely would be worse off were he to depend on his own limited resources. John Cooper observes that, in this,

> Glaucon mimics Thrasymachus and calls such people "weak" and "no true men" (359b1–2)—if they were really strong and self-reliant, as true men should be, they would find the means to get away even with openly flaunting their disregard for the terms of the agreement, if their pursuit of their gratification made that necessary.[6]

Socrates' reply addresses one part of the challenge but not the other. He insists that Glaucon and Adeimantus recognize the difference between desires and *needs*, arguing that communities were formed not for the purpose of gratifying hedonic motives but to supply what each person actually requires if life is to be sustained. From this understanding it is but a few steps—though neither sure nor short—to the conclusion that the possession of virtue is itself a basic good.

On the question of fortunately being the right sort of person, the Socrates of Plato's *Republic* is explicitly hereditarian, as when he proposes that the class of Guardians must come about through eugenic schemes. The Hesiodic "men of gold, men of brass, men of iron" is called a convenient fiction, but the plan to breed Guardians is decidedly not offered as myth. The complex matter of phenotypic heritability aside, Socrates may speak for legions when concluding that nurturing can do just so much, and that, absent the right constitution, the ceiling on virtue is set rather close to the floor. As with Helen's physiognomy and Einstein's brain, candidacy for praise and blame, on this account, would seem to some uncertain extent determined.

Free Will and Determinism (Again)

As if it were necessary to say, this *quaestio vexata* is not to be settled here. One plausibly aspires to no more than clarifying the question and then working out the graver implications. There are five reasonably defensible positions on the issue, as well as numerous shadings of each. First there is the resigned admission of failure in principle to produce a decisive argument on either side of the issue. Kant's antinomies reign here, relieved only by his famous dictum, that, for purposes of morality, it is sufficient that freedom be "thinkable" rather than provable. In his Preface to the second edition of the first *Critique*, he puts it this way:

> Morality does not, indeed, require that freedom should be understood, but only that it should not contradict itself, and so should at least allow of being thought, and that as thus thought it should place no obstacle in the way of a free act (viewed in another relation) likewise conforming to the mechanism of nature.[7]

Then there are the two comparably radical positions: those of radical autonomy and radical determinism. The defender of radical autonomy requires some means by which actions arise from conditions or states or powers that are not themselves "determined" by sources external to the actor's own agency. The defender of radical determinism must offer explanations that do not presuppose an audience whose powers of choice undermine the thesis itself. As a way out of the difficulties borne by these radical positions, there are versions of "compatibilism," of which Kant's is a special case.[8] The usual forms of compatibilism would eat their metaphysical cake and have it, too. Finally, there are versions of what might be called the "unintelligibility thesis," according to which the very question of whether or not the will is free is either meaningless or based on an essentially lexical mistake. John Locke defended this position, and his argument will be examined later in this chapter.

Perhaps the most economical statement of radical determinism is Galen Strawson's rendition of what he has called the "Basic Argument":

> (1) Nothing can be *causa sui*—nothing can be the cause of itself. (2) In order to be truly morally responsible for one's actions one would have to be *causa sui*, at least in certain mental respects. (3) Therefore nothing can be truly morally responsible.[9]

The basic argument is adopted by those who require of any mental or moral science that it be consistent with what is taken to be the authoritative science; namely, physics. The tradition here is venerable and largely unbroken. David Hartley was among the first and by any account the most rigorous of the defenders of the basic argument in the Enlightenment. Expressly committed to Newtonian science and what he took to be its unavoidable implications for a science of mental life, he summarizes the authorized position succinctly:

> By the Mechanism of human Actions I mean, that each Action results from the previous Circumstances of Body and Mind, in the same manner, and with the same Certainty, as other Effects do from their mechanical causes; so that a person cannot do indifferently either of the Actions A and its contrary a, while the previous Circumstances are the same; but is under an absolute Necessity of doing one of them, and that only. If by Free-will be meant a Power of beginning Motion . . . according to the Opinion of Mechanism, as here explained, Man has no such power.[10]

It nearly goes without saying that the entire thrust of a voluntarist or an incompatibilist theory is that persons are, indeed, the causes of their intended actions, fully possessed of the power to begin a course of action, so the Basic Argument begins with a major premise that begs the question at issue. In opposition to it one might stand with Edward Pols and contend that

> the causes of what the mind does are to be found by attending to the mind itself. [Its] achievements are adequately explained only if we are prepared to say that *mind itself* performed them.[11]

But the Basic Argument is powerful, the major premise compelling, and able defenders present in numbers. In *The Non-Reality of Free Will*, Richard Double asks straight out if the "positive and negative exemplars of freedom . . . stand for distinguishable non-linguistic classes of types of entities" and concludes that they do not.[12] There is therefore no need to evaluate arguments for or against freedom and determinism, for these very arguments are based on categorical distinctions that are ontologically empty. Double presents a wide variety of challenges to the concept of free will, most of them leading not to a refutation of libertarianism but to the conclusion that the concept itself is incoherent or intractable. Against moral realism, he avails himself of the old standby, color: "The fact that we *see* the color blue does not provide any weight for the direct realist's theory over indirect realism."[13] He then adds the now-conventional proviso that "the *moral* . . . cannot influence behavior unless it works through some psychological mechanism."[14] As noted in chapter 1, however, the fact that we see the color blue provides as much weight for the direct realist's theory as that theory requires. As for the allegedly required "mechanism," a comment is in order here and then further consideration later in the chapter.

The determinist thesis depends on notions of causation, usually of a mechanistic sort. There is, however a nonmechanistic sense of determination that can be extricated from any given theory of causality. Richard Sorabji has provided an illuminating discussion of this in his analysis of Aristotle's position on the question of determinism. Finding Aristotle to be an indeterminist, Sorabji notes that the connection drawn by Aristotle is between determinism and *necessity*, rather than determinism and *causation*. One can hold the thesis that the relationship between x and y is one of necessity, such that, given the occurrence or presence of x, it follows of necessity that y occurs. But this can be asserted without holding any additional thesis about causation. Understood this way, there may well be a necessary relationship between some feature of a person and that person's course of action, but without this relationship in any way compromising the person's moral responsibility. Sorabji goes on to say that

> I have not defined determinism as a view which denies us moral responsibility. The latter idea, often known as "hard determinism," is comparatively rare, and was rarer still in antiquity.[15]

Staying with Aristotle further, but here to address the supposed impossibility of the causa sui, consider his well-known examination of the sense in which someone's death is "fated." We find this in his *Metaphysics* (bk. VI, chap. 3):

  a. If the man eats spicy food he will be thirsty.
  b. If thirsty, he will leave the dwelling and go to the well.
  c. If he goes to the well now, highwaymen will be there.
  d. If he arrives when they do, they will kill him.
  e. He eats spicy food.[16]

Here, then, is the scenario that permits Aristotle to ask whether the man's death is the inevitable outcome of a chain of factors such that its occurrence is rigidly determined. In analyzing Aristotle's arguments, Richard Sorabji has challenged Cicero and others who find a "hard determinism" in the works. At 1027b12–14 Aristotle takes the decisive step; in Sorabji's words, "the meeting at the well has no cause at all," and this because the man's thirst had nothing to do with the meeting. That is, the highwaymen's arrival and the man's thirst are utterly independent events. This absence of a cause "saves the meeting from being necessary."[17] As Sorabji notes in this same connection, Aristotle exempts rank coincidences from any and every causal matrix and surely would reject the proposition that what is caused is (therefore) necessitated.

How, then, does Aristotle come to terms with the "causa sui" conundrum cited by Galen Strawson? In the *Nicomachean Ethics* he deals with it straightaway. The drunken offender may be out of his wits owing to alcohol but it was in his power not to get drunk in the first place.

> If a person does what knows will make him unjust, he will be unjust voluntarily. It does not follow, however, that, if he wishes, he will stop being unjust and be just. For neither does the ill person become well like this; but he is ill voluntarily by living incontinently and ignoring his doctors, if that was what happened. At the time, it was open to him not to be ill, but it is no longer once he has thrown away his chance.[18]

For Aristotle, life presents innumerable choice points and, at each one, the course of action is open. Choices made thereupon may foreclose future choices such that, in time, with the earlier chances having been thrown away, one has, as it were, made one's future. Summarizing the argument, Sorabji states that "voluntariness involves not only the absence of certain excusing factors, but also its being *up to us* to act or refrain".[19]

It is clear from many passages in Aristotle's ethical and psychological works that he takes the actor himself to be the cause of the action; the actor as a deliberative, rational being with goals and powers. If, in the course of an inattentive and squandered use of options, the actor has predisposed himself in a wayward manner, he is not only no less responsible but is ever more responsible for what might seem like a "fated" end. Here we find not events without causes but events that are personally caused. The cause of the action is the will of the actor and the "cause" of the will is the actor himself.

Causation, however, as it operates in the conventional sense captured in Galen Strawson's position, persists as a most perplexing concept, no clearer at all for the habitual reference to "mechanisms" of one or another sort, often by a kind of airy implication. Indeed, "mechanism" in compatibilist and determinist theories functions as something of a deus ex machina, without much effort expended in explanations of just how the thing is supposed to work. Then, too, there is that most fundamental ontological question as to just how many different kinds of "stuff" occupy reality. Voltaire's amazement presumably would be abated if he accepted the proposition that not everything in the universe is merely physical, and that some entities, namely *moral* ones, have the special property of self-governance (autonomy). To accept this, however, is to accept dread dualism, an option no more appealing to Voltaire than to most of today's philosophical practitioners. Tied to this, in ways subtle and significant, is the suggestive question as to whether the truth of moral freedom would ipso facto vindicate dualism.

On this knotty question of causality, adherents of both radical theories face a hardship. Defenders of radical autonomy seem to allow a swinging gate without hinges, while defenders of radical determinism affirm a thesis so at variance with the daily and even momentary experiences of the human race as to appear to be less than fully sincere. Recall that when Boswell tried in vain to enlist Dr. Johnson into the debate he was greeted with the flat reply, "Sir, we know we have free will, and that puts an end on it."[20]

Where one billiard ball, striking a neighbor, imparts motion to the latter without any consideration of volition entering into the event, it would be strange to say that a person in the market for an automobile finally acquired a Fiat without any consideration of volition entering into the event. In ordinary nonphilosophical discourse, it would be more apt to say that the motion of the second billiard ball was caused by the first, but that the acquisition of the Fiat expressed the buyer's wishes (or even whims). In the former case, motion was inevitable; in the latter, the outcome was subject to choice. Where the ball could not have done otherwise than move, the customer could have had a change of mind or simply the power to resist initial impulses.

Here, then, is the classical distinction between a *cause* and a *power*, a distinction that tapped the energies of Hobbes, Locke, Hume, Reid, Mill—the list is lengthy. Several of the more influential proposals will be considered. If constitutive luck is at the bottom of things praised and blamed, then it is in virtue of being a link, even the first link, in a causal chain that culminates where it does *of necessity*. After all, there's a difference between random events (e.g., the emission of radioactive particles) and intended actions. The latter are understood as initiated with some end in view, but it is not the end that works backward in time to trigger an event that might bring it about. Rather, there must be some state or condition within the actor that narrows the field of attention and renders certain courses of action more salient or compelling than others. These states and conditions are inextricably bound up with the very nature—the very "constitution"—of the actor. Fish can live under water but not out of it. The type or kind of entity one is, therefore, establishes certain needs and conditions of survival, these then causing sensations, thoughts, or plans of a given sort which in turn impel actions coherently related to the antecedent conditions. To act in a certain way, then, is to instantiate a certain type of being, in a certain condition or state, such that the best explanation of the action is in terms of the constitutive nature of the actor in combination with circumstantial facts. Of the many who have defended such a thesis, both Hobbes and Locke were especially influential. It is useful, then, to begin with a brief review of Hobbes's *Leviathan* (1651), pt. II, chap. 21, "Of the LIBERTY of subjects."[21]

Hobbes and Locke as Compatibilists

There is a clear difference between the sense in which dead matter is influenced by the laws of gravitation and the sense in which, say, one is influenced by municipal parking ordinances or by an armed robber. It has been argued by many, over a course of centuries, that a completely determined cosmos is nonetheless compatible with a species of freedom; that is, freedom from duress, threats of harm, legislative impositions, physical barriers to movement and action. What such a cosmos is not compatible with is really existing, authentic free will.

As there are so many and various defenses and criticisms of compatibilism, it is wise at the outset to make clear the version that will be subjected to appraisal in these pages. To make this clear, it is also necessary to contrast it with its incompatibilist alternative. Mark Heller's economical summary of one version of compatibilism serves the present purposes:

> Consider the following relatively simple statement of what it is for an action to be free.
>
> (FA) Necessarily [S's action A is free if and only if: S wanted to do A, S would do A, and if S wanted to refrain from doing A, S would refrain from doing A]
>
> If FA is true, then so is compatibilism, because FA allows for S's actions to be free even if S's desires are completely determined by previous events—as long as S's actions follow from her desires they are free actions, regardless of how S came to have the desires she has.[22]

This version of compatibilism would admit as an instance of FA an action arising from a narcotically or hypnotically induced desire, or one brought about by direct stimulation of targeted regions of the brain. Indeed, it might well admit actions performed in the face of coercion and threats of gross bodily harm, assuming that it is the desire to avoid these that is satisfied by acts of compliance. Such instances ground a notion of "freedom" clearly at odds with ordinary understandings. What one generally has in mind in regarding an action as free is that the entire sequence of internal conditions and external options culminating in the action did not render that particular outcome determined by anything other than that actor's own powers of agency. The difference between what is taken to be an addiction and what is understood to be a very strong inclination is that the latter can be resisted whereas the former is understood as arising from an essential alteration of the consumer's basic physiological processes. All this is to say that, even at the outset of an analysis of determinism and libertarianism, it is clear that there are weak and strong versions of the competing theories, and that a criticism that may seem fatal to one version might well be absorbed nonfatally by another.

A classical version of compatibilism was framed by Thomas Hobbes, whose thesis was the specific target of Cudworth's counterproposals. Liberty and freedom for Hobbes are nothing more than the absence of opposition to motion and thus can be ascribed equally to living things and dead matter—as aptly to a river constrained by its banks as to a person constrained by chains. Alas, "that which is not subject to Motion is not subject to Impediment."[23] As it is the person who moves, it is meaningless to speak of a free "will" or free "desire." What faces opposition is the behaving person, a conclusion that Locke will endorse and enlarge. On this understanding,

> *Liberty* and *Necessity* are *Consistent*; As in the water, that hath not only *liberty*, but a *necessity* of descending by the Channel: so likewise in the Actions which men voluntarily doe; which (because they proceed from their will) proceed from *liberty*; and yet because every act of mans will, and every desire, and inclination proceedeth from some cause, and that from another cause, which causes in a continuall chaine (whose first link is the hand of God the first of all causes) proceed from *necessity*. So that to him that could see the connexion of those causes, the *necessity* of all mens voluntary actions, would appeare manifest.[24]

If Hobbes's thesis is redolent of the challenges laid down by Glaucon, Adeimantus, and Thrasymachus, Hobbes's own perspective was beholden less to the past than to the leading-edge science of his day, to the new science of Galileo and its mechanistic foundations. Any moralist or political theorist thus committed will find his subject matter in varieties of motion itself. The larger objective of such a theorist is a scientific psychology of the physiological-behavioristic sort, for the subjects of the science are the external and internal conditions that render specific actions inevitable.

The skeletal version of this psychology is summarized in *Leviathan* (pt. 1, chap. 6). It is reductionistic, for, following Galileo's "resolutive-compositive" method, Hobbes must begin by breaking down complex behavior into its constituent parts and their position within the overall causal chain. Following this scheme, he locates the initial source of all voluntary movement in what he calls "endeavours," "the small beginnings of Motion, within the body of Man."[25] These are of two forms, either toward or away from things.

In the former case, the endeavours are expressed as appetites; in the latter, as aversions. Here, then, is an early form of "hormic" or drive-based, behaviorism, prefigured in ancient Greek philosophy by Epicurus and his disciples. Could the chain of events from the earliest endeavour to its succeeding links be disclosed, the veritable necessity of the behavior would be manifest.

One can only wonder how Hobbes's "endeavours" are to be understood, though the need for them is transparent if the "resolutive" phase of the program is not to be drawn into an infinite regress. In more modern times, there were two psychological theories approximating this phase of Hobbes's scheme, one advanced by William James and another by Clark Hull. James and Hull differ in so many respects that it is hazardous to cite them in the same paragraph, but there are good reasons for so doing. In James's attempt at a coherent theory of volition, however, there is a Hobbes-like starting point—similar to the "endeavours"—whereupon authentically agentic powers are engaged. In Hull's drive-reduction theory, a thoroughgoing Hobbesian mechanistic psychology is retained from start to finish. The similarities are not accidental, James's "functionalist" psychology being an unintended harbinger of behaviorism.

In *Psychology, Briefer Course*, James identifies the conditions necessary for there to be volition at all: "*A supply of ideas of the various movements that are possible, left in the memory by experience of their involuntary performance, is thus the first prerequisite of the voluntary life.*"[26]

The organism, biologically and behaviorally active, is predisposed to any number and variety of stereotypical patterns of action. As these occur in their various combinations and with varying strength and frequency, they are included in the memory stores of the system that, later, can be tapped by one who now *intends* to achieve certain goals. Where there is no stored movement-pattern, but there is nonetheless a goal, the actor can do no more than *wish*, "but if we believe that the end is in our power, we *will* that the desired feeling, having or doing shall be real."[27]

In James's theory, the actor comes to have active powers, powers of deployment and restraint, that are volitionally pulled from the storehouse of movement-patterns built up over the course of time. As the buzzing world of physical stimulation is filtered out by the percipient who *selects* what is of interest in it, so, too, is the thick inventory of behavioral possibilities inert until the agent, with an end in view, picks out the ones required by the task at hand. Hobbes's "endeavours," on the other hand, remain the atomistic first-terms in a deterministic series in which active power, selectivity, intention, and authentic volition have no real part or place.

Hull's theory as with Hobbes's, is a drive-based theory of action, the "drives" being such sensible states as hunger and thirst, but these reflecting what at the molecular level are basic tissue-needs.[28] In Hullian terms, Hobbes's "small beginnings of motion" would be states or conditions of the body not sensed as such by the actor but giving rise to sensations capable of impelling action. The state of the tissue determines the quality and intensity of the drive, the latter typically but one of a number of such drives of a competing or an augmenting nature. If all such states are known and quantified, the necessity of actions heretofore considered voluntary would become clear, to paraphrase a basic tenet of Hull's theory.

Restricted to basic modes of adaptation, integrally related to survival itself, the thesis succeeds at the level of common sense. To see someone running toward the sink and thrusting his hand under the cold water is to witness an event whose volitional attributes cease to be mysterious once one learns that the actor has just been burned and is in great pain. The actor *chooses* to put the injured hand under water, but the choice is directed by a state of affairs that is virtually determinative. By the same token, the consumption of food and liquid, the heating of houses, the forming of friendships—the myriad undertakings of a lifetime—arise from needs, desires, motives, and aspirations such that knowing all of these renders the activities themselves intelligible and reasonable. Were it otherwise the conduct would seem to be, and would be, simply bizarre.

No defender of radical autonomy (often referred to as "incompatibilist freedom" owing to its rejection of compatibilism), however, has ever suggested that autonomy requires the rejection of causal efficacy. Rather, the defender of autonomy locates the efficacy within the actor as agent and not as patient. To be autonomous is to be self-directed, not undirected. One of the leading contemporary advocates of incompatibilist freedom, Robert Kane, makes the point by identifying the actor as having "ultimate responsibility."[29] If Hobbes can avoid the dilemma of infinite regress by postulating "endeavours," the defender of autonomy is at liberty to choose his own starting-point, which typically is taken to be the agent's own will.

John Locke extended the Hobbesian conception of volition in a manner consistent with an overall Newtonian psychology as developed in *An Essay Concerning Human Understanding*.[30] The main lines of analysis are set down in Book II, Chapter XXI, "Of Power." Locke distinguishes here between active and passive powers, the former having the ability to cause changes, the latter referring to the capacity to be changed. Our active powers are of two sorts, those that pertain to the course of our thinking, and those that pertain to the course of our bodily actions. In both instances, the power to initiate and direct actions is, says Locke, "that which we call the *Will*."[31] The power can be present without being applied. The term Locke reserves for the actual application of the will is "volition" or "willing." The mind's will to deploy or withhold power is then said to be voluntary such that "whatsoever action is performed without such a thought of the mind, is called *involuntary*."[32]

Locke then accounts for the ideas of liberty and necessity as arising from the experience everyone has of these powers and their deployment both in the matter of thought and of action. What it means to be free, then, is to be able to direct one's thoughts and actions according to the preferences of one's own mind. In a labored passage in which Locke draws out the implications of his analysis, he argues that one may have the power to direct one's thoughts and actions but lack the power to bring about the desired ends. That an action is voluntary is not the same as its being at liberty. Where there is no thought or volition there is no liberty. Nevertheless, there can be thought and volition without there being liberty. In Locke's own example, a man may go to sleep only to awaken in the company of a friend he has longed to see. He chooses to remain with this person and converse at length, unaware of the fact that he is locked in the room and could not leave even if he wished. What can be said in this instance is that the man remains in the room voluntarily, but is not at liberty. Thus,

> liberty is not an idea belonging to volition, or preferring; but to the person having the power of doing or forebearing to do, according as the mind shall choose or direct. Our idea of liberty reaches as far as that power and no farther.[33]

Locke now can declare the utter impropriety of the question of whether the will is free, being akin to the question of whether sleep is swift or virtue square! Liberty is not an idea that attaches to the will but to the ability of the *person* to achieve desired ends. Both liberty and the will are powers, so it is idle to ask whether a power has a power. The root question is therefore not whether the will but the *man* is free, possessed of the power to attain desired ends as these are conceived in self-directed thought and realized through voluntary actions.

More to the point at issue, is the actor *free to will*? On this question Locke and Hobbes converge in their respective analyses. An action for Locke is free when it depends on the actor's volition, not the actor's preferences. As he says, a man at the edge of a precipice may prefer to jump upward to a height of twenty yards but cannot do it. What he can do is choose to jump or not jump. As leaping downward is in his power, he may be at liberty to do this. Clearly he is not at liberty to jump *up* twenty yards. Willing, as Locke has argued, is an act of the mind productive of certain thoughts and actions. So the right answer to the question of just what it is that determines the will is, alas, the mind itself.[34] The states of mind that thus determine the will are finally states of desire and it is these that determine the will to frame the thoughts and action-patterns occasioned by conditions of pleasure and pain. In a passage that summarizes what is now called the internalist theory of ethics, Locke concludes:

> Let a man be ever so well persuaded of the advantages of virtue, that it is as necessary to a man who has any great aims in this world, or hopes in the next, as food to life; yet, till he hungers or thirsts after righteousness, till he *feels an uneasiness* in the want of it, his *will* will not be determined to any action in pursuit of this confessed greater good."[35]

What Locke is at pains to avoid is the invocation of occult powers floating freely above the plane of experience, thought, and feeling; powers that Gideon Yaffee has dubbed *the illusive Something*.[36] Yaffee records Locke's cautious and limited libertarian position which would chasten that "inquisitive Mind of Man" leading him to believe "that a Man is not free at all, if he be not as free to will as he is to act what he wills."[37] Again, it would require some sort of "illusive Something," on this account, to support that "liberty of indifference" by which willed actions were brought about by nothing but an unhinged freedom.

As with the "endeavours" of Hobbes, the Lockean hungers and thirsts, the feelings of uneasiness, are the necessary and proximate causes of the will's determinations. What Bentham will later call the twin masters of pleasure and pain are identified by Locke as the very stuff of moral attributions. Granting that pleasure and pain are aroused in mind and body to varying degrees by "the operation of certain objects," "what has an aptness to produce pleasure in us is that we call *good*, and what is apt to produce pain in us we call *evil*."[38]

Far from being a constraint on liberty, these very determinations of the will stand as "the end and use of our liberty," for what is liberty for if not the deployment of our powers of thought and action in pursuit of happiness? Lest there be any doubt as to the reach of happiness in this Lockean scheme, he bravely discloses its limits: "God Almighty himself is under the necessity of being happy!"[39] To be spared the impulses to pleasure, the impulses to avoid pain, is to court self-destruction: "Is it worth the name of freedom to be at liberty to play the fool, and draw shame and misery upon a man's self?"[40]

Rounding out this section, a return to Hartley is useful for he speaks more directly to contemporary philosophers with, a neurocognitive orientation. Hartley is comfortable with, and even confident of, volitional accounts of actions:

> "If Free-will be defined the Power of doing what a Person desires or wills to do, of deliberating, suspending, choosing, etc., or of resisting the motives of Sensuality, Ambition, Resentment, etc., Free-will, under certain Limitations, is not only consistent with the Doctrine of Mechanism, but even flows from it."[41]

That is, given the antecedent motive or desire, the ensuing action aptly answers to it in a way that renders the chosen course of action not only consistent with a mechanistic theory but an obvious implication of it.

Compatibilism and Internalism

Internalism has a long pedigree and many contemporary defenders. Defined in the most general terms, it is the thesis according to which one who has a reason to act is, by that fact, motivated to act. In the strong form, internalism supposes that the connection between having good reasons for action and having the corresponding motive is one of necessity. Internalists acknowledge that there are common violations committed, in that persons often hold something to be very important, conferring great value on it, and nevertheless feel no direct motive to act on its behalf. But advocates of internalism regard these exceptions as evidence of insufficient rationality in the circumstance. Robert Johnson, in a critical appraisal of the thesis, summarizes the internalist's treatment of the exceptions thus:

> The plausibility of internalism is no more diminished by the fact that values do not always produce their expected motivational responses than the plausibility of dispositional theories of colour is diminished by the fact that colours do not always produce their expected visual responses. . . . The plausibility of the internalist doctrine thus rests on its conditional formulation: that it is valuable for you to perform some action entails that *if you were fully rational* then you would want to perform it."[42]

Johnson detects a fallacy in this conditional formulation of the thesis. Consider an action of the sort "making oneself more rational." Suppose now that the actor is fully rational. In that case, there would be no motive for rendering oneself *more* rational, though one would continue to have good reasons to be rational and to value rationality highly. There is a rupture here between (a) having good reasons or according something great value and (b) having motives impelling rationality-enhancing actions. Johnson argues further that efforts to repair the rupture are costly to the doctrine's greatest strength; namely, "showing how reasons can both explain and justify actions."[43]

All this is to offer one conventional account of internalism and an example of what may be certain problematic conditionals. The main point, however, is to convey the internalist's answer to questions as to how reasons bring about actions. Actions are *explained* by connecting reasons to motives, and are *justified* by establishing the rational and intelligible relationship between the action performed and the motive to which it is responsive. If this solves the dilemma of the utterly "free will," it also introduces a deterministic element that might otherwise be a bar to ascriptions of moral standing. The tension between actions being thus determined by reasons, motives, and desires and their being free requires some form of relaxation. It is seemingly relaxed by versions of compatibilism. If an "elusive Something" is to be avoided, some ostensibly less elusive something must function as a mediator between the reason for acting and the action. Hobbes's "endeavours" and their kin have been invoked by scores of theorists unwilling to weigh the possibility that the mediational mechanism is at least as elusive a something as anything it would replace. What, after all, is gained by denying that a reason for action can result in the action, but is nonetheless able to generate or somehow cooperate with something called a "desire" that possesses just that "something" needed if an action is to materialize?

The impulse behind compatibilist "solutions" is not difficult to locate. It springs from the confident first-person knowledge of our actions being under our own control and answerable to our own aims and purposes, but all this in the face of a cosmos whose operations, one and all, express fixed causally determinative laws. More than even this, the (allegedly) radical versions of autonomy seem to require actions tied to nothing but a species of whim, the will swinging as it were on an unhinged gate. In his *Essays on the Principles of Morality and Natural Religion*, Lord Kames stated the case against such autonomy forthwith: If, indeed, one's actions are not determined by one's desires and motives, but are instead the result of unconstrained liberty, then

> such a liberty must signify a power in the mind of acting without and against motives, a power of acting without any view, purpose, or design, and even of acting in contradiction to our own desires and aversions, and to all our principles of action, and is an absurdity altogether inconsistent with a rational nature.[44]

Against this, Kames would defend the deterministic internalist thesis, insisting that every choice and inclination must be answerable to basic motives and causally brought about by them. Kames speaks here for many theorists, spread evenly over the history of moral thought, who regard alternative formulations as bearing the heavy burden of the *causa sui* conundrum. Not to have motives and desires must, on this understanding, result in "acting without any view, purpose, or design," a manifest absurdity, "altogether inconsistent with a rational nature." As Kames puts the matter, one might regard such actions as the product of madness!

A more influential version of compatibilism was advanced at length by Jonathan Edwards in his *Inquiry*.[45] As with all forms of compatibilism, Edwards's rendering supposes a necessary connection between antecedent conditions and subsequent actions, but preserves liberty in the face of such necessity. How he does this is instructive.

In light of his avowedly religious mission, specifically to oppose certain Arminian heresies, Edwards first considers the question of divine foreknowledge and its implications. He devotes many pages to scriptural evidence of this foreknowledge, but all this for what turns out to be an essentially logical argument of the following form:

1. Whatever has already taken place must stand now as a necessary fact for, "having already made sure of existence, it is too late for any alteration of possibility . . . it is now impossible that it should be otherwise than true that that thing has existed."[46]

2. If there is divine foreknowledge, then it is now a necessary fact that at some past time there was this foreknowledge. Thus, it is now impossible that it should be otherwise than true that this foreknowledge has existed.

3. Whatever is "indissolubly" connected with what is necessary is itself necessary.

4. Certain foreknowledge of action A necessitates the occurrence of action A, such that action A is not only determined but necessarily determined to be what it is.

Although not central to issues under consideration in this chapter, the question of "divine foreknowledge," as a bar to freedom, does provide a useful route to matters that are of concern here. With the concept of divinity removed, it remains one of the implicit (and often explicit) claims of determinism that any course of action is fully predictable once there is sufficient knowledge of facts and ruling laws or principles. The alleged connection between foreknowledge and determinism is, however, largely illusory. If Harriet's date of birth is known independently by one who nonetheless asks her for it, her response can be predicted with certainty, but is no less freely given.

Among the questions that so plagued Boethius as to drive him to seek consolation from Philosophy, it was just this: If God is omniscient and thus knows the future, then the future is determined, for if it is correctly and certainly known that x will occur, then the occurrence of x is necessitated. But what Boethius learns from Philosophy, as she speaks and sings her replies, is that any number of events can be fully foreseen *and* freely brought about. She illustrates this by noting the skill of the charioteers as they guide their teams. If such actions were compelled by necessity the whole point of cultivating a skill would be empty. Nevertheless, onlookers well know how the charioteers will perform. Such an event, even though foreknown, is free.[47]

Returning to Edwards, his further task now is to redeem the "liberty" of compatibilism in the wake of his successful defense of determinism. He must do so, however, even as he opposes Arminianism's radical defense of a will so free as to defy all foreknowledge. With Locke, Edwards affirms what might be called the ordinary understanding of liberty; that is, "the power, opportunity, or advantage, that any one has to do as he pleases," but then adding, "without considering how his pleasure comes to be as it is."[48] To be at liberty, then, is to be able to pursue a desired course of action and attain what is attainable through one's own actions. The course of action itself is, on this account, determined by the desire or motive. It is, at least to this point, irrelevant how the desire itself came about, for the actor's liberty refers only to the freedom to satisfy the desire in question. If thirsty, is one free to drink? If hungry, to eat? If cold, to warm oneself at the fire? Edwards is satisfied that this sense of freedom is really all the word has ever signified.

What, then, of the motives and desires which, if utterly beyond the personal resources of the actor, would determine actions against the wishes of the actor? On Edwards's account the question itself is absurd. To what can "the wishes of the actor" refer if not to occurrent desires, motives, and aims? On the very first page of his *Inquiry*, Edwards regards the meaning of the word "will" to be nothing but that by which the mind chooses anything such that "an act of the *will* is the same as an act of *choosing* or *choice*."[49] The very concept of a "will" includes that of choice and thus of freedom.

Complications arise, of course, so refinements must be grafted onto the basic argument. In many instances there are competing desires. All of them cannot be satisfied and some may be in direct conflict with others. The person addicted to alcohol desires it, but may also desire to be purged of the vice so that a reasonable life can be undertaken. Owing to the addiction, the actor may plead a form of what Edwards calls "moral inability." If actions are determined by antecedent motives and desires, and if every vice is recognized as owing to motives and desires of the wrong sort, how can anyone be held responsible for vicious actions?

As with compatibilists before and after, Edwards would have it both ways. In the matter of so-called moral inability, he notes that

> no inability whatsoever, which is merely moral, is properly called by the name of *inability*; and . . . in the strictest propriety of speech, a man may be said to have a thing in his power, if he has it at his election; and he cannot be said to be unable to do a thing, when he can, if he now pleases, or whenever he has a proper, direct, and immediate desire for it.[50]

Desires and motives are present in the mind, the strongest determining the will of the actor. Edwards's theory is not of the mechanistic sort, for his conception of "motive" covers the full and varied range of states, habits, and desires that incline the will in one direction or another. What finally determines the will is what is judged to be most agreeable; what is judged on the whole to be *good*. Nor does he accept what might be called purely physiological (let alone Freudian) motives, for a motive must be that which is "*extant in the view or apprehension of the understanding*, or perceiving faculty."[51] A motive cannot be unconscious, for it is tied to a perceived goal or state of affairs judged to be agreeable, to be the greatest apparent good. Whatever overcomes the actor beyond the range of his powers cannot be taken as a motive proper. One able to lift no more than one hundred pounds does not "desire" to drop a weight of two hundred pounds but does so per force. This now sets the stage for Edwards's understanding of "necessity" and then the compatibilitist conclusions.

How is the term "necessity" to be understood? Edwards quickly notes that mere synonymy affords no explanation. To say that "necessity" means "couldn't be otherwise" is to say the same thing twice. Nor is any progress won by including notions of inevitability, ability, impossibility, and the like. There is also a confusion of the issue spawned by the failure to distinguish between philosophical or metaphysical necessity on the one hand, and that concept of necessity that bears directly on the issue of freedom of the will. Philosophical or metaphysical necessity refers, says Edwards, solely to "the certainty that is in things themselves, which is the foundation of the certainty of the knowledge of them."[52] To say that the law of contradiction is necessarily true is to say that it is *certain* that a thing cannot simultaneously be and not be. At work here is not simply something we know to be certain, but something that—owing to the intrinsic certainty—*can* be known with certainty. Of such things it can be said that they are, in the philosophical or metaphysical sense, necessary, and may be so as a result of relations of three distinct sorts: The connection between subject and predicate in any proposition, between, say, *x* and *y*, is necessary when affirming one while denying the other leads to contradiction and absurdity; or again, the connection between *x* and *y* is necessary when *x* implies *y* and *x* has already come to pass; or again, the connection between *x* and *y* is necessary when this connection is itself connected to other relations that are themselves necessary.

What remains for Edwards now is to make the distinction between these senses of necessity and what he calls moral and natural necessity:

> By *natural necessity*, as applied to men, I mean such necessity as men are under through the force of natural causes; as distinguished from what are called moral causes, such as habits and dispositions of the heart, and moral motives and inducements.[53]

Moral necessity can be as absolute as natural necessity, for a given pattern of motives and desires may be so firmly disposing as to render the subsequent actions fully predictable. Nonetheless, this is assuredly not at the expense of liberty, for liberty refers specifically to the power to act on one's choices and desires. What is generally meant by "coercion" is the application of measures such that one's desires are thwarted. These measures may establish a veritable *natural* necessity that no one is at liberty to oppose. But if by *moral* necessity no more is meant than the necessary connection between one's actions and "habits and dispositions of the heart," then liberty itself virtually requires such a connection. At the core of the concept of liberty is the recognition that some things cannot be opposed or prevented *by us*, which is to say that their status or occurrence is utterly independent of our desires and choices. These fall beyond the sphere of freedom.

Is there any room left for the notion of a self-determining will? None. A totally unconstrained will, far from grounding praise and blame, would nullify all the moral categories. It would be only in willfulness itself that there would be the freedom otherwise required of moral judgment, for not even the consequences of willfulness could be subject to moral scrutiny.[54] Rather, it is patent that no action of moral consequence ever has as a required feature that it be unhinged from any and every motive, desire, aim, and disposition. Edwards argues that whatever comes to be does so in virtue of causal antecedents and conditions, except that which has existed from all eternity. Human actions come to be and therefore are not causeless. They are causally connected to habits, motives, desires, and dispositions. These, too, have not existed from all eternity. Some are tied to basic biological requirements; others to custom and socialization; others to habitual modes of gratification.

As with so many earlier and later commentators—including most contemporary philosophers—Edwards seems unable to locate a *person* between motives and actions; or, if there is someone or something mediating these "causes" and "effects," it is something either passive or powerless. The phenomenology of choice, however, is at variance with this account, and the account only repairs itself at the price of circularity. Faced with two options—wishing to preserve one's health but also preferring not to exercise—John collapses into the overstuffed chair and clicks the remote-control buttons. Wishing to preserve one's health but also preferring not to exercise, Jill puts the remote-control device in the drawer, dons a pair of running shoes and takes off for the trails. The different actions are then "explained" on the basis of motivational strength: John's motive to rest was greater than the motive to promote good health, but the opposite was the case for Jill. And the evidence for this conclusion? John watched television while Jill trotted off into the night. The account leaves no room for what John and Jill might offer as a counter explanation; namely, that, both of them, in the circumstance, just *decided* to do what they did. The account leaves no room because, as a mechanistic, causal account it *cannot* allow noncausal explanations. Note that the latter include indifference, whim, distraction, resolution, commitment, devotion—states of an agentic nature that are "causal" only in the sense that persons are *responsible* for much of what they do.

A more economical, if unusual, version of compatibilism had already been propounded by Leibniz in his *Discourse on Metaphysics* (1710). Leibniz distinguishes between rational and factual truths. Rational truths are governed by the Law of Contradiction and are thus both certain and necessary. It is a truth of reason that two things equal to a third are equal to each other. Although factual truths are not *logically* necessary, they are nonetheless necessitated by Leibniz's principle of "Sufficient Reason." Once one has the complete picture of the world as given, the events in that world hold together in a special way. Brutus does not stab Caesar as a result of logical necessity, but Brutus *necessarily* stabs Caesar, for the act in question is part of the complete concept of Brutus. It is an event that enters into the root ontology of Brutus. Accordingly, owing to the fact that the event is not logically necessary, Brutus acts freely. Leibniz summarizes his theory this way:

Our will as contrasted with necessity, is in a state of indifference, being able to act otherwise, or wholly to suspend its action, either alternative being and remaining possible . . . it is, however, true, and has been assured from all eternity, that certain souls will not employ their power upon certain occasions.[55]

It is as if the events in the world have been scripted, such that the participants do freely what the author of the narrative requires. The narrative makes inevitable what the characters, in their self-reflecting preparations, freely adopt as their course of action.

Kant would be led to compatibilism by a different route, one essentially dictated by his division of reality into "phenomena" and "noumena," and his distinction between "intelligible" and "natural" causes. At the phenomenal level, every event presupposes a causal antecedent that it follows as a rule (Kant's *Second Analogy*), and this must be at the foundation of experience itself. Every experience is thus caused, and caused in the manner of all natural phenomena. But freedom obtains in the noumenal realm: the realm of things in themselves such that there is no contradiction in affirming causal necessity in the matter of all experience and freedom in the intelligible realm of *reasons*.[56] As rational beings, we occupy the intelligible realm within which the "laws of freedom" render actions explicable. As physical beings, we occupy the natural realm within which causal laws are determinative. Hence, compatibilism. Thus,

as a rational being, and consequently as belonging to the intelligible world, man can never conceive the causality of his own will except under the Idea of freedom; for to be independent of determination by causes in the sensible world . . . is to be free. . . . A rational being counts himself, *qua* intelligence, as belonging to the intelligible world, and solely *qua* efficient cause belonging to the intelligible world does he give to his causality the name of *will*. . . . But *the intelligible world contains the ground of the sensible world and therefore also of its laws*.[57]

Kant goes on to discuss *the antinomy of freedom and necessity*, noting that neither freedom nor necessity can be concepts of experience. Nothing in the purely contingent world of experience can convey the concept of necessity, which, accordingly, can be known only a priori. In the realm of experience, however, everything is known to arise from antecedent causes and thus to be subject to the laws of nature. Accordingly, the concept of freedom cannot be transmitted by such causally determined events. The concept of nature itself is, however, grounded in experience and comes under the aegis of the understanding. The result is what Kant calls the "dialectic of reason":

The freedom attributed to the will seems incompatible with the necessity of nature; and although at this parting of the ways reason finds the road of natural necessity much more beaten and serviceable than that of freedom for *purposes of speculation*, yet for *purposes of action* the footpath of freedom is the only one on which we can make use of reason in our conduct. . . . Reason must therefore suppose that no genuine contradiction is to be found between the freedom and the natural necessity ascribed to the very same human actions; for it can abandon the concept of nature as little as it can abandon that of freedom."[58]

Kant's compatibilism is the resolution of a patent antinomy. Reason can no more abandon the concept of nomic necessity as it obtains in nature than it can abandon the concept of moral freedom as it operates at the level of chosen courses of action. Freedom cannot be "proven," of course, at least if proof is to be of the empirical, covering-law variety. What can be subsumed under an iron law of nature is what is precisely *unfree*. And what is accessible to experience, being part of the sensible world, is by its very nature subsumable under just such laws. For all moral purposes, it is sufficient, then, that freedom be thinkable, though unprovable. As a concept of reason it grounds moral judgments and permits ascriptions of praise and blame. Necessity, as a concept of reason, grounds scientific understanding and permits explanations of natural occurrences. The two concepts must be compatible, for neither concept can be abandoned.

Compatibilism and Alternate Possibilities

Compatibilist theories, diverse though they are, weigh the competing claims of determinism and moral freedom according to the availability and the power of choice. Freedom contrasted with coercion seems to require that, in a given context, an action is free only to the extent that a different action could have been performed; that is, that the actor had open at least one other course of action in addition to the chosen one. It is this option that is routinely identified as the essential condition for moral freedom. More than thirty years ago Harry Frankfurt put the issue on new footing by posing instances in which persons are rightly judged to be responsible, although in fact there could be no alternative whatever to the outcome in question.[59] It was Frankfurt who labeled the traditional view *the principle of alternate possibilities* (PAP) and formulated it thus: "PAP: *A person is morally responsible for what he has done only if he could have done otherwise*."[60]

Examples offered as refutations of PAP, some quite graphic, have multiplied over the years. Frankfurt's own example features Smith who has had electrodes implanted in his brain by Black, a nefarious neurosurgeon. If activated, a charge would be delivered to regions of the brain causing Smith to perform a certain act. This is paradigmatic and one is free to pick any desired behavior on the part of Smith that, if not chosen by Smith, would be elicited by stimulation of Smith's brain. For example, we can imagine a case in which Smith serves on a committee whose members signal approval of a motion by raising their right hand. As Smith's vote is essential, Black will see to it that Smith will vote for the motion, just in case Smith fails to do so voluntarily. As it happens, Smith does choose to vote for the motion, though *he could not have done otherwise*. Accordingly, Smith is fully responsible for an action that could not have been different from what it is.

In cases such as this, it is possible to predict unerringly what the action will be, no matter what the actor chooses to do. Therefore, the actor does not have the allegedly necessary power to have done otherwise. Other contingencies can be grafted onto the basic paradigm. Thus, Walter Glannon adds yet a third party. Now Smith wants to assassinate the President. Smith's surgeon friend, Dr. White, wants the same. Just in case Smith wavers, White puts electrodes in Smith's brain, thereby being able to have the deed done while remaining blameless. Another of Smith's friends discovers White's plot and so informs Smith. Now Smith has a very clever idea: He can *not* perform the act, thus causing White to activate the device. The net effect is that the President is assassinated but now, the plot revealed, it is White and not Smith who is held responsible.[61]

Considerable attention has been given to Frankfurt-type challenges to PAP, but there is ample room for doubts as to whether they actually reach the target. No matter how imaginatively such scripts are composed, they all suffer from the same defect: the failure to distinguish moral ascriptions based on outcomes with those based on intentions. The linchpin in the scripts and opposing scripts is, of course, the sense of "done," as in "could have *done* otherwise." It is always reasonable to wonder whether Oedipus engaged in an incestuous relationship with his mother, having killed his father. The reason for the perplexity is that the concepts of "incest" and of "killing" are typically bound up with assumptions of relevant knowledge and desire. One can consistently assert that Oedipus is responsible for killing Laius without agreeing that Oedipus is responsible for killing his father. One can consistently assert that Oedipus willingly was intimate with Jocasta but was not willingly intimate with his mother.

So, too, with wanting and intending the death of the President. Such an intention would constitute grounds for moral appraisal independently of the subsequent *act* of assassination and thus indifferently with regard to whether the act is ever performed. The juridical picture here is different from the moral one. Of course, predictability and responsibility are not unambiguously related in such cases. As R. M. Hare has noted, actions are subject to moral appraisal just in case the agent could have acted otherwise, but the action itself nonetheless may be entirely predictable.[62] Indeed, too much weight is attached to predictability in relation to questions of moral freedom. To ask those in an audience to raise their hands if they have blue eyes is to be in a position to make reliable and even perfect predictions but without in any way infringing upon the freedom of those who do and those who do not thereupon raise a hand.

Returning to PAP, others have noted that there are hidden ceteris paribus clauses in Frankfurt-type cases and that, when these are exposed, the instances are far less vexing. Alan White illustrates the point with a gambling casino fixing the roulette wheel so that losses are especially likely in the later games. The player, however, owing to a run of bad luck earlier, never gets far enough into the game to sustain the prearranged great losses. Clearly, we would not absolve the house merely because its intentions were never realized. White concludes,

> We require in general that our morally responsible actions are not merely our own, but *fairly* so, apart from a conspiratorial set of even actually otiose circumstances that would otherwise guarantee a particular kind of outcome. So PAP remains a necessary condition for full moral responsibility in that wider sense."[63]

Joseph Campbell has raised still other objections, contending that "free will" refers to unimpeded cognitive and agentic powers. As the parties in Frankfurt-type situations have these powers, they are thereby holders of "free will," though they lack any course of action that is incompatible with determinism.[64] Rounding out the dispute, Michael McKenna has rejected this on the grounds that Campbell's critique pertains not to one's ability to do otherwise but to the different notion of what it means to act freely. As Frankfurt-type cases do not question the possibility of acting freely— only the possibility of doing otherwise—Campbell's criticism is found wanting.[65]

Peter van Inwagen has been one of the most influential defenders of strong voluntarism. Van Inwagen takes moral responsibility as arising from the consequences of one's actions. A particular action is explained and understood in terms of the antecedents that bring it about. As a result, just in case the actor does by choice what, in fact, would have been brought about anyway, the Frankfurt conundrum is irrelevant. That is, if Smith votes as a result of his own deliberation and free choice, he is responsible for the consequences of the vote—though in fact he could not have but voted for the motion.[66] In response, Frankfurt has rejected the premise that responsibility is tied solely to consequences. Laura Ekstrom, however, has made out a strong case for the failure of Frankfurt-type examples to invalidate the principle of alternate possibilities and thus one of the foundations of incompatibilist freedom.[67]

One of the more original approaches designed to accommodate the complexities associated with PAP and moral responsibility has been advanced by John Martin Fisher and Mark Ravizza.[68] The central concept in their work is that of a "guidance control mechanism," which, at first blush, seems more applicable to the behavior of robots. But the "guidance" referred to in their theory is (a) one that ties actions to reasons for acting, where the tie is of the right sort; and (b) one that intelligibly connects the actions themselves to actual events in the world. And the "mechanism" in the theory is anything but mechanical, for it refers to practical reason. There is in the theory the requirement of authenticity, in that the "mechanism" must be the actor's own, as must be those deliberations that culminate in actions. On the Fisher-Ravizza account, moral responsibility is established just in case the overall process culminating in the action is "guided" by the "mechanism" in the right sort of manner. Taking the PAP example given above, if Smith has authentic reasons for casting his vote, thereupon signaling the vote with the correct action, and doing all this in contexts in which such behavior is expected and appropriate, Smith is fully responsible. Note that, understood in these terms, Smith's responsibility is utterly independent of whether or not there was an alternative. What makes one responsible for acting is, according to the "control" theory, the actual process leading up to and including the action, not the presence or absence of some different alternative course of action. Being morally responsible does not entail the power or freedom to do otherwise. Rather, commenting on Frankfurt-cases, Fisher and Ravizza conclude,

> The relevant sort of control need *not* involve alternate possibilities. The suggestion, derived from the Frankfurt-type cases, is that the sort of control necessarily associated with moral responsibility is *guidance control*.[69]

Daniel Dennett has enriched the debate further by contending that in fact we can never know under any realistic set of conditions whether someone *could* have done otherwise than he actually did and, in any case, nothing of consequence would be gained by such knowledge. Given the person's history of experiences, genetic makeup, prevailing internal states, prevailing states of the physical world, and the binding laws of physics, Smith scratches his nose. What sense would it make to say that, under all of these conditions, both internal and external, should they in fact be replicated, Smith "could" do otherwise? Indeed, what sense would it make even to think that such conditions ever could be duplicated? For Dennett, it is sufficient that much of what we do is predicated on the idea of its being done freely, and this conduces to states of affairs that are pragmatically desirable. Less a *pax philosophica*, Dennett's position is a rehearsal of garden-variety determinism, but with Darwinian selection pressures favoring certain modes of cognitive representation and emotional response.[70]

There is ample room for conviction on both sides of the Frankfurt line. Much of the long debate on this issue remains largely unaffected by Frankfurt examples. It was, after all, Aristotle who made responsibility conditional on the source of the action being internal to the actor. Presumably the mere location of stimulating electrodes would not be sufficient to satisfy this requirement! What, however, of a kind of mindless agency: agency in the sense of actually performing actions that serve a purpose, but without any consciousness of such purposes?

It is again Daniel Dennett's deployment of the "intentional stance" that raises interesting questions. As he defines it, the intentional stance "is the strategy of interpreting the behavior of an entity (person, animal, artifact, whatever) by treating it *as if* it were a rational agent who governed its 'choice' of 'action' by a 'consideration' of its 'beliefs' and 'desires.'"[71]

Suppose the intentional stance is brought to bear on the phenomenon of self-replication on the part of macromolecules. It is this process that results in the complex functions and overall design of all biological systems. Thus, the process as judged from the intentional stance satisfies what one generally takes to be evidence of actions toward an end. These same systems, properly organized and most fully evolved, are the very ones permitting learning, memory, perception, cognition, emotion—the entire range of psychological processes by which a rational agent chooses an action on the basis of considerations, beliefs, and desires. Understood in these terms, the macromolecules no less than the actor are performing actions and, if only in the most primitive sense, are displaying *agency*, although, as Dennett says, they "know not what they do."[72]

The incompatibilist libertarian, needless to say, would dismiss this entire line of reasoning as beside the point at issue. Whatever merits the intentional stance might have in deciding whether agency is ascribable to macromolecules, it is surely not the stance occupied by anyone agentically engaged in achieving goals and realizing personal aspirations. Persons on such a mission do not act *as if* they had beliefs and desires, but *because* they have them. The stance, then, could only be applied strangely in the introspective case where it would suggest nothing less than a worrisome dissociative disorder. Persons do not act *as if* they believe something, nor do they adopt a belief so as to be able to attempt actions that presuppose it. Perhaps more central to the point under consideration, it is simply not credible to ascribe agentic actions to entities that "know not what they do."

When we undertake any action, no matter how trivial, the very process of "undertaking" establishes at once a cognitive awareness of the thing to be done and a belief on the part of the actor that indeed it can be done. Implicit in any such undertaking is the awareness on the part of the actor of certain powers or abilities. This was the topic Thomas Reid chose for what was perhaps his final philosophical composition and, with customary clarity and economy, he put the case this way:

> Every voluntary exertion to produce an event seems to imply a persuasion in the agent that he has the power to produce the event. A deliberate exertion to produce an event implies a conception of the event, and some belief or hope that his exertion will be followed by it. . . . The consequence is that a conception of power is antecedent to every deliberate exertion. . . . I am inclined to think that our first exertions are instinctive, without any distinct conception of the event that is to follow, consequently without will to produce that event. And that, finding by experience that such exertions are followed by such events, we learn to make the exertion voluntarily and deliberately, as often as we desire to produce the event. And when we know or believe that the event depends upon our exertion, we have the conception of power in ourselves to produce that event."[73]

Reid's understanding here is strikingly similar to William James's, as cited earlier in this chapter, and calls for some elaboration. Against Locke, Reid denies or at least strongly doubts that one's active power is an object of sense or of consciousness. In this, Reid agrees with Hume. But against Hume, who then "rashly concluded that there is no such conception in the human mind" Reid makes clear that the very initiation of an action presupposes just such a conception.[74] If, however, it arises neither as a percept nor as a conscious experience, what is its source? Reid cannot be sure and is here as elsewhere loathe to theorize in the dark. During some interval between conception and childhood there emerges a conception of personal active power on the part of the actor. Before this, there would appear to be an ensemble of instinctual patterns of behavior, common throughout the animal kingdom and tied to the basic requirements of life. Through repeated emissions of these patterns of behavior, a reservoir of experiences is built up such that the actor learns which of the patterns leads predictably to a given outcome. It is this, then, that establishes the actor's conception of active power. Thus, it is not an innate concept magically present in consciousness, nor is it something sensed or perceived, for power as such is not an object of experience.

Dennett's intentional stance, on this account, is hopelessly beside the point. Unless the performing robot has beliefs, its behavior alone cannot support the claim that it possesses any active power whatever. Unless the robot has the cognitive resources by which to frame possibilities, its performance cannot support ascriptions of intention. The thesis of incompatibilist freedom requires active powers, the cognitive resources needed to frame means-ends sequences, and the actor's deliberate choice or selection of a course of action *because* it is expected to achieve the desired end. It should be clear, then, that incompatibilist freedom runs counter to both the *as if* depictions of the intentional stance and to radical versions of the proposition that has all choices determined in ways incompatible with freedom. By the same token, determinists reject the proposition that choices are not rigidly determined by antecedent and causally efficacious events. If only by default or for purposes of argument, one more engagement with compatibilism recommends itself.

"Motivation" and Causation: Hume and Mill as Compatibilists

It is not at all clear that any part of an Edwards-type analysis is able to preserve the liberty presupposed in ascriptions of praise and blame. It is not at all clear that the compatibilist arguments of Leibniz and Kant succeed any more completely, even if Kant's is formally and metaphysically richer than the others. In the end, Kant's "solution" is a metaphysical truce at the end of a war of attrition. As we simply *cannot* abandon either the concept of nomic necessity within the natural world or the concept of freedom within the domain of intelligible actions, we must accept that in some unknowable way the two concepts are compatible. It is far from obvious, however, that any ultimate validity attaches to a concept solely owing to our inability to abandon it. An incompatibilist reply to Kant might take this form: There are not two distinct "realms" of reality, nor are there two equally valid standpoints, one natural and the other intelligible. Rather, there is one cosmos and everything having bona fide ontological standing is to be found within it. As it happens, there are not two *standpoints* but two ontologically distinct genres of entities, one physical and one moral. They are not comprehended in the same terms, understood in the same way or similarly constituted. The reason we cannot surrender or abandon the concept of freedom is that it arises from what are the real moral properties of the world of actions. As such, it is incompatible with any monistic ontology that denies the reality of just these properties.

At a less elevated metaphysical level, there is another difficulty associated with compatibilist and incompatibilist positions, this one based on a widespread but unexamined notion of just what a motive or desire is and how it could be *causally* efficacious in bringing about a given action. A brief consideration of prevailing views of motivation is in order if what seems to be the circularity of compatibilist and determinist theories is to be exposed. A serviceable introduction to this is given by returning to the compatibilism advanced by Hume and Mill, this time by way of analyzing their understanding of causality itself.

Surely one of the most controversial and celebrated features of Hume's philosophy is the "constant conjunction" theory of causal concepts:

We are never sensible of any connexion betwixt causes and effects, and that 'tis only by our experience of their constant conjunction, we can arrive at any knowledge of this relation. Now as all objects, which are not contrary, are susceptible of a constant conjunction, and as no real objects are contrary; I have inferr'd from these principles, that to consider the matter *a priori*, any thing may produce any thing, and that we shall never discover a reason, why any object may or may not be the cause of any other.[75]

Consistent with his empiricism, Hume reasons that the origin of the concept of causation must be in habitual modes thought, for there is nothing apparent in the external world that would pick out the "cause" of events. What perception reveals is no more than spatial and temporal contiguity between event *A* and event *B*. No third term, no "cause," is seen in such occurrences. Rather, it is a fixed feature of mental life that, when conjunctions of this sort are invariant, the sequence generates the idea of causality. As every idea is but the melding of sensations, held together by the Humean laws of association, the idea of causality is reducible to constantly conjoined perceptions. On this understanding of causation, to say that a relationship holds *of necessity* can mean no more than that the terms are either (merely) logically related or that they have been conjoined in experience *without exception*.

Hume's moral theory and its place within the tradition of British Sentimentalism has been illuminated by Paul Russell in a major book on the subject and in a number of essays.[76] What is made clear in these studies is that Hume's compatibilism is not of the "compulsion" but of the "regularity" genre, which is to say that it is his theory of causation that grounds the moral theory. Indeed, as Russell has convincingly shown, Hume's reliance on the regularity theory of causation can only create problems for a compulsion thesis that calls for the very mechanistic modes of causality that Hume rejects.

John Stuart Mill adopted and developed Hume's empiricistic and thoroughly psychological approach to moral and political issues. Regarding the free will–determinism issue, Mill traced opposition to the deterministic theory precisely to traditional but defective notions of causation. The traditional view, as Mill reviews it, thinks of causes as occult or mysterious forces somehow making something else happen; getting a grip on something and requiring it to behave in a predictable manner. Accordingly, we resist the notion of our own actions being "determined," for we have no experience or sense of a power of this sort acting on us; and, when we do, we identify it as coercive. What is objectionable, therefore, in the Doctrine of Necessity is not limited to its undermining of morality. What is objectionable extends to its seeming to be factually false.

Mill examines the matter specifically in Book VI, "On the Logic of the Moral Sciences," in *A System of Logic*. He declares himself loyal to the doc-

trine of necessity, but, faithful as well to Hume's philosophy, he finds in
this no bar to accepting moral responsibility. The two are readily seen as
compatible once the older and defective notion of cause is emptied of superstitious and mysterious elements and is replaced by the only notion of
"cause" validated at the level of experience; that is, *constant conjunction.*
Everyone (claims Mill) is strongly inclined to believe that, were we to know
everything about a person's past—his character, his motives and desires—
we would be able to predict his actions under specified conditions. That is
to say, there is nearly universal agreement that actions arise from various
conditions and states and that knowing these renders the actions predictable, though no less "free" for all that. Foreknowledge is not incompatible
with freedom. Nonetheless,

> the doctrine of causation, when considered as obtaining between our
> volitions and their antecedents, is almost universally conceived as in-
> volving more than this. Many do not believe, and very few practically
> feel that there is nothing in causation but invariable, certain, and un-
> conditional sequence. . . . Even if the reason repudiates, the imagina-
> tion retains, the feeling of some more intimate connection, of some
> peculiar tie or mysterious constraint exercised by the antecedent over
> the consequent.[77]

And this is the rub. Once the metaphysics of causation is required to
include "some peculiar tie or mysterious constraint," it is in the court of
personal experience that the Doctrine of Necessity is convicted of falsehood.
As no one *feels* such a tie or constraint, no one accepts that the chosen
course of action has been "caused" by anything but the will itself. Reid
had made abundantly clear—so much so that his critique had the ring of a
truism—that nothing in mental life matches up, property-for-property, with
anything in the physical realm. As Dugald Stewart, his friend, student, and
successor in the Scottish Enlightenment, calmly noted, "It is now, I think,
pretty generally acknowledged by physiologists, that the influence of the
will over the body, is a mystery which has never yet been unfolded."[78]

Mill was wary of all reductionistic programs and thus found safe moorings
in a theory of causation stripped of metaphysical (let alone *physical!*) properties. Nonetheless, his version of determinism is not at the expense of morality, for he includes among the determinants of action not only the character of the actor but this character as to some extent *self-formed.* Roger Crisp
has underscored this important side of Mill's moral psychology:

> Mill sees morality as concerned not only with the regulation of actions,
> but with the self-education of the sentiments. This is so not merely
> because the character one has affects the actions one does, which in
> turn affect the level of happiness overall. . . . Rather, self-education is
> important in coming to understand the nature of happiness itself, and

is itself a constituent of happiness. . . . Mill saw Bentham as a child with a child's limited imagination, and believed that the most important sources of happiness lay in the adult world of noble morality and the arts.[79]

Recognizing this to be at variance with strict determinism, Mill looks for places in which such personal responsibility can be coherently assigned and finds it in the domain of experience itself. He makes the distinction between others necessitating a course of action rather than merely setting up conditions that call for one course of action as opposed to another. It is not the ends but the means that can be manipulated to bring about behavior in another. In the same way, a person can make use of personal experiences in a manner capable of forging a different character. It is when past experience results in feelings of disappointment, pain, and failure that new initiatives may be attempted:

> Our character is formed by us as well as for us; but the wish which induces us to attempt to form it is formed for us; and how? Not, in general, by our organization, nor wholly by our education, but by our experience—experience of the painful consequences of the character we previously had, or by some strong feeling of admiration or aspiration accidentally aroused.[80]

There is nothing vulgar in Mill's version of utilitarianism, but there is also far too much conceded to the moral and aesthetic sides of life for the theory to be a robust alternative to traditional moral thought. Once character, self-education, and nobility become virtual *constituents* of happiness, utilitarianism can fit comfortably on the same shelf of books that feature the ethical treatises of Aristotelians, Stoics, Epicureans and even liberated Kantians. This is abundantly clear in chapter 3 of Mill's *Utilitarianism*, where he distinguishes between external and internal sanctions. Rewards, punishments, fear of God, the favor of our fellows—these and other inducements comprise the external sanctions. But of the *internal* sanctions, Mill has this to say:

> The internal sanction of duty, whatever our standard of duty may be, is one and the same—a feeling in our own mind. . . . This feeling, when disinterested, and connecting itself with the pure idea of duty, and not with some particular form of it . . . is the essence of conscience. . . . The ultimate sanction, therefore, of all morality (external motives apart) being a subjective feeling in our own minds."[81]

For Kant, of course, the ultimate sanction is the categorical imperative itself, but what Mill describes here is so close to the Kantian "good will" that the two theories begin to converge rapidly. This is not a criticism but the adumbration of a theory whose patron was far too wise to confine the important human desires to mere comfort.

On the specific question of the adequacy of Mill's compatibilism, it is sufficient to say that it cannot rise higher than the adequacy of that theory of causality on which it depends. Treatises on this subject abound. For present purposes it is sufficient to record a healthy skepticism toward the "constant conjunction" account. Thomas Reid was among the first to dismiss it on conceptual, psychological, and scientific grounds. Conceptually the account leaves no room for a distinction between causes and reasons. Whatever "cause" is behind the universal law of gravitation, it will not match up with one's reasons for acting and with the belief that the course of action has some chance of success. Psychologically, we readily distinguish between causal sequences and mere conjunctions, no matter how constant the latter might be. No one thinks of the day as "causing" the night. Moreover, we readily distinguish causes from *active powers* in that the latter permit us not only to bring about certain outcomes but to forbear from doing so. Scientifically, it is simply absurd to regard the lawful dependencies found everywhere in the natural world as amounting to no more than faithful coincidences.

This much granted, there still is a need to identify just what is necessary or sufficient to initiate and direct a course of action if that course of action is to be subject to moral scrutiny. Current internalist "causal" theories of action, whether of the Hume-Mill variety or otherwise, require actions and choices to be shaped and directed by internal states of desire and motivation. The assumption is that, were it otherwise, choices and actions would remain free-floating and inexplicable. Underlying this conception of the causes of choice and action, and presupposed by it, is a broader and typically physiological theory compatible with more general causal theories of purely physical events. Just as mechanical advantage is increased by a system of pulleys or by levers, so too, on this assumption, does a choice or an action become ever more likely as some similar advantage is conferred by prevailing physiological or predetermined genetic processes. The most basic of these processes are those directly associated with survival; processes engaged by threats to the physical integrity of the organism or to the perpetuation of the species. As the latter cannot be a consideration of the individual organism or animal, it must be secured by way of impulses and instincts that answer to the needs of the individual in a way that furthers the survival of the collective.

Presumably (such theories conclude), the processes of learning, socialization, and acculturation then broaden the range and quality of desires and choices by connecting certain options to the most basic needs. As a trite example, one works for paper currency not because the paper has any intrinsic value but because, in a given culture, it has derived value from its reliable association with such necessities as food and shelter. All this in place, it is now (allegedly) possible and plausible to explain choice A as "caused" by conditions of desire and need—motivating conditions—directly addressed by one course of action and not by alternatives.

Apart from the fact that very few actions, under normal and long abiding conditions, are ever initiated under such taxing and portentous conditions, there is the insuperable problem of linking *any* condition of the body to a process of deliberated choosing, where the ultimately chosen course is guided by general moral precepts. It is doubtful in the extreme that one who has engaged in criminal or villainous conduct did so because he couldn't find the sort of maxim that would have inhibited one set of actions and triggered another. That is, it is doubtful in the extreme that the best explanation of praiseworthy or blameworthy behavior is one that locates sources of mechanical or biological advantage, more or less bypassing the actual moral struggle typically associated with actions warranting great praise or general condemnation.

Before considering the adequacy of such theories, it is worth recalling that one of the putative fathers of modern experimental psychology—and one who actually named the specialty of "physiological psychology"—Wilhelm Wundt, recognized that the issue of free will was far too complex to be absorbed into the framework of biological processes. In the third volume of his *Ethics* Wundt reserves whole chapters for the topics of the moral and the social will, the "causality" of the will, and related subjects. A committed voluntarist, he argues that the concept of freedom requires more than the power of choice; it requires a genuinely free choice, the defining mark of which is "reflective self-consciousness," which is

> a consciousness of one's own personality together with all those characteristics which result from the past development of the will. To reflect concerning oneself means to be conscious of one's personality as determined by previous volitional development; and to act with reflection is to act with a consciousness of the significance which the motives and purposes of the actions have for the character of the agent.[82]

Wundt's defense of moral freedom is not at the expense of causality but is constructed on the foundation of what he calls "psychical" causality. He regards as a dangerous and widespread mistake the attempt to restrict all modes of causality to the natural-physical or "mechanical" forms.[83] The success of such reasoning would be at the expense of all of psychology itself and, to that extent, self-defeating, as the reasoning on which it is based can only be understood through the very modes of psychic causality. That some species of determinism is at work is clear to Wundt, who further specifies,

> not determinism in the mistaken sense of applying the naturalistic concept of cause to the will and undertaking to predict the action from its conditions, but in the sense of maintaining the absolute sway of psychical causality and explaining events that have actually occurred by referring them to their causes. Without psychological determinism of this sort there can be no psychology, no science of mind whatever.[84]

The moral side of the person is the character of the person, the outcome of a psychological determinism, and something crystallized over the seasons of life as a result of education, experience, and so forth. To this point, Wundt might be seen as tracing along lines set down by Hume and extended by Mill, now needing only a version of associationism to complete the deterministic sketch. Even constitutional factors are included in the account of character, now rendered by Wundt in explicitly Darwinian terms:

> The empirical character . . . is involved in the ceaseless flux of psychical development. Its germ lies hid in the earliest tendencies of the individual consciousness, an inheritance from our ancestors, unfolding in the individual life, and destined to be transferred, enriched with new tendencies, to future generations.[85]

Also noted in Wundt's account, in part by way of Kantian inspiration, is an ideal *intelligible* character, impervious to life's fluxes but also never actually found in the life of actual persons. There is, however, an interim process, not wholly external and ceaselessly changing, not the stable self-determined ideal. The empirical character is, indeed, at first the product of external influences.

> We soon find, however, that the most important factor in the process is the exercise of will. . . . While external education begins the process of character-building, self-education completes it.[86]

Not only is there irreducibly *self*-direction but also the shaping, nurturing, and enriching powers of what Wundt dubs the "social will." It is a corrective to those abstract theories based on some never existing *individual* driven by utterly egoistic motives. Both Hume and Kant feature such entities, though in different ways and toward radically different theoretical conclusions. But, says Wundt, "all these fictions must vanish before the simple fact that the isolated individual man whom they presuppose does not exist and undoubtedly never has existed as a fact of experience.[87] That motives arise from, or actually include, sympathetic feelings is not denied by Wundt. Rather, they are expanded by him to include *motives of the understanding* that arise when the facts of perception are refined and evaluated by deliberation.[88] This is no barrier to motives being the cause of action, unless of course "cause" is mistakenly confined to some sort of mechanical operation. In Wundt, then, there is yet another form of compatibilism; one that rejects the hegemony of physicalism. Consequential actions arise from the deliberated choices of the individual, these choices expressive of a formed and ever-forming character, itself to some extent a self-creating entity. For a being with reflective self-consciousness, the sentiments and sympathies, the feelings and impulses, are never merely "states." They are rich in meaning and in moral significance, for the process of reflection includes centrally considerations of principle.

Mechanisms, Real and Imagined

Of the veritable library of Wundtian contributions, his ethical discourse would be largely neglected by the very profession claiming him as a father. Psychology, in its putatively scientific manifestations, would feature "drive-reduction" theories of motivation throughout most of the of the twentieth century. Mill's close friend, Alexander Bain, would speak for the future (but not for Mill) when, in his *The Emotions and the Will* (1859), he wrote patiently of that dated doctrine of two substances, "a material united with an immaterial in a certain vaguely defined relationship," and then noted that all this is "in course of being modified at the instance of modern physiology."[89] What physiology already makes clear in the matter of the determinants of actions is presented with controlled confidence: "Various motives—present or prospective pleasures and pains—concur in urging me to the act; the result of the conflict shows that one group is stronger than another; and that is the whole case."[90]

Clark Hull, now nearly as forgotten in psychology as Bain, produced books, articles, research studies, and a flock of disciples in support of the thesis just summarized. A growing body of research gradually exposed the failure of the particulars of Hull's program, and then the inadequacy of the entire theory. Any number of "drives" had to be added to hunger, thirst, and sexual activity to get the data to agree with the overarching assumptions. Soon there were "curiosity" drives, "affiliation" drives, "self-presentation" drives, and many others. Nonhuman primates were prepared to starve when given a choice between food and the ability to view the activities of others through a small window. That human beings displayed a continuing history of self-denial, of a willingness to die for love or honor, to accept impoverishment in order to erect a cathedral or oppose tyranny would have to convince all but the converted that a biologically based drive-reduction theory was not going to yield convincing or even plausible explanations of momentous undertakings. That such a theory was able to explain the choice of water over food after periods of dehydration seemed to some to be less promising than trivial.

At the end of the day, all internalist theories of action are a species of drive-reduction theory in that some impelling state of affairs is posited as the necessary causal antecedent of choice or action; then, the success of the action, by altering the previously impelling state of affairs, completes the sequence. The system must have the starter's pistol at the outset (a Hobbesian "endeavour," a Humean pleasure or pain) and a finish line down the road: one or another condition of "drive" is the fired shot, its reduction the broken tape. But actions understood as warranting praise or blame are those tied to principles marking out what are taken to be virtues and vices. Yet no one becomes, as it were, "satiated" by virtue. Few if any would conclude the day by noting that they had done nothing vicious for hours or weeks and now, "satiated" by virtue, must answer the summons to vice!

There are various ways of avoiding the problems tied to the standard internalist view. One attractive alternative, indebted to Ryle, does not so much deny internal causes of action as to render them otiose. Actions can be explained according to the outcomes they realize without including any hypothetical state of desire, want, belief, or the like. A bimetallic strip can be incorporated into a heating system such that the ambient temperature is regulated. True, the burner comes on and goes off as a result of the two metals having different coefficients of expansion. To explain the performance of the heating system in terms of "maintaining a specified average temperature" assigns no desires to the bimetallic strip, even if the states of that strip causally bring about the specified average temperature.

Arthur Collins has argued in favor of this approach to explanation, observing that "the thought that there is always a desire or something like a desire involved in actions, as a candidate causal factor, is not suggested in the least by the phenomenology of action."[91] When we consult the phenomenology of action what is typically apparent is that actions have ends in view. The requirement that every explanation be causal, coupled with essentially mechanistic conceptions of causality, sustains an otherwise hopelessly incomplete drive-reductionist account of every action.

Collins offers an amusing summary of how such an account takes care of even the least momentous of events, turning on a light: granting that a person wishes to have the light on and, seeing a switch, concludes that flipping it will result in the light going on. One could explain all of this by citing a causal law linking desire (an internal state) to the mobilizing of behavioral resources (also internal states), the public outcome being the overt behavior of flipping the switch. Using Collins's own example, one could find in such an explanation a parallel with, say, the desire to hoist an engine block on to a workbench. To achieve this, it is necessary to put a jack under the engine, the jack here being the mechanically enabling means by which to bring about the desired event. What Collins offers here is a parallel between a jack and a desire, each of them causally necessary to overcome the inertia or drag in the system. As it then makes sense to say that the engine could be placed on the workbench "if I could put a jack under it," Collins reduces the causal theory of desire to claims of the sort "I could have the switch flipped in no time if only I had a cause like wanting the light on." He concludes that

> it seems reasonably certain that "I wanted the light on" is never offered as a causal explanation for switch-flipping. If this is so, then there is really no serious competition for the teleological interpretation of reason-giving explanation.[92]

If the drive-reduction version of behavioristic explanations is defective, the purer descriptive behaviorism advocated by Collins is deficient. In the moral sphere, what finally moves one typically is neither the urgent demands of the body and things tied to bodily ease or pleasure, nor a specific goal or end for which the teleological account is sufficient. With respect to the latter, it is enough to recognize that actions guided by moral considerations are typically beholden to a principle rather than a "goal." Just as it would be peculiar in such contexts to hear the agent say, "If I could just adopt that principle I'd be able to offer assistance to one in need," it would be no less so to hear the agent say, "I offered assistance to one in need as a way of achieving a goal." Surely, adopting the right principle is an essential feature of moral life, and surely the morally aware person has such life as a goal. But the phenomenology of action, to use Collins's useful phrase, is far more textured, pliant, and *personal* than would be allowed even by a "teleological" behaviorism.

As for drive-reductionist accounts, the facts are often such that quite the contrary is the case. What finally *moves* one to choose and then to act on that choice is a judgment, Wundt's "motives of the understanding." True, a desire is to be satisfied by the chosen course of action. But the desire itself is generally not a bodily impulse or corporeal state of affairs, and when it is one of these the actor recognizes (through deliberation) that the ends in question are different from *moral* ends. It would be absurd to suggest that one seeks justice in precisely the way one seeks a cold drink on a hot day. Impulses and states of desire require little if any deliberation and scarcely need a higher principle as a justification. A thirsty person drinks not because it is "right" but because drinking slakes thirst. Does a thirsty person steal to slake the thirst? Alas, the answer to this question depends on whether, in the end, the thoughtless urgency of tissue will trump the developed and fundamentally different desires of a deliberating moral being. Where the conditions of the body are of such intensity as to render action essentially a reaction, the person is typically judged as having been compelled or coerced and thus not fully responsible in any morally significant respect. Clearly, where the drive-reduction model works best is precisely where moral ascriptions appear to be either irrelevant or improper.

It is instructive to return once more to Hume's philosophical psychology, not only because of his priority in the school of compatibilists but because of his rejection of reasons even as possible sources of action. He states the case unequivocally and, by now, famously:

> Since reason alone can never produce any action, or give rise to voli-
> tion, I infer that the same faculty is as incapable of preventing volition,
> or of disputing the preference with any passion or emotion. This conse-

quence is necessary. 'Tis impossible reason cou'd have the latter effect of preventing volition, but by giving an impulse in a contrary direction to our passion; and that impulse, had it operated alone, wou'd have been able to produce volition. Nothing can oppose or retard the impulse of passion but a contrary impulse. . . . Reason is, and ought only to be the slave of the passions, and can never pretend to any other office than to serve and obey them."[93]

Here again is a classic version of the internalist thesis: Actions are brought about and, as such, must be responses to efficacious antecedent events. No reason, as such, can move a muscle or cause the eye to blink. Rather, some motive force impels action. Within the animal economy, this force is given the name of passion or emotion or desire. Whether the course of action is x or y depends on the strength of the passion inclining each course, the stronger prevailing.

Against all this, and obvious from the conduct of others and from the thinnest introspective inquiry, is the fact that one is moved to act by words and taunts, by challenges and appeals to honor, by what one takes to be a good reason for action after due deliberation. It is equally obvious that the mere pattern of sound vibrations does not disclose what within the rhetorical performance is causing resolute commitments to action. The noncognitivist might insist that the power of rhetoric is just the power of exciting the passions, but this misses an essential first step; namely, the requirement that the actual account be of such a nature as to excite passion. Rhetoric does not move one to action the way sound waves impart motion to a loudspeaker. The power of rhetoric is the power of persuasion, itself comprehensible only at the level of rational appraisal. This power is a matter of undeniable fact and any general theory of human action must be able to account for its efficacy. One such theory was developed by Aristotle. It offers a particularly useful guide through the complexities of moral evaluations and warrants some measure of elaboration.

How Rhetoric Moves to Action: A Gloss on Aristotle

There is a somewhat pernicious confusion surrounding the notion of rhetoric, as in the phrase "That's just rhetoric." There is something of an aversion to exhortations, discernible in Ayer's remarks about the "exhortatory." It is the social constructionist who would have all values arise from the shifting predilections of the local culture, those who take the "discursive turn." Accordingly, the social constructionist is much less likely to dismiss any performance as "mere" rhetoric. As all moral appraisals on this account are discursive practices by which a given social world preserves itself and justifies itself, there is, alas, nothing "mere" about rhetoric. The social constructionist goes on, however, to conclude that there is no certain external standard that can be applied across cultures for the purpose of grading or ranking, only standards developed within the given culture by which to determine if the practices are succeeding *for them*. On this account, rhetoric is a device, a tool by which social cohesion and compliance are forged and maintained. The art and science of praise and blame can be understood without assuming the objectivity of the ascriptions themselves. So, even where the power of rhetoric is recognized, there is still the strong tendency to regard its content as subjective, situated, artifactual. If, after all, praise and blame are but local sign posts to direct traffic within morally independent duchies, then once again only a descriptive anthropology is needed to cover the subject completely.

To be sure, and however understood, praise and blame are rhetorical instruments. To understand their essential nature requires a fuller appreciation of rhetoric itself. At the least, it calls for distinctions between mere exhortations (as in cheerleading) and the serious mission of rhetoric within civic life; distinctions between mere opinion and what might actually be expected to move an audience to action.

In the ancient world, the young man who would develop his own powers of persuasion took instruction from the Sophists who promised disciples success in all forms of verbal combat. In Plato's *Sophist* the competing claims made against and on behalf of such sophistical instruction are examined. Here as in other dialogues there is close examination of the nature of knowledge and of real being, the extent to which one is able to know anything as in itself it really is, and whether language is able to represent or express the truth. If, as Sophists such as Protagoras insisted, "Man is the measure of all things," then the knowable realm is not filled with ontological absolutes awaiting discovery or philosophical illumination; rather it is filled with discursive *productions* awaiting some sort of contextual analysis or grammatical deconstruction. Depending on which of these ontologies is taken to be valid, it is either the philosopher or the sophist who warrants full if only hopeful allegiance. Thus, in the *Sophist*, young Socrates asks the Stranger from Elea whether he and his famous teachers, Parmenides and Zeno, are regarded in Italy as philosophers, statesmen, or sophists. It is a question that permits the Stranger to examine just what the sophist does, why he does it, and how immune his art is to the criticisms it routinely elicits.

Against the charge that the Sophists create false images and thus delude their students, the Stranger conducts a brief inquiry into the nature of icons of any type.[94] To call something an "image" of something else, one must mean there is a likeness between the two: a likeness brought about by the duplication of proportions and the careful copying, one-to-one, of the features of the original. But if this were done perfectly, there would be no basis on which to call one "original" and the other a "copy" or image or icon. Indeed, for there to be the latter, there must be a difference between it and the original. But in this case, the "image" will be a true copy of something else; or, put more aptly, will itself be an original.

The same line of reasoning can then be applied to discourse, for it, too, serves as an image of sorts—an image of an image. Now it may be asked whether discourse can be about nonbeing (about that which has no ontological standing) or only about being. If our discursive references are only about that which has being, then every such statement will be true, for there will be a real something to which each referring sentence is tied. If, however, there is falsehood and deceit, it must come about by way of referential discourse about nonbeing. As the latter is manifestly the case, the Stranger locates the sophist in that clear-cut realm wherein there are only idols and fancies or where there can be nothing said that is mistaken.

In his close study of this dialogue, Stanley Rosen observed,

> On either alternative, it follows that the distinction between truth and falsehood is impossible to maintain. We have no discursive access to the original or to genuine being, except in the sophistical sense that every statement is true. Philosophy is then assimilated to sophistry. The sophistical thesis is thus the assertion that man produces being in his capacity as talking animal.[95]

The dialogue concludes successfully for young Socrates who, in silent attendance, learns from the Stranger that the sophist has mastered the art of causing others to contradict themselves; an art human and not divine, for not natural; the art of word-juggling, itself a form of icon-making that strips ontology of natural kinds. The philosopher, on the other hand, makes images of what is real, thereby uncovering the truth of things as these may be known by the soul. (It is scarcely necessary to point out the extent to which this sophistical achievement has shaped any number of contemporary treatises on the nature of morals!)

Both philosopher and sophist exert themselves on the souls of their students, for both must avail themselves of those psychological powers and faculties by which one can be moved and taught in the first place. Accordingly, long before Aristotle would give the subject its disciplinary form, rhetoric was understood by the Sophists and by Socrates as an applied psychology whose efficacy depended entirely on the adequacy and soundness of the foundational subject. Nonetheless, it was Aristotle who most thoroughly examined the sources of rhetorical influence and first refined the subject, as he did so many others, into a systematic body of knowledge and theory; a "technical study," as he says, whose subject matter is "the modes of persuasion."[96]

For present purposes only books I and II of the *Rhetoric* need be considered, these treating of modes of persuasion associated with the spoken word. The factors identified by Aristotle as supplying rhetoric with its persuasive force are the character of the speaker, the mental or affective state into which auditors might be moved, and the actual logical or evidentiary resources contained in the rhetorical performance.[97] These establish the conditions of success needed by the rhetorician. These might be classified as the conditions of credibility, receptivity, and proof.

Although these conditions are distinguishable, they are nearly invariably interrelated and, to some extent, interdependent in practice. Consider only how the audience's mental or emotional or moral state might incline them to misjudge the character of the speaker; or how the evidence and logical rigor of an argument might alter the emotional tone of an assembly. Yet again, the command of relevant evidence and the precision and judiciousness with which it is deployed by the speaker may cause auditors to impute an exceptional character to him. Nonetheless, and against the opinions prevailing among writers on rhetoric in his own time, Aristotle takes the character of the speaker to be the primary source of rhetoric's power of persuasion. In other words, there is already something of a moral calculus in place before rhetoric can even begin to work on the moral sensibilities of auditors. Put another way, morality cannot be "mere" rhetoric, for rhetoric itself presupposes and depends on evaluative standards that must be met if there is to be any chance of rhetorical success.

In observing this, however, Aristotle finds something both odd and irksome. After all, under ideal conditions those perceived to be of upstanding character, those who are "good men," should enjoy neither more nor less credibility than what the actual words warrant. Persuasion, he says, "should be achieved by what the speaker says, not by what people think of his character before he begins to speak."[98]

Aristotle offers illustratively the deliberations of the judges of the Areopagus and other courts in what he calls "well-governed" states. In such settings disputants are simply not allowed to talk about nonessential matters. "This is sound law," he says, for it is wrong "to pervert the judge by moving him to anger or envy or pity—one might as well warp a carpenter's rule before using it."[99] There is a theoretical issue here, and a seeming paradox tied at once to considerations of a purely formal nature and at the same time to others that are personal, political, and ethical. One should be persuaded by the quality of an argument and should be otherwise immune to the repute or established honor of the speaker. But the latter proves to be the major source of rhetorical influence.

In light of this, one might be confused as to how Aristotle meant the subject of rhetoric to be understood. Is it an effective device by which to achieve ends otherwise blocked by purely judicious reasoning? Is it a way to move those whose passions are easily stirred? Is Aristotle to be counted among cynical and even Machiavellian experts informing those who would aspire to high office just how to manipulate an audience? Indeed, there is much in the essay that presents itself as just such a "how-to" manual. There are, however, constant reminders in the same pages of the qualities of the virtuous person and the emotions and dispositions of the vicious. Examin-

ing these passages one is inclined to regard the *Rhetoric* as a means of knowing oneself, knowing one's vulnerabilities in the face of masters of persuasion. Taking both aspects of the work at once, one does find the elements
of paradox, for the same essay seems to recommend what it condemns.

How is the paradox, if there is one, to be unraveled and settled? To begin,
the *Rhetoric* is concerned with a special kind of art that must guide us, as
Aristotle says, where we have no other art or systematic knowledge on which
to rely.[100] As persuasion itself enters into nearly every aspect of social life,
rhetoric is omnipresent. Thus, a taxonomy is needed just to organize the
subject, but this very taxonomy depends on that most general of the perspectives to be found in Aristotle's nonlogical treatises; that is, the ethological
perspective. The way to go about defining and identifying the principle
forms of rhetoric is to examine its various aims and occurrences where it is
explicitly practiced. To know what it is intended *for*, and to know the causal
modalities on which it depends, is finally to understand what kind of art or
science it is. This part of the inquiry is essentially value-neutral. One can
examine the purposes of a trireme and the mechanical and dynamic principles by which it becomes seaworthy without approving of such acts of war-
fare or piracy as might be perpetrated by the crew. At this point, then, we
are best served by reviewing the taxonomy.

Aristotle partitions rhetoric into three branches. With his characteristic
zest for categorization, he distinguishes between and among what he calls
the deliberative, the forensic, and the epideictic forms, each operating within
a definable temporal sphere. Deliberative rhetoric urges action or forbear-
ance and thus seeks to influence the future, chiefly by appeals to prudence
and utility. Forensic rhetoric, on the other hand, is the rhetoric of prosecu-
tion and defense, the rhetoric of adjudication, based on events that have
already taken place and which now cry out for justice. Epideictic ("showy"
or "flowery") rhetoric differs from both of these. It is the rhetoric of censure
or encomium, the rhetoric of the here and now, seeking to honor or to condemn. If praise and blame are understood as rhetorical endeavors in this
richer and more precise sense, then they are at once deliberative, forensic,
and epideictic: they would influence the future by serving as teachers of
prudence and utility; they would aid in the punishment of offenders by
underscoring the nature of the misdeed; they are of the very essence of
encomium and censure.

The time frames and the ends sought by the three forms of rhetoric differ.
We often honor those who throw caution or prudence to the wind and engage in heroic actions that later warrant great praise even by those who first
judged the effort to be futile or foolish. Similarly, one might win at litigation
on a minor technicality, but thereby secure justice in a manner that is worthy
of censure. These specific matters aside, Aristotle encourages us to consider
in the most general terms the basis on which we should be urged to do
anything at all, or on which urgings are likely to be heeded. Just what is the

most general objective of exhortations? Unsurprisingly, for Aristotle this turns out to be *happiness* and its constituents.[101] Whether the rhetoric is deliberative, forensic, or epideictic, it must finally resonate with commonly held desires and values among which Aristotle includes good birth, good friends, wealth, worthy children, health, beauty, honor, and a happy old age, adding a measure of good fortune or luck.

Clearly, no reasonable person would urge others to neglect or undervalue these, nor would an audience be easily moved to action were these and kindred possibilities not at stake. But once "happiness" or the good life is taken to be the end or target or goal of an activity (and rhetoric is no exception), the nature of happiness itself must be clarified, as well as the nature of that beneficiary or seeker who would find happiness in one or another form of life. Whether we examine individual persons or entire governments, says Aristotle, their qualities "are revealed in their acts of choice, and these are determined by the end that inspires them."[102] When rhetoric is able to move them to choose, their choices reveal not only the power of rhetoric but something fundamental about those moved by it. So the subject of rhetoric turns out to be more than an examination of the modes of persuasion. It is also, and perhaps more importantly, a means by which to evaluate the qualities, chiefly moral, both of those who exert and of those who respond to rhetorical influences. It becomes part of that enlarged and *characterological* psychology found throughout Aristotle's political and ethical compositions. In these respects, it offers a more complete picture of the function and nature of praise and blame. These, too, become part of the overall project that aims at a flourishing form of life.

If the character of the speaker is often singularly effective in persuading others, it is of importance for the rhetorician to know how character and honor and nobility are comprehended by others. This is especially so where the rhetoric is epideictic. Just what is that excellence of character (*aretê*) that so fully establishes an allegiance on the part of those who behold it? The general view, says Aristotle, is that it is what finds one "providing and preserving good things."[103] Persons of normal judgment and perception regard as excellent those whose efforts bring about and nurture that which is good. For the multitude to reach this judgment, however, it is necessary that they regard these consequences as intended. Adventitious good offers no basis for praise or honor. Thus, when the character of the rhetorician is sufficient to win others to his cause it must be a character reflecting, or thought to be composed of, certain dispositions. Aristotle lists them: justice, courage, temperance, magnificence, magnanimity, liberality, gentleness, prudence, wisdom—in a word, just the virtues extolled in both the *Nichomachaean* and *Eudemian Ethics*. To be sure, it is easier for the rhetorician to move an audience by ascribing such virtues to himself or to the audience itself. As Socrates noted, it isn't difficult praising Athenians before a group of Athenians![104] Lest Aristotle's observation here be taken in a cynical vein, however, note that only those won over to such virtues will be moved by those allegedly possessing them. The fool is not attracted to wisdom, nor the small-minded to magnanimity. Again, the observation establishes one of the grounds on which to assess the moral qualities of both speaker and audience. Those who are moved by guile and pretense, or by expectations of what the virtuous judge to be mean and sordid, present the objective observer with all of the evidence needed to reach a sound judgment as to the worth of the collective.

To make such judgments, however, one must have access to more than the actions themselves or even their consequences. Good persons can bring about the undesirable inadvertently. The same is true of foolishness and small-mindedness or other vices, great and small that, like their virtuous opposites, are grounded less in the act than in the dispositions that give rise to it. This is an important aspect of praise and blame: the degree of each is typically a measure of the judged intentions rather than the actual consequences of the actions of another. As Aristotle notes, "The worse of two acts of wrong done to others is that which is prompted by the worse disposition. Hence, the most trifling acts may be the worst ones."[105]

The mission of rhetoric in such cases is clear, at least within the forensic domain where punishments would otherwise be mechanically tied to physical actions and material injuries. To fail to examine the underlying dispositions—the character of the actor—is to treat such behavior as merely a bare fact with no meaning beyond itself. Understood this way, however, rhetoric itself has a certain reflexive property in that it seeks to bring about otherwise refractory actions, and can do so only by appealing to certain dispositions. The rhetorician finds the principle to which the relevant dispositions are attached and in this way brings about a desired response on the part of those sensitive to the appeal.

To refer to what moves others is to refer to some cause of activity. Aristotle subscribes unequivocally to an internalist theory of action in that he takes actions as caused by motives, states and conditions within the actor. His theory of rhetoric is centrally a theory of action, the underlying causes being seven in number: *chance, nature, compulsion, habit, reasoning, anger,* and *appetite.*[106] Other candidate causes of action prove to be mere correlates. Thus, young men might act out of strong passions, but it is the anger or the appetite, and not their youth, that *causes* the action. What chance brings about has only an indeterminate cause and must be without purpose. Nature, as Aristotle would have it understood in this context, yields utterly determined and uniform outcomes, more in the manner of instincts and reflexes, and thus beyond the reach of rhetoric. As for compulsion, there is no need for rhetorical persuasion once one has put a gun to the head of another. Nor is it necessary to offer rhetorical inducements for actions that have already become habitual. If, then, the rhetorician is to induce action, he must achieve his aims by appealing to what is the rational, affective, or appetitive processes in his audience. Again, what is promised is what is, or is taken to be, a source of happiness; what is promised is what is *pleasant*; or what will reduce or terminate suffering or grief; or what will secure that which is commonly desired, either for its own sake or for its usefulness.

The actions that rhetoric would elicit, however, have consequences not only for the actors but for those toward whom the actions are directed. As a result of this, the rhetorical context is one in which considerations of justice often arise even when the context is not forensic. Justice for Aristotle is not univocal. It refers both to statutory requirements and to abiding principles of equity; to what is local and expressible in writing, and to what requires deeper and more intuitive sources of judiciousness; to understandings that might be implicit in the legislative intent but might also reach cases never envisaged by the lawgiver.

In this the paradox dissolves further, for we see that forensic rhetoric, far from being a manipulative ploy operating extralegally, is in fact a much needed device for enlarging the juridical context to include principles of equity. What the assembly must be made to understand is what an act betokens about the actor himself. The punishment, if there is any, for injuries caused by accident or inadvertence is to be far lighter than that arising from turpitude and malignant intent. Thus, in drawing attention to what an evil person really was seeking to achieve—even where the offense itself is minor and its immediate consequences trivial—the rhetorician leads his auditors, by argument and empathy, toward conclusions faithful not only to the facts but to their significance. Thus, even in instances in which a man has acted rashly or intemperately and should therefore receive punishments or rebukes, it is equity, as developed by the rhetorician, that would

> ask not what a man is now but what he has always or for the most part been. It bids us to remember benefits rather than injuries, and benefits received rather than benefits conferred.[107]

This same rationale operates in other rhetorical contexts as well, for, in assigning praise or blame or in urging others on toward a nobler or happier state, one must identify what may only be implicit or even lacking in the aspirations and deliberations of one's audience. In these more general contexts, the rhetorical devices will be those Aristotle called "nontechnical"; devices not formally logical, not closely tied to evidence, eyewitness accounts, and written or uttered oaths and contracts.

In these same general settings the rhetorician must be informed as to how such nonrational or, as the current term is used, noncognitive factors as anger and appetite move us. As an internalist, Aristotle examines the relationship between emotions and motives that serve as the efficient causes of behavior, and the moral weight of the actions thus generated. One of his choice exemplars in this connection is anger. To understand his treatment of it in the *Rhetoric* is to understand his general position on the emotions.

To begin, Aristotle recognizes that the emotions and appetites are endemic to animal life and are utterly natural. They have the instrumental function of impelling actions typically associated with self-preservation and propagation. The question as to whether anger or affection or shame or fear is good or bad, right or wrong, praiseworthy or blameworthy, is unanswerable, therefore, for the emotions qua emotions can have no such properties. It is only when their objects or sources are identified that moral appraisal becomes possible. To know, for example, that one is experiencing the emotion of love, and to know no more, is a morally neutral fact with no more significance than an itch or toothache until it is discovered just what or whom is the object of this love. Only then is it possible to judge the moral quality of the person. To know how someone is "disposed" to love is part of knowing what sort of person that someone is. The moral quality that can be assigned to affective states is determined by an analysis of the agent's disposition(s) (*hexis*). Properly recast, therefore, our moral ascriptions will be of the form "Smith has a good (or bad) disposition to anger (or love, or shame, or fear, and so on)." The virtuous man is angered by villainy; the great-spirited man has contempt for small-mindedness, the rash man lacks all fear where fear is in order.

The dialectical relationship is again apparent in Aristotle's briefer discussions of pity and indignation. Pity is the pain we feel when an evil befalls one who does not deserve it. Indignation is the pain we feel when good fortune befalls another who does not deserve it. In both cases, we may be said to have a good hexis for the felt emotion. Both of these feelings, says Aristotle, "are associated with good character."[108] Tranquility in the face of injustice, to paraphrase a political slogan of not too many years ago, is no virtue.

The emotion of anger finds a special place in Aristotle's *Rhetoric* because it is most closely associated with the gaining and preserving of honor, with avenging injuries, and with the burdens faced by those who would have prudence prevail in times of unrest. Anger thus figures centrally in the three main branches of rhetoric; the aforementioned deliberative, forensic, and epideictic.

Perhaps more than any other emotion, it is anger that the rhetorician must understand most fully, for it is the very grounding of *blame*. What this points to is a feature of praise and blame frequently overlooked when their moral content is studied. In his detailed analysis of Aristotle's *Rhetoric*, Eugene Garver highlights the often neglected link:

> We make our discourse ethical by making our ethos argumentative. Ethos is an incidental result of argument in the same way that *phronEsis* is an incidental result of ethical virtue and happiness an incidental result of virtue."[109]

Discursive practices can attain no moral status as long as they aim at preserving the status quo. It is only when the "discursive turn" is in the direction of argument—in the direction of a rhetorical mode of suasion for the purpose of correcting and refining the given—that it rises to the level of a virtuous practice and can promise, as an incidental result, happiness itself. It is not discourse qua discourse that establishes the foundations of morality. It is a special and critical mode of discourse, a rhetorical and dialectical mode, the point of which is finally a *criticism of life*. Far from preserving the given, rhetoric properly understood seeks to transform it. Far from being a record of prevailing habits and cultural attachments, it is the engine of moral progress, when not the springboard for revolutions. This leads to a conclusion about the motive power of rhetoric somewhat different from prevailing theories, whether cognitivist, noncognitivist, externalist, or internalist.

Determinism, Compatibilism, and Constitutive Luck Revisited

Determinism bears a distinct and distinguishable relation to the concept of "necessitation." To regard an event as determined is, among other considerations, to regard it as essentially required by the determining factors such that, when these factors are present, the event *necessarily* ensues. Hume's "constant conjunction" thesis is no exception here. Even if Mill can insist that all one means by a necessity is an unfailing association in experience, the idea of necessity asserts itself. The constant conjunction thesis is a theory regarding the psychological grounding of the concept of causation, not a theory about causes. So too is it not a metaphysical but a psychological theory of necessitation.

Too often those who defend compatibilism and more severe forms of determinism seem to require that, where antecedent events necessitate a given outcome, authentic and deliberative agency need not be invoked. The tendency is strong, even if a reasonable counter to it was offered by Joseph Butler more than two centuries ago. In his *Analogy* he depicts an argument between a fatalist (necessitarian) and a defender of moral freedom. He stages the colloquy within a house, noting that the disputants must agree on this much: that the house arose from an architectural plan devised by the architect. Thus, both fatalist and libertarian accept the fact of the house and the conceptual requirement that it realize a design. The only bone of contention, then, is not whether there was design, deliberation, and agency, but whether the architect did what he did *freely* or as a result of necessity. Accordingly, the fatalist's assertion that the house arises from or by necessity can only mean, according to Butler, "by an Agent acting necessarily," and that nothing in this precludes the elements of intelligence, intention, and design. So, even if fatalism were granted,

> it would just as much account for the formation of the world as for the structure of a house, and no more. Necessity as much requires and supposes a Necessary Agent, as Freedom requires and supposes a Free Agent.[110]

On what grounds, then, would Butler choose between the two accounts? Alas, on the grounds on which a tolerable form of life becomes possible. For just in case the offspring of the fatalist were confirmed in the theories of his parent—coming to regard himself as utterly determined in his thoughts, actions, and aspirations, and thus beyond the reach of moral appraisal—this offspring would find no habitable spot within the world of social beings. "And therefore, though it were admitted that this opinion of Necessity were speculatively true, yet, with regard to practice, it is as if it were false, so far as our experience reaches; that is, to the whole of our present life."[111]

It was C. D. Broad's judgment that Butler had utterly demolished the egoistic theory of ethics by exposing its defects at the level of human psychology. In his usual feisty fashion, Broad concluded that, notwithstanding Butler's success, the theory remains the favorite among

> bookmakers and smart young business men whose claim to know the world is based on an intimate acquaintance with the shadier side of it. . . . Still, all good fallacies go to America when they die, and rise again as the latest discoveries of the local professors. So it will always be useful to have Butler's refutations at hand."[112]

Where others would search for telling arguments for or against determinism, Butler rests his case on the wide and required experiences of those who would actually take up residence in the world and strive for a coherent and productive life amidst others. In any dispute between those possessing what is and must be merely speculatively true and those adopting a thesis on which an acceptable form of life depends, reasonableness itself (if not logic) embraces the latter.

With all due respect paid to Butler and to C. D. Broad, the staying power of egoistic theories depends on more than the alleged importation of fallacies by American professors! The defender of such theories need only insist that, whatever the rider on the Clapham omnibus might believe to be the source of altruistic behavior and morally principled conduct, the actual source is self-interest. Accordingly, at a more rigorous level, it becomes clear that the issue of freedom in an otherwise determined world calls for nothing less than a full-blown moral theory that goes beyond speculation regarding what most persons know or feel in the matter of morals. An economical defense of this view has been advanced by Michael McKenna, who argues that, even if free will and determinism cannot be reconciled, moral responsibility and determinism can.[113] We have seen that there are different arguments tending toward this conclusion, some of them not compatible with others. Moving, then, beyond Butler, even while mindful of the persuasive pragmatic test to which he would expose competing theories, we turn to theories regarding the relationship between moral responsibility and the seemingly determined world in which agency expresses itself. There are on offer a number of the required "full-blown" theories, but none so complete and air-tight as to arrest criticism and continuing debate.

Robert Kane has written extensively in defense of incompatibilist freedom, while providing scrupulously fair presentations of competing views and their limitations. He has drawn attention to different kinds of freedom, insisting that, though all may be desirable, there is one that is *worth having* more than the rest, and that is *free will*.[114] Possession of this confers ultimate responsibility on the actor, rendering actions an authentic, self-defining, self-affirming expression of one's very self. What ultimate responsibility entails is that events and states of affairs are actually brought about by what the agent willingly did or failed to do; more,

> if the agent is personally responsible for X, and if Y is a sufficient reason (ground or cause or explanation) for X (assuming relevant laws), then the agent must also be personally responsible for Y.[115]

Central to moral responsibility is not simply the possessory condition that establishes the relation between agent and act as "his"; rather, the relation must be possessory in the intimate and authentic sense of "his own." The relationship is akin not to having a tooth, but to having a *toothache*. Not only is this something known and possessed by direct acquaintance, but it is something over which one has incorrigible epistemic authority.

But is this relationship ever present? Is it ever the case that the agent is so authentically free that the course of action undertaken is uniquely *his own* in the sense of being uniquely caused by him as a free agent? The very question resurrects Mackie's depiction of moral entities as "queer," for what could be more odd than that which is at once real and uncaused, knowable but privately possessed? What confers the unwanted property of oddness, however, is nothing in our actual experiences. Rather, it is the dominant theory regarding experience itself, the theory advanced by Locke and brought to full maturity by Hume and by Mill. It is customary to refer to it as "empiricism," but this is misleading, for the theory makes provision only for a certain class of experiences and is largely indifferent to a radically different but significant class.

Locke answered his own question as to how the mind becomes furnished with the word "experience," but he devoted nearly all of the *Essay* to our experiences of the external world. When Hume got around to adding the interoceptive dimension, his labor was expended chiefly on the passions, these being the springs of action. Even within the school of empiricism this bias and its awkward progeny were sources of concern.

Thomas Reid, as noted earlier, and the "*ideologue*," Maine de Biran, were the most astute critics of the tendency. It was Reid who argued that no number of mere pairings ("constant conjunctions") of external events could of themselves give rise to the notion of a causal relationship. Rather, the imputing of causal dependencies to such external events must be an inference drawn from our awareness of our own powers. Thus, from the direct knowledge one has of one's own ability to bring about certain events (e.g., raising one's hand), one infers that regularities in the external world express the operation of an otherwise hidden power. Reid reasoned that our awareness of ourselves as possessing active power—the power to do or to forbear from doing—arises early in life. One might surmise that even in fetal life the movement of the thumb to the mouth is evidence of such primitive knowledge. Clearly, it is not by observation or by trial and error that one comes to know that one is the source of one's own movements.[116]

Maine de Biran, a fellow *ideologue* of Destutt Tracy, is now as unread as he has long been untranslated. But he was widely regarded as a leader of French philosophy for a century following his earliest publications (1812), and described by Henri Bergson as "our Kant."[117] It was Biran, perhaps more than any other writer within the empiricist tradition, who drew attention to two subtle but powerful features of the interoceptive world of experience: first, it is only by selection and volition that the external senses come to be directed toward one object or source and away from others. Secondly, unlike the ephemera of external sights and sounds, the interoceptive processes are continuous and thus provide the very context by which the percipient can have awareness both of his own continuity and the subject of these experiences. Biran would record in his diary on May 6, 1816, his own appraisal of how his *Essai sur les fondements de la psychologie* of 1812 helped to resolve the free will-determinism issue: "I have proved that our experience of selfhood is nothing but one of the liberty and the power to act, to perform an action independent of all causes other than the will."[118]

It is a fact of introspection that I am able to darken the world by closing my eyes; that I can reduce the visible size of an object by holding it at a greater distance; that I can hear one of two simultaneous conversations by choosing to listen to one and ignore the other. The access the external world has to the realm of consciousness is at the discretion of the percipient. That this same percipient remains erect in posture, directs his gaze, tenses and relaxes muscles to meet the burdens of gravity—all of this and ten thousand other intended actions are the required performances of daily life, all reliably experienced from within, all operating continuously even as the external senses shut down. On this basis there is, indeed, that very "liberty of indifference"otherwise incomprehensible on the assumption that only impressions and passions comprise the realm of possible experience. Whether one looks toward the light of day or into the darker reaches of the cave is not "determined" by the external world or an internal sentiment.

What Reid and Biran offer is a more complete and credible psychology; a psychology informed by daily experience and conformable to the actual record of striving, selecting, and attending actions that fill the unforgiving minute. The mind can only be furnished by the experiences one chooses to have, chooses to assign importance to, chooses to retain and rehearse and record. There is, then, at least this much of a rejoinder to the tabula rasa school and its noncognitive supplements.

Constitutive Luck and Its Beneficiaries (Victims)

Whatever the fate of theories of incompatibilist or compatibilist freedom, or those of hard or soft determinism, there is every reason to expect that praise and blame will be deployed according to the introspective lights of actors, witnesses, and victims. There is something utterly *natural* about holding persons responsible for their actions and about harboring sentiments that match up with rational assessments of praiseworthy and blameworthy conduct. As discussed above, Aristotle's *Rhetoric* presents an outline of the emotional appeals to action and the interplay of social, personal, and affective factors. Some of these same factors are treated in Peter Strawson's highly influential "Freedom and resentment," briefly cited in the preceding chapter, in which the role of praise and blame is understood to be far-reaching.[119] In that address Strawson predicts that moral ascriptions would not be withheld or significantly altered just in case some powerful new defense of determinism were to be advanced by philosophers or scientists. The reason is found within what Thomas Reid would have taken to be our natural dispositions and those first principles of morals; natural dispositions that figure in that *natural language* by which others comprehend our most basic needs and expectations. In Peter Strawson's terms, the very possibility of a social life carries with it a cadre of reactive attitudes expressive of gratitude, resentment, love, hurt feelings, disapproval, and forgiveness among many others. As these are central to the very possibility of interpersonal relationships and all that arises from social and civic life—forming nothing less than a natural endowment—they are not hostage to metaphysical or moral theories.

Exceptional persons often have identifying and relevant attributes on which exceptional achievement may even heavily depend. Obesity and cross-country running are an unpromising tandem. Mongolism and theoretical physics are as well. So what if both the greatest achievements and the most dreadful actions are but heritable deviations waiting to be unearthed? And what of all the outcomes between these poles? Should there not be a kind of moral handicapping for those receiving less from the lottery?

Perhaps it is now clearer to see that the notion of "constitutive luck" exemplifies what Wundt referred to as the "mechanical" species of determinism, in that it takes achievement and failure to be relevantly, if not solely, caused by natural constitutional factors. One's personal worthiness, for praise or for blame, is thereupon diminished precisely to the extent that desirable or admirable or repulsive attributes are genetically predisposed.

In its radical expression, however, this line of reasoning suffers from the self-refuting nature of the parent theory. For to accept the deterministic theory is to accept further that, whether or not one does accept such a theory—whether or not one is disposed to advance such a theory—is also determined by constitutional factors over which one has no control. In the end, we have no means by which to subtract out, as it were, the genetic predisposition to accept or reject propositions of a certain kind from their intrinsic truth or epistemic worth. The determinist who implores us to accept determinism on the strength of the arguments favoring it implicitly ascribes to us the power to choose one argument over another, and to do so solely on the basis of the quality of the argument. Thus, to argue for the adoption of such a theory is to deny its validity.

If this is one of the textbook defects of radical determinism, it is a defect shared by the "constitutive luck" thesis, for there is no reason to assume in advance that the constitutional factors that determine the quality of body and mind will not also determine how body and mind react to their respective "adequate stimuli." If constitutional factors causally yield creative genius, they surely must be at the bottom of deductive and inferential reasoning, the weighing of evidence, the development of arguments, and ultimately the epistemic and doxastic states one occupies.

We see, then, that one of the liabilities of this whole drift of thought is that it turns out, perhaps surprisingly, to be utterly inconsequential. Like the parent and radical version of determinism, it transforms all of the important terms of the debate into inevitabilities, leaving disputants in a condition of fatalistic hopelessness, though curiously unaffected by the truth of the thesis. One either agrees with the theory or rejects it because *one must*, and that's the end of it. This consequence was recognized and analyzed by Aristotle who put these words into the mouth of an ancient advocate of "constitutive luck":

> A man needs to be born with moral vision, so to speak, whereby to discern correctly and choose what is truly good. A man of good natural disposition is a man well endowed by nature in this respect; for if a thing is the greatest and noblest of gifts, and is something which cannot be acquired or learnt from another . . . a man will (have it) . . . bestowed on him at birth.[120]

Having summarized the theory thus, Aristotle then goes on to conclude that, if it is true, there can be neither virtue nor vice, since "for both the good man and the bad man alike, their view of their end is determined in the same manner, by nature. . . . All their actions of whatever sort are guided by reference to their end as thus determined." Aristotle will have none of this, concluding that the "natures" in question pertain to matters of character, and that persons take a share in the responsibility for the formation of their own characters.

But then is nothing to be said for constitutional factors and the genetic processes from which they presumably arise and on which they depend? The question calls for a distinction between being able to say nothing at all, and being able to say nothing of *moral* significance. Needless to say, no one is morally responsible for what one cannot control, influence, or alter. Nor is one blameworthy for failing to do either what no one can do or what, in the circumstance, the actor is plausibly regarded as having been unable to do. The sense in which it is not entirely to basketball legend Michael Jordan's *moral* credit that he can do what he does is precisely the sense in which it is not to his moral discredit that others cannot. Moral discourse and reasoning are about choices and intentions. They are about actions and achievements only to the extent that these instantiate or verify the actual aims of the agent. From a moral point of view, there is only one constitutive factor that needs to be consulted in attempts to assign moral standing to actions or events: one must be constituted in such a way as to be able freely to frame alternative courses of action and to recognize the harms or benefits likely to arise from choosing one or the other. The freedom to frame or to will an outcome is not the same as the ability to do it; it pertains only to the ability to wish it.

The possibility of moral worthiness is in the last analysis a threshold consideration rather than a matter of superiority or defect. There must be just enough rational and self-reflective power—enough *free will*—for the being in question to be able to choose freely and to base the choice on a principle or maxim, the moral quality of which can be discerned by a rational being.

What is to be said finally about so-called selfish genes and sociobiological accounts of morality; about the heritability of psychological phenotypes or, in the older idiom, the instinctually barbarous tendencies of the human species? At the purely technical level, nothing much needs to be said. Heritability is a measure of sample variance and permits statements to be made only about the extent to which nongenetic manipulations are likely to alter the sample variance. If it says something about how, for example, measures of altruism or introversion or I.Q. are distributed, it says nothing about Smith's saintly mission, Jones's shyness, or Pascal's legendary cleverness.

It is, however, not merely that heritability refers to sample variances and not to individuals that excludes it from judgments and explanations in individual cases. Clearly, to judge any person on the basis of "traits" shared with other members of a given gene pool exemplifies that very *phratric* justice from which the ancient Greek world was liberated by Solon. More to the point is the difference between being *inclined* and being *determined*. Anticipating Leibniz and perhaps influencing him, Thomas Aquinas defended the distinction in the *Summa Contra Gentiles* (chap. 85), in relation to astrological determinism. One may be inclined by natural (planetary) forces but not determined by them unless that outcome itself is not a matter of choice but of instinct.

By way of conclusion, it is instructive to consider the Thomistic theory of the will as developed in eight Articles in Question VI of the *Summa Theologiae*[121] Thomas understands that the determinist and the compatibilist agree that the will is directed toward goals and is impelled by desires. The determinist denies that freedom enters into this at any point; the compatibilist grants that there is "choice," but that it is determined by the internal conditions of need, desire, and the like. The core question, then, is whether desires *necessitate* the will's deployment.

Addressing this question in the Second Article, Thomas Aquinas, again prefiguring Leibniz's argument, contrasts the contingent with the necessary adherence of one thing to another. Consider things that can be known. Some intelligibles adhere of necessity to first principles such that their denial would constitute a logical contradiction; for example, that two things equal to a third are equal to each other. Some intelligibles adhere only contingently to first principles. Where adherence is of necessity, the intellect itself assents of necessity, this determined not mechanically but logically. Turning next to volition, the framework now in place, Thomas contrasts those particular goods that have a necessary connection with happiness with those that do not. The latter can be missing and one still can be happy. On this understanding, the will adheres *necessarily* to that which has a necessary connection to happiness. This necessary adherence is built into the very logic of the case and is not explained by appeals to "mechanism."

Not surprisingly, Thomas Aquinas takes "seeing God" as that which is foundational for all true happiness. For one who has seen "God in His essence," the will necessarily adheres to God. But the Thomas Aquinas who connects our duties to our nature is never indifferent to constitutive factors capable of directing and also defeating the will. Influenced by Aristotle's ethical treatises, he distinguishes between compulsions and coercions on the one hand, and choices one would have wished not to have to make. Under compulsion or coercion,

> the will does not consent, but is moved entirely counter to that which is done through compulsion; whereas what is done through fear becomes voluntary because the will is moved towards it, although not for its own sake, but . . . in order to avoid an evil which is feared.[122]

This profound theological element can be withdrawn for philosophical purposes and replaced by secular candidates for "the good life," the argument itself remaining intact. In this form, the argument can be directed at notions of "constitutive luck" and genetic determinism. That Helen of Troy was the beneficiary or the victim of her own beauty does not settle, but rather raises the moral question; namely, whether it is ever right to praise or blame on the basis of attributes falling outside the volitional resources of the target. That Einstein was (somehow) genetically empowered to achieve that which falls beyond the general run of intellectual resources again leaves open the question of whether Einstein should be praised or blamed: praised for making good use of these resources or blamed for doing too little with them. Clearly, there is no gene that expresses itself in the form of revolutionary contributions to *Physics Review Letters*; nor is there a gene that sets the course for a thousand warships.

Necessity inheres in logical relations, not psychological relations. Following Swinburne and the standard view, we can reserve praise for those who overcome limitations and withhold blame from those who cannot, provided the limitations are not self-imposed. We can praise those who resist strong impulses toward wrongdoing, without forfeiting that very axiology by which actions are recognized as wrongful.

In reserving necessity to logic and mathematics, one is drawn again to consideration of moral realism, to notions about the alleged "queerness" of moral properties, to the widely perceived differences between moral science and natural science, to determinism as a metaphysical presupposition and determinism as the best explanation of observed facts. William Wallace has written an insightful precis on certain habitual contemporary notions about natural science that may, in fact, constitute a bar to richer understandings. Noting the tendency to treat causation and necessity as more or less synonymous, Wallace writes,

> Coupled with this, scientific knowledge is thought to be necessary and universal, allowing for no exceptions, and thus to be attainable only where complete certitude is possible. Such views of science and causality . . . work against the understanding of nature.[123]

This much is the case in our examination of what Wallace calls the *outer* dimension of nature. When attention turns to the *inner* dimension—which reveals just what it is that makes something the sort of thing it is—we discover

> particular natures found in the universe that enable things to be classified into natural kinds. . . . Questions relating to nature in this second sense turn our thought within, to a consideration of the intrinsic factors that enter into the individual's composition.[124]

It is in this sense of *human* nature that one has reason to expect defining properties not obscured by the accidental features bequeathed or painted over by merely contingent or ephemeral occurrences. "Fitness for the rule of law" is an economical way of capturing among the most defining of the properties. Law itself is predicated on the facts of human nature, including such facts as the potential for venality and moral weakness. Law is predicated, too, on the conceptually necessary assumption that beings fit for the rule of law can conform their conduct to legal proscriptions. Were we all saints, no law would be necessary, and were we merely physical systems whose actions—*reactions*—were causally determined, no law would be intelligible. The law is put in place *because* we are moved by anger or avarice or envy or frustration or lust. Far from ignoring these products of our physical natures the law offers one method for controlling them and converting them to better purposes. On the moral side of the ledger, these same physical, and to some extent inherited, tendencies are the very grist on which the moral mill must do its work. Indeed, had we been constituted as perfectly moral beings, there would be no moral work to be done!

Who should have won the prize at Troy? Should it have gone to the best horseman, the best man, the one favored by the gods or the one just lucky enough to have been pulled by the fastest horses? One answer that recommends itself is that the race belongs to the swift, defined as the one who arrives first. We reserve the right to temper our admiration of winners with an awareness of the role of good fortune; to penalize those who play fast and loose with the rules; to exercise sympathy where a bad run of luck impedes the worthy; and to harbor ideals according to which, in the end, only good things happen to the good.

Meanwhile, both the rule of law as well as duties to oneself and others are grounded in the assumption of authentic moral autonomy. It is this assumption, and not any contingent physical or physiological fact, on which the presumption of moral equality rests and, with it, nearly every canon of justice. This recognition is not at the expense of the explanatory power of causality.

Clarke vs. Hobbes and Leibniz

When Thomas Reid pithily declared the cause of an action to be the will of the actor, and the cause of the will to be the actor himself, he summarized whole volumes devoted to the essential and self-forming nature of character. He also drew attention again to the difference between a cause and a power, and a mere power and an *active* power. In these respects, he carried on the case for voluntarism that had been made a half-century earlier as Samuel Clarke, in his Boyle lectures (1704), tested the deterministic metaphysics of Hobbes and Spinoza. Against the proposition that every effect presupposes an antecedent cause, Clarke's reply is that this cannot always be an *external* cause for "there must of Necessity be Somewhere a Beginning of Operation or a Power of Acting . . . and that this Power may be, and is in *Man*."[125]

The proposition itself leads to an infinite regress in which the first term in the causal sequence would have to be *nothing* if a self-causing entity is denied. Against the supposition that the laws of material causation must apply to human actions, he contends that thought and volition do not inhere in matter and thus "are not concluded under the Laws thereof."[126] The category of matter is exhausted by the properties of mass, figure, and motion, none of these matching up with any feature of thought or volition. Against that form of compatibilism that would have actions determined by the immediately preceding judgment, Clarke again finds the thesis curiously trivial:

> There are some other Arguments against the Possibility of *Liberty*, which Men by attempting to answer, have made to appear considerable; . . . As for Instance, those drawn from *the Necessity of the Will's being determined by the last Judgment of the Understanding*; and from the *Certainty of the Divine Prescience*. As to the former. . . . this is only a Necessity upon Supposition; that is to say, a Necessity that a man should *Will* a Thing, when 'tis *supposed* that he *does Will* it . . . (and) If upon *Other Accounts* there be no Impossibility, but that the Actions of Men may be free; the bare *Certainty of the Divine Fore-knowledge* can never be proved to destroy That Freedom, or make Any Alteration in the Nature of Men's Actions.[127]

On the first point, Clarke is content to show that the vaunted discovery that an action is causally dependent on the judgment immediately preceding it is but a rewording of just what it means to say that the actor did what he intended to do. On the second point, Clarke reminds the reader that to know with certainty what one will do cannot render the action more or less free. To know with certainty just what every feature of the action will be is the same as saying that it will suffer no alteration of any kind whatever. The certainty of foreknowledge is not what causes the certainty in things. To know with certainty that Smith has drawn the fourth ace is to know that Smith will win the hand. But it is not the certainty of the knowledge that yields the certainty of the outcome. Volitional actions express an active power, unchanged and no less free just in case the action itself is predicted with certainty.

Clarke would offer comparable criticisms of Leibniz's special brand of determinism, that entailed by his theory of preestablished harmonies and a divinely ordained cosmos that, thus ordained, it is the best possible. We shall consider Leibniz in this connection again in the next chapter. Here, in concluding the present chapter, Clarke's distinction between passive matter and the active powers of moral agents is worth repeating. The Leibnizian metaphysics is a *necessitarian* variant, and compatibilist in that the actor's "free" action is included in the preestablished design. In his Fourth Reply to the letters from Leibniz, Clarke observes that Leibniz's theory leads to universal necessity and fate, by supposing that motives have the same relation to the will of an intelligent agent as weights have to a balance, so that, of two things absolutely indifferent, an intelligent agent can no more choose either than a balance can move itself when the weights on both sides are equal. But the difference lies here. A balance is no agent but is merely passive and acted on by the weights. . . . But intelligent beings are agents . . . they have active powers and do move themselves, sometimes on the view of strong motives, sometimes on weak ones, and sometimes where things are absolutely indifferent. In this latter case, there may be a very good reason to act, though two or more ways of acting may be absolutely indifferent.[128]

Clarke, this celebrated and nearly official spokesman for the Newtonian science, eschews the application of this science to a moral domain in which passivity is replaced by active powers, and where deliberation is able to impel a course of action even in the face of contrary motives, weak or strong.

As Reid would argue, the evidence we have of such power within ourselves is as compelling as that which grounds belief in the external world. It is neither more nor less "psychical" or subjective as evidence, and is under no greater burden of justification than avowals of pains. The ultimate defense of moral realism is that our moral powers are as real and as natural as are the musculo-skeletal operations engaged by them; operations that would be usually unintelligible except as explained by the former. The ultimate defense of moral realism, then, is in the actual *effects* arising from our moral judgments and aims.

Clarke would be no more inclined to think of the contents of moral perception as "queer" than of the effects of gravity. This is an important point warranting further discussion. In the letters passing between them, Leibniz held up the concept of gravity as a species of occult force, the attraction between bodies seen as a miraculous cause. Clarke will have none of this and will echo the distinction Newton himself makes in his *Opticks* between our knowledge of causes and the law that expresses the relationship between a cause and its effects. Referring to gravitational attractions, Newton puts the matter this way:

How these Attractions may be perform'd, I do not here consider. What I call Attraction may be perform'd by impulse, or by some other means unknown to me. I use that Word here to signify only in general any Force by which Bodies tend towards one another, whatsoever be the Cause. For we must learn from the Phaenomena of Nature what Bodies attract one another, and what are the Laws and Properties of the Attraction, before we enquire the Cause by which the Attraction is perform'd.[129]

Having quoted this passage, Clarke then criticizes Leibniz as being unreasonable in calling "gravity" an unphilosophical term, a miracle, "after it has been so often distinctly declared that by that term we do not mean to express the cause of bodies tending toward each other, but barely the effect or the phenomenon itself."[130]

In this exchange, Clarke anticipates the commonsense realism of Thomas Reid and opposes attempts to conflate physics and metaphysics. If there is to be a proper philosophical understanding of morals, it begins with the observation of those effects that are brought about by attachment to principles, freely chosen and rationally defended. Where the actions and principles stand in the relationship of lawful regularity, and where the agent has no doubt whatever as to conduct expressing the chosen course of action, Leibniz's form of necessitarianism is refuted. To be sure, if objects attracted each other solely as a result of a preestablished harmony (*harmonia praestabilita*), divinely intended, the term "gravity" would refer to a miracle and would indeed be an odd term for philosophical purposes. But as it refers to no more than the attractive phenomena themselves, and expresses no pretended knowledge of causes, it is a fit term for purposes of natural philosophy.

The case against incompatibilist freedom, however, doesn't end with such arguments against necessitarian and deterministic challenges. For even if these fail the combined tests of pragmatism and credibility, the moral skeptic still has a formidable argument against the libertarian and moral absolutist, an argument based on the notion of chance and luck, pure and simple, the topic of the next chapter.

3.

MORAL LUCK, MORALITY, AND THE FATES

> One's history as an agent is a web in which anything
> that is the product of the will is surrounded and held up
> and partly formed by things that are not, in such a
> way that reflection can go only in one of two directions; either
> in the direction of saying that responsible agency is a fairly
> superficial concept, which has a limited use in harmonizing
> what happens, or else that it is not a superficial concept, but that
> it cannot ultimately be purified—if one attaches importance
> to the sense of what one is in terms of what one has done and
> what in the world one is responsible for.
> —BERNARD WILLIAMS, *Moral Luck*

On Being Lucky, Morally Speaking

What is it that qualifies events or conditions as "luck"? Robert Kane offers this definition of what he calls "the luck principle":

> If an action is *underdetermined* at time *t*, then its happening rather than not happening at *t* would be a matter of *chance* or *luck*, and so it could not be a *free* and *responsible* action.[1]

The plays of Sophocles and Euripides feature persons caught in these webs of their own characters, of things done to them, of lives that thus seem fated. They seem somehow to be "chosen," and in ways that defeat their every effort. Oedipus, more on the basis of a coin-flip than by design, took the road to Thebes rather than Daulis, and that would make all the difference. In "The Knight's Tale," Chaucer reminds the ministre general that

> the destinee that executeth in the world o'er all,
> The purveyance which God hath seen beforne,
> So strong it is, that tho' the world had sworn
> The contrary of a thing by yea or nay,
> Yet sometime it shall fallen on a day
> That falleth not oft in a thousand year.[2]

As noted in chapter 2, Aristotle seems to have been of a different mind on all this, and Emerson, after giving due honors to the subtle and powerful effects that fate has on us all, nonetheless concludes reassuringly:

> We stand against Fate, as children stand against the wall in their father's house, and notch their height from year to year. But when the boy

grows to man, and is master of the house, he pulls down that wall, and builds a new and bigger. 'Tis only a question of time. Every brave youth is in training to ride and rule this dragon.[3]

In his widely cited *Mortal Questions*, Thomas Nagel devoted a chapter to the subject of "Moral Luck" that consistent with the passage from Bernard Williams in the epigraph to this chapter, underscored the variety of unintended but morally charged outcomes that deliver praise or blame to the participants.[4] Nagel actually outlines four categories of luck: circumstantial, constitutive, luck in antecedent circumstances, and lucky outcomes. Constitutive luck was examined in the previous chapter, as was luck in such antecedent circumstances as birth within a nurturing family or early schooling of an indifferent or even pernicious nature. What needs to be examined, then, is that "circumstantial luck" that would pick one out of many in ways that elicit praise or blame. And, as the lucky outcome (e.g., the luck of the draw) is itself circumstantial, Nagel's four categories can be reduced to three, the focus now on circumstantial or, more commonly, "moral luck."

Consider the driver who, perhaps no more negligently than thousands of others, drives faster than the speed limit, only to run over a child who suddenly appears in front of the vehicle. Here is an event made tragic by no more than the unlikely presence of a child in the road; perhaps a child pursuing a ball that took an unexpected bounce. In such instances, the very sense of the term "luck" points to what defies the central tenets of determinism, but this is of no solace to the defender of libertarianism. Rather, what luck reaches are just those outcomes falling beyond the ambit of both the rigid laws of science and the best laid schemes of mice and men. This much acknowledged, there is generally little or no lessening of praise or of blame for those targeted by good or bad luck, and this requires the attention of the moral theorist. Is blameworthiness lessened by a bad turn of luck? Is no praise to be accorded one who bets on a long shot? Is no blame to be assigned to one who bets on a long shot?

Luck was considered in chapter 1 as part of the criticism of moral realism and objectivity. In chapter 2 the theory of constitutive luck was examined within the larger context of determinism. In this chapter moral luck is offered as the other side of the coin, the side featuring events seemingly so unrelated to desires, intentions, and antecedent conditions as to leave no room whatever for moral ascriptions of any sort. This needs to be qualified, however, for in this chapter instances are discussed in which there may well be relevant desires and intentions, but where the outcomes nonetheless cannot be reasonably anticipated, or where the outcomes are tied to desires and intentions formed in the person by (lucky?) conditions that many would regard as partly, if not fully, exculpatory.

There is need for a further qualification, this one pertaining to what are actually mistakes, as contrasted with good or bad luck. It is ever more common in recent years to hear public officials and celebrities seek pardon for moral faults on the grounds that they "made a mistake." This is an abuse of language when it is not a transparent attempt to deceive. To make a mistake is to have accepted a way of doing things or to have adopted a widely held value or principle but, in the process of completing a task or applying the principle, to have done so ineptly. With moral faults, it is the aim or principle itself, adopted at the outset, that is subject to blame and would remain subject to blame whatever the consequences. There is, then, a fundamental difference, both conceptual and factual, between mistakes and moral faults, and it is illicit to absorb the latter into the category reserved for the former. Luck can become intermixed, however, with both. One can mistakenly place a wager that nonetheless proves to be a winner. One can undertake a wrongful course of action that nonetheless produces a happy ending. As previously noted, one of the problems of consequentialism is that it is unable to offer morally informing and distinguishable appraisals in such circumstances.

Returning to the unlucky driver, we condemn one (who condemns himself, as well) who, in running through a stop sign, maims a child. As a matter of fact, moral arguments aside, the same condemnation is seldom visited upon the many who drive in the same manner but (luckily) are spared such an outcome. Now, it may be said that what is condemned is recklessness itself, the tragedy serving as but a harsh reminder of what it is about recklessness that makes it condemnable. Recklessness may bear an element of undifferentiated intent. To be reckless is to be disposed toward high-risk behavior, without intending harm to any specific person but with indifference to the safety of all. On this understanding, some go so far as to deny that there is ever genuinely "inadvertent" recklessness at all. James Brady, for example, noting the difference between recklessness and negligence, classifies the negligent as taking insufficient care. The reckless, however, possess an awareness of the risks courted by their conduct but remain indifferent to them.[5]

There is much to recommend in this thesis but there are still all too many occurrences pointing to some sort of mindless lottery that picks out winners and losers. Added to the actor's burdens is the apparently widespread phenomenon of what has been called "hindsight bias." Where risky actions actually do result in harm, there is a strong tendency to regard the risk as much greater (in hindsight) than it actually was before the fact.[6] Moreover, although there are complex statistical techniques within decision theory for estimating or otherwise quantifying risk, these are not available to ordinary persons at the moment the routine duties and activities of daily life are undertaken.

Even when time and resources permit the calculation of risk, the morally right course of action is often not transparent. Kenneth Simons illustrates the point with his example of "the mythical Ford Pinto." Engineers discover that the fuel tanks on 12.5 million vehicles now in service can be strengthened at a cost of $11 each, the likely consequence being the prevention of 180 deaths from burning. Now the arithmetic is done:

> Calculating a unit cost of $200,000 per death, $67,000 per injury, and $700 per burned vehicle, the manufacturer concludes that the total cost of preventing the injuries is $137.5 million, while the accident losses that the precaution would prevent amount to $49.5 million. Accordingly, the manufacturer chooses not to take the precaution.[7]

The example can be further complicated by the decision to invest the savings in highway safety programs actuarially calculated as saving 3,400 lives. In the end, statistically based decisions of this sort must be hostage to myriad conditions—personal, atmospheric, mechanical, contextual—laced through with good and bad luck. Apart from this, there is still the question of whether, having based the decision on risks and costs, the manufacturer should be judged as "negligent," just in case the unfortified tanks actually do result in burn-deaths.

Notwithstanding the benefits of a utilitarian calculus, nagging questions remain as to how to incorporate "unlucky" outcomes into a defensible theory of praise and blame. Take two actors, one negligent and one reckless, each of them failing to perform some action that would make a tragic outcome less likely. Fate intervenes in such a way that one of them—it doesn't matter which one—pays the price either for reckless or for negligent behavior. The death of the child in the aforementioned example, whether by negligence or by recklessness, showers blame on the driver, whether negligent or reckless. Granting that the law is able to distinguish between the two cases, how should the moral distinction be made? More generally, why should anyone be targeted for moral appraisal when the decisive circumstance is that of being in the right (wrong) place at the right (wrong) time?

Once again, such questions can be reduced to an exercise in descriptive psychology. As with "hindsight bias" studies, one might undertake research to determine the general a priori and ex post facto judgments of moral fault when negligent or reckless actions result in harm. To determine the degree of "bias" in such judgments, however, there must be an objective standard, presumably based on calculations of risk. Yet, in instances of the interesting sort, such calculations are either impossible or incredible. What is the likelihood of a ball taking an erratic bounce on a paved sidewalk just after a brief thunderstorm? What is the likelihood that a child will pursue the ball into the street? How many vehicles, on average, use that street during those hours and after thunderstorms? Surely the point is made.

It is comparably unrealistic to think that drivers are driving with such questions in mind, or that parents—having performed such obligatory calculations—share the blame for not keeping their child indoors in light of prevailing conditions and the host of joint probabilities. Issues such as these may provide social scientists with any number of leads for interesting empirical studies, but the issues themselves must finally be understood through an essentially philosophical and conceptual analysis. Only then can the actual practices of praising and blaming be evaluated. It is notable that we tend to overestimate the prior risk when the actions actually do cause harm: useful knowledge, lest mere impressions of risk be converted into graver punishments for what is incorrectly judged to be flagrant recklessness. However, the moral argument for obliging actors to consider the gravest consequences that could result from their actions must be richer than warnings as to the ex post facto impressions others might form. As will be shown, this very argument draws strength and force from moral luck itself.

One way out of the bind is to insulate moral responsibility from any and every kind of luck on the grounds that what gives an action or event moral weight makes no contact with what would constitute its being lucky. In this vein, philosophers such as Brian Rosebury have contended that a principal feature of all moral dilemmas is epistemic. Therefore, to the extent that "luck" falls beyond the epistemic powers of the actor, its incorporation into such dilemmas profoundly misrepresents the essence of the matter.[8]

Although there is much to recommend in such arguments, they are nevertheless subject to being answered by the addition of "epistemic luck" into the overall account of moral luck. Andrew Latus employs just this manoeuvre, not in an attempt to settle issues raised by the notion of moral luck, but rather to illustrate that the concept is quite resilient in the face of a wide range of criticisms.[9] Great discoveries in science and medicine have been based on lucky guesses. Those who guess right, it might be argued, deserve little if any praise, and those who guess wrong should be similarly exempt from blame. Guessing is just that: It is guessing as opposed to hard-won and tested knowledge. From an epistemological point of view, it is not unlike betting on the long-shot that just happens to win.

Luck, Fate, and Determinism: The Stoic Compromise

It is clear that a metaphysical argument supporting either incompatibilist freedom or hard determinism inevitably must address the role of luck or chance. In some respects, the burden is heavier for hard determinists whose theory leaves precious little room for surprises. But the "hard voluntarist" also must grapple with lucky and unlucky elements in the actor's undertakings and achievements.

The hard determinist these days, owing to developments in the physics of the very small, can seek safe moorings in "uncertainty," a ubiquitous feature of particles and their interactions. The moorings, however, are less safe than they may seem. Although ubiquitous at the level of subatomic particles, uncertainty of the Heisenberg variety does not obtain at the level at which morally consequential events occur. By the time one enters the world of the visible—the world of the grape seed—uncertainty in the behavior of physical entities is on the order of one part in a thousand trillion. Something more relevant is needed for the determinist. A sensible place to look is in the school of ancient philosophy that was uncompromisingly deterministic while eschewing moral skepticism.

Among the ancients, it is the Stoics who adopted versions of determinism comparable to those now on offer. Critics, then as now, regarded the theory as so fatalistic as to make any and every initiative jejune at the outset. Determinism, after all, leaves little doubt as to what it affirms: Whatever takes place—given the laws of physics, in conjunction with all antecedent and concurrent conditions—could not have been otherwise.

If all that happens is thus determined, why bother to do anything at all? This reading of Stoicism attaches the school to what its ancient critics called "the Lazy Argument," an argument for a resignation indistinguishable from morbid sloth. Had this been really faithful to Stoic teaching, however, it would surely be odd to find major figures in the school so busy in the world, so committed to the framing of legal codes, so participatory in civic life.

Susan Sauve Meyer has clarified the Stoic conception of determinism, extricating it from vulgar forms of fatalism and the Lazy Argument. Without a doubt, the Stoics rejected the possibility of causeless occurrences. Their metaphysics assumes a system of nature in which (often in the person of Zeus) the unfolding of all the seminal principles (*spermatikoi logoi*) "constitutes the course of the universe from its beginning to its ultimate conflagration."[10]

Events might be fated, however, while still requiring that certain conditions be met, and these conditions often include the specific actions of persons. Thus, *if* it is fated that Smith will win a boxing match, it is patently necessary that Smith have an opponent, the two of them now co-fated. In many instances, human decisions become necessary in just this way in the fated outcome. Applying this to the illustration of bad moral luck, one might say that if it had been fated that the child would die at that precise moment, then it was also necessary that that driver had previously decided to exceed the speed limit, and at the crucial moment, had also decided to look away from the road.

There is an important distinction made in Stoic thought between those causes identified as "proximate" and those that are "primary." Meyer takes her example from Cicero.[11] A traveler is robbed by a highwayman. Owing to his expensive dress, the traveler becomes the predictable target of a robbery. One of the *proximate* causes of the event, therefore, is his wealthy appearance. But the *primary* cause, which is internal to the source of the action, is in the robber himself. The idea that one's character is one's destiny is compatible with such an understanding of causality and, as discussed in connection with Aristotle in the matter of determinism, compatible with his conception of responsibility, as well. Thus, in the example of the driver and child employed in this chapter, the proximate cause of the tragic event is the child running into the road, but the primary cause is the negligent or reckless disposition of the driver.

Certain of the Stoics and, later, the neo-Platonists would see no way out of the matter except by assuming some ageless and scripted plan realized through the earthly doings of seemingly autonomous actors. Cicero's traveler is robbed as a result of two causal modalities; one proximate and one primary. But if the latter is the assailant's defective character, it, too, must have arisen from proximate and primary causes, the latter in this case presumably being some sort of native tendency or disposition. An omnipotent and omniscient deity would be regarded as behind all of these conditions and would, therefore, be the ultimate cause of all things. Aristotle, as noted, would have none of this; not because he rejected the thesis that would have the cosmos expressing the design of a cosmic designer, but because he rejected the thesis that an intelligence of this nature would busy itself with highwaymen and well-dressed travelers.[12]

Defenders of neither hard determinism nor incompatibilist free will are likely to rely for support on distinctions between proximate and primary causes and the room they allow for active participation within an otherwise determined space. If the driver's negligence or recklessness has arisen from deliberate, authentic, self-formed, and free patterns of conduct, then moral responsibility is preserved at the expense of hard determinism. If negligence and recklessness are the consequence of causal factors over which the driver had and has no direct, authentic, and free control, then the very grounds of moral responsibility are removed. And, if the entire episode is "just one of those things"—a mere happening that no one could foresee and that could have picked out nearly anyone to be agent or patient—neither hard determinism nor hard volitionalism has a convincing account to offer. The driver's inclinations, taken as primary causes, are readily absorbed by a radical determinism. As for the incompatibilist-libertarian, there is little to choose between events that are fated and those that are co-fated. If the child's running into the road is determined by the joint conditions of wanting the ball and the ball's odd bounces; if the death of the child is jointly determined by all of this and the driver's negligent or reckless disposition; and the latter is determined by the driver's overall psychobiological constitution, then *there is no one to blame.*

Lucky Outcomes, But Do Consequences Matter?

Bad moral luck is thought of as warranting some measure of forgiveness, the actor now thought of as having a valid excuse. In *A Plea for Excuses*, the ordinary language philosopher J. L. Austin explored how excuses, as contrasted with justifications, function in the language.[13] Smith claims his actions are *justified* by invoking a principle or by citing conditions that establish his actions as correct, prudent, dutiful, and so forth. Smith seeks to be *excused* for an action acknowledged as wrong but mitigated by factors understood to be relevant to blameworthiness. In some instances, "fate" is taken to be just such a mitigating factor. Thus, "inevitably" a piece of that fine china was going to break, no matter how carefully cared for. That is, even when persons are scrupulous and vigilant, *things go wrong* and, when they do, the appropriate response is that of resignation rather than recrimination. There are, however, counterinstances in which the outcome is understood as evidence that one has, so to speak, tempted the fates. How one who runs a stop sign and runs down a child is judged depends to some extent on the sort of person that driver is taken to be. Behind this fact stands a general and defensible precept; that is, that "fate" ultimately exposes character itself. Here one is tempted to stand with the ancient tragedians: one's character just *is* one's fate.

If, as noted, there are too many particular instances raising doubts about so broad a generalization, there are others in which luck works to reveal the hero among us, and still others in which luck stands in service to the vicious among us. The Stoic notion of events being co-fated is exemplified in every act of heroism for, without the challenging event, there can be no hero. Granted, valor was shown by many at the Battle of the Bulge and all earned the decorations subsequently awarded. But those assigned to positions behind the lines of battle also might have had heroism within them, though never given the opportunity to display it. Suppose Achilles and Hector had lived long and uneventful lives in an age of peace. What names then would have been sung by Homer?

If there is a background moral theory that paradoxically generates, and is also embarrassed by, the problem of moral luck it is one or another version of "consequentialism." Whether in its refined utilitarian or its so-called vulgar form, consequentialism reserves moral appraisal to the foreseeable and actual occurrences in the world. Eschewing the burdens of mind reading, the consequentialist looks not to the motives, dispositions, or character of the actor, but to what follows (or is likely to follow) from the adopted course of action. Utterly outcome-based consequentialism must confine judgment to happenings, but inevitably is tested by any number of such happenings in which the role of luck has been decisive.

Consider blameworthiness associated with unsuccessful attempts to commit a crime; or criminal attempts that succeed, but not in the intended manner. Steven Sverdlik, skeptical about the concept of moral luck, offers these instances to support the argument that there is something counterintuitive in the notion that only consequences matter.[14] The law is not indifferent to criminal intent, even when the desired outcome is not achieved. Needless to say, from a moral point of view, the intention to cause harm is blameworthy whether or not it is fulfilled. The grounding of moral appraisal is clearly deeper than consequentialists are wont to acknowledge and is capable of taking notice as to whether and how luck might figure in outcomes.

In this same connection, consequentialism suffers from the added defect of allowing no relevant distinctions between intention and foresight. If what matters are consequences, the moral quality of an event must remain the same whether achieved by design or resulting from inadvertence.[15] Judged in consequentialist terms, there would be no morally significant difference between someone failing to clear ice from the walk owing to a failure to envisage untoward consequences, and one leaving the ice on the walk *so that* the neighbors might be harmed.

Consequentialism also fails to provide a credible means by which to make moral distinctions between actors impelled by fundamentally different desires but behaving in an otherwise similar fashion.[16] Smith flags an oncoming vehicle for the purpose of hitching a ride. Jones does the same, but for the purpose of causing an accident. In both cases, an accident ensues. If the moral gravamen of an action is nothing but the consequences arising from it, such paired cases are morally indistinguishable.

Recently Roger Crisp has identified still other problems with consequentialism when applied to accomplishments.[17] Consequentialism's defining tenet is that

> the best state of affairs, or history of the world, is that containing the most overall well-being. Any action is to be judged morally only by its contribution to bringing about the best state of affairs.[18]

Given this standard, the source of good (or bad) consequences is irrelevant, for only the net effects matter. Where accomplishments are considered, however, praise is properly bestowed on those who actually achieve the praiseworthy end and not indifferently on the basis of the net good effects thereby brought about. As Crisp says, "Outcome-assessments of accomplishment . . . rely on the notion of agent-causation."[19] Furthermore, accomplishment is understood by way of features that are internal to the activity itself. Quoting Crisp again, "The contribution of Michelangelo's accomplishment to his well-being depends on the fact that it was *he* who painted the Sistine ceiling."[20]

We see, then, that neither the theory that would have one's character forging one's fate, nor that of cost-benefit consequentialism is plausible when applied across the rich range of events in the world of actors and actions subject to praise or blame. Against the tragedians, one might present ample evidence of luck pure and simple, such that something terrible (wonderful) was going to occur at that moment, no matter who happened to be there, and no matter how developed (depraved) the character of the actor. Against consequentialists, one easily distinguishes one who has set out to run down a child from one who does so owing to distraction; or to simple negligence; or while in a drug-induced hallucinatory state; or under hypnotic suggestion. A theory that makes no morally relevant distinctions across such a range of predisposing factors is woefully incomplete. Each of these factors—character, motivation, distraction, negligence, mental disorder—calls for still further analysis. In the end, it is *character* that is proposed as the grounding of all valid ascriptions of praise and blame, but character less in the sense envisaged by the ancient tragedians than by Aristotle.

Further groundwork must first be completed. Character, even if self-forming, is also influenced by others, by circumstances, even by episodic events. Some or all of this might be subsumed under the heading of "luck," such that one's character would stand as just another lucky or unlucky outcome.

Moral Luck, Social Conditioning, and Character

The concept of character—of one's "personality" or notions to the effect that "that's the sort of person Smith is"—are invariably included in estimations of blameworthy or praiseworthy actions. If or when the fundamental attribution error is, indeed, an error, it is pardonable on the grounds that so much of daily conduct does express intentions, desires, and inclinations. Unarguably, one's character is to some extent formed and nurtured and otherwise subject to contextual factors at once numerous and powerful. Whether and to what extent one is a responsible participant in one's own character formation needs to be incorporated into any general theory of morals.

To begin at the beginning, consider early childhood in a family unable or unwilling to provide proper guidance. Here we have what, in Nagel's account, would be bad "antecedent luck." Consider further development within an entire culture of neglect. Susan Wolf has argued that many social pressures and defects over which a child has no control may well lead to mental illness; further, that formidable social pressures can make otherwise decent persons comply with and execute the laws of a ruthless government.[21] Others have argued along just these lines, contending that character itself is, in some complex manner, constructed out of the accidents of family affiliation, the genetic lottery, the shaping conditions in that part of the real world into which this same genetic endowment is deposited. Edward Sankowski summarizes a prevalent view within moral philosophy when he questions the validity of autonomy-based ascriptions of blame. Posing instances in which a blamer represents the judgment of an authoritative community that supports a theory of strong autonomy, and in which the blamed comes from a community supporting a theory of minimal autonomy, Sankowski concludes that, "there will be hesitation, doubt, puzzlement, about the justifiability of blaming the agent for an action."[22]

This last consideration raises the question of "collective guilt." Is it ever right to blame persons for the unavoidable associations entailed by country of birth? Gregory Mellema has considered the question in detail, weighing the merits of collectivist and individualist arguments.[23] He advances a limited defense of the notion of collective responsibility, while acknowledging that a person does not always have a choice in the matter of being part of, or parted from, a given collective. Where Hobson's choices face the actor, considerations of duress may remove the subsequent actions from the category of blameworthiness but, again, whether or not such choices are faced may often be a matter of chance.

Even where one's character keeps one mindful of one's duties, there are often conflicting duties. The decision to favor one over the other may be blind to outcomes that are themselves matters of chance. In *Moral Luck*, Bernard Williams illustrates the determinative efficacy of "luck" in human affairs.[24] He offers a hypothetical Gauguin who turns away from the cares of the world in order to obey his muse. His commitment to art, at the expense of everything else, may be seen as creating a hardship on friends and family, removing Gauguin from service to God and country, finding him otherwise taxing the resources of the community and so forth. In a word, Gauguin's duties to art are at the expense of many other significant and recognized duties, but ones judged by Gauguin as of lower standing.

At the time Gauguin launches this singularly devoted life, neither he nor anyone else can predict the long-term consequences. It is not as if the right calculation of "utilities" might inform Gauguin or others on the spot as to whether the chosen course is the morally right one. Williams here reveals yet another dilemma faced by consequentialists; namely, in most settings the actions expected to have weighty consequences cannot always and accurately be informed with respect to just which consequences will, in fact, ensue. So neither Gauguin nor anyone else can say whether his decision will in the long run repay the world so richly as to compensate for the previously neglected responsibilities.

As the world tends to judge such persons, the moral appraisal of Gauguin's decision presumably awaits the artistic achievements of a lifetime. In such a case, many would forgive or even applaud his resignation from the world of civic and domestic duties. Yet these very achievements depend centrally on the element of native talent or genius, which can be discerned, if ever, only after the fact (by the judgment of posterity) and thus cannot supply a justification at the time the new life is chosen. Even if the required gifts are there, Gauguin might slip on the ice and become comatose, or might develop a brain tumor that robs him of sight. He might live in a world that loses its taste for art, or at least for his sort of art, and thus earn the scorn of those who judge his efforts as negligible. The point, of course, is that the final moral standing of Williams's Gauguin appears to be so plagued by contingencies over which the artist has no control that it would be idle to hold him responsible.

Williams offers as another illustration of his main point a different Anna Karenina, one whose fatal devotion to Vronsky is thoroughly defeated by his accidental death, or even his suicide. Whatever might have been said about the decision Tolstoy has her making, the overall moral assessment of her life surely would have been different just in case Vronsky died soon after their liaison was established, or if she had become incapacitated by disease, or if one of them had been kidnapped, and soon. As none of these conditions falls within the ambit of the actors' direct control, any of them can locate the actors in a moral space not of their choosing.

Coming to Terms with Moral Luck

Clearly, no simple or single path will lead one through the thickets of luck to an end point at which full moral responsibility is evident. Though faithful to the impressive array of lucky conditions and circumstances summarized above, I will attempt to show that the ingredient of luck spares no actor the burdens of moral conflict and moral judgment. I will argue that, to take one example, the moral value of Gauguin's decision can and should be assessed prior to and independently of such artistic achievements as might be claimed on his behalf at a time after the decision. In such instances, Gauguin's rejection of primary duties will be seen as a moral fault, and the quality of moral faults is unaffected by anything taking place after the fact. This argument is consistent with those that would have crimes graded not according to the severity of the outcome but in proportion to the *risk* implicit in the act.[25] Later in this chapter the concept of "risk" will be expanded and deepened.

To launch the argument I begin by partitioning moral luck into two distinct but not exclusive categories that may be labeled "event-luck" and "nurturance-luck." As the terms suggest, one may be the beneficiary or the victim of a rare event, such as having the winning lottery ticket or being suddenly confronted by a child appearing in the headlights. One also may benefit or suffer from relatively sustained conditions of nurturance or neglect throughout the formative periods of physical and social development. The two categories may well not exclude each other, for at least some of the events one is more or less likely to confront depend to some extent on how and where one is positioned in society. Thus, assuming that one might luckily be in the company of those able to offer attractive employment, such event-luck is more likely to take place in settings in which we find those who have been beneficiaries of thoughtful, caring, and wholesome nurturance. Nonetheless, these two forms of luck are different and call for separate analysis. Before considering event-luck, it will be useful to examine the more complex conditions of nurturance-luck, for these are routinely included in pleas for excuses and exonerations.

Nurturance-Luck

Susan Wolf has described JoJo, "favorite son of Jo the First," the father being
a malign dictator presiding over an impoverished population. Having love
for his son, Jo the First showers the boy with affection and provides him
with a good education. Predictably, JoJo becomes a loving and faithful son,
his role model being Jo the First. On attaining rule later in life, JoJo carries
forth his father's programs, these, in Wolf's graphic example, "including
sending people to prison or to death or to torture chambers on the basis of
the slightest of his whims." Given JoJo's background and the special nurturing conditions of his childhood, Wolf concludes that

> it is dubious at best that he should be regarded as responsible for what
> he does. For it is unclear whether anyone with a childhood such as his
> could have developed into anything but the twisted and perverse sort
> of person he has become. But note that JoJo is someone whose actions
> are controlled by his desires and whose desires are the desires he wants
> to have.[26]

Compatibilists have readily acknowledged that persons act on the basis of
motives and desires, freely choosing from available alternative courses of
action those likely to realize their motives and satisfy their desires. The typical compatibilist account, however, then takes the motives and desires to be
the causal antecedents of the actions, and established either by the actor's
overall biogenetic makeup or by a process of socialization and conditioning.
Susan Wolf's character is one she would understand as having a "deep self,"
as she calls it, so shaped by early life as to qualify JoJo, in the relevant respects, as "insane." Rejected, of course, is the counterproposal that would
explain even JoJo's actions as *free, for all purposes, of moral judgment*.

Against such a counterproposal stands an array of defeating conditions.
Robert Young has partitioned these into conditions established by others as
a way of effecting compliance and conditions within the actors themselves.[27]
The first class includes wants and desires arising from inducements in the
form of threats and promises to those known to be vulnerable; brainwashing,
subliminal advertising, hypnosis, indoctrination, and/or psychosurgery. The
second class includes neuroses, psychoses, pathological urges, and/or uncontrollable impulses. If defeating conditions were all of this ilk, the incompatibilist defender of freedom would have a fairly direct rebuttal. If, for example, one accepts the claim that JoJo is actually insane, then by definition
his actions cannot be taken as the product of rational deliberation. Surely
our freedoms can be curtailed and even fully subverted by forms of coercion,
insanity, surgery, and drugs. There are weighty arguments against the proposition that JoJo's upbringing has rendered him insane, but if in fact his insanity is stipulated then he would no longer be in the pool of actors whose

judgments and actions could be used in support of incompatibilist freedom. What is left over once Young's macabre inventory is recorded and set aside is the free and fully lived life of all who are not victims of total insanity, coercion, and the like.

What JoJo is allowed, on Susan Wolf's rendition, is a framework of authentic motives and desires, but now giving expression to a "deep self" grossly distorted throughout early development. Understood in these terms, the life of JoJo is seen to be exceptional, the deliberated aims of a lifetime corrupted into nothing less than a form of insanity by an evil parent. But the defenders of determinism do not reserve the causal power of socialization to extreme cases. As Young notes,

> The real problem comes with the inclusion in the list of defeating conditions of causes which do not involve the intentional instilling in, or the manipulation of wants of one agent by another. For, says our critic of compatibilism, humans develop socially and psychologically in an environment not of their own making and with a given genetic endowment. They acquire their wants through a process of socialization and social conditioning. . . . This makes nonsense of the idea that our convictions, motivations, preferences, principles, ideals and the like are truly ours.[28]

Young's own conclusion is that compatibilism can survive this criticism on two general grounds. First, there are many routine actions—for instance, deciding to raise one's hand—for which social conditioning and the like would be superfluous as explanations. As he says, it would be "to collapse the distinction between our wantings and cravings." Second, though there are actions impelled by social conditioning and kindred forms of manipulation, it is a goal and achievement of forms of psychological therapy to expose this fact and, in the process, liberate the patient from it. On both grounds Young believes the case has been made for at least some motives and desires to be authentic and therefore compatible with compatibilism.

Here again, though the analysis is suggestive, it is still exposed to a telling determinist-incompatibilist counter; namely, that the first of Young's grounds begs the question, and the second points to a *causally* efficacious way of installing or replacing motives and desires. The determinist is under no obligation to accept the proposition that the simple act of raising one's hand—of *deciding* to raise one's hand—is exempted from the domain of biosocially determined patterns of behavior. Nor is the determinist likely to accept that the modalities by which psychotherapy is in some sense liberating are exceptions to the ultimate modality, which is causal. Predictably, the analysis is exposed as well to counters from the incompatibilist defender of free will. If there are certain agentic powers, such as deciding to raise one's hand, that fall outside the deterministic framework of socialization and biogenetic determinants, then these powers point to all the autonomy required by the defender. Further, if psychotherapy is in some respects able to liberate one from unthinking fidelity to conditioned beliefs and aspirations, it must be different from socialization itself and must yield a state of freedom, again of the required sort. In all, then, the ostensibly reasonable middle course faces hardships at least as daunting as those confronted by more radical alternatives. There is also the special hardship of what is perceived as a vacillating inconsistency to which the radical alternatives are relatively immune.

Let it be granted that early childhood is perhaps *the* critical period within which basic values are inculcated, tastes and preferences shaped, general attitudes and dispositions subjected to approval and disapproval. There are, after all, such critical periods associated with the widest range of behavioral, perceptual, cognitive, and linguistic functions. Conditions of enrichment or deprivation during these periods have their greatest and most enduring effects. The specific stages of development propounded by such theorists and Freud, Piaget, Erickson, and Kohlberg are controversial among specialists, but there is widespread agreement that human development includes periods of greatly heightened receptivity to external influences. Nurturance matters.

This much granted, the core question reasserts itself: are the outcomes of these admittedly powerful nurturing influences essentially immune to authentically personal initiatives of the sort required by free will–incompatibilists? From the perspective of praiseworthy and blameworthy actions and lives, there is the related question: where one has been either the beneficiary of good or the victim of bad nurturance-luck, should there be a corresponding diminution of praise or blame? Neither moral nor legal judgments are indifferent to background and contextual factors, some of such a nature as to be mitigating or even fully forgiving.

The law traditionally relies on the legal fiction of the "reasonable man" in reaching conclusions as to how persons should be expected to act in the circumstance. Far less common in law, however, is attention to the distant nurturing conditions that surely had something (even much) to do with the course of life on which the defendant entered. Some would take this to be a serious limitation in juridical reasoning: just the sort of blind spot that a robust moral theory exposes and seeks to correct. This feature of adjudication, however, is not evidence of ignorance or indifference. It is not an accidental or inadvertent feature, but one built into the very concepts of legislation and adjudication.

The enactments of a legislative body are grounded in necessary but typically unstated assumptions. One of these is that what the law requires is possible. Laws that command cannot without contradiction compel the impossible. Tied to this is the assumption of competence on the part of those judged to be fit for the rule of law. This is the basis on which the "legal infant" is largely exempted from the law's punishing sanctions as well as the fullest range of its entitlements. The right to vote is not withheld from children because they cannot read or mark a ballot, but because they lack what are taken to be the requisite cognitive powers by which a vote deserves to be counted. It is not at all surprising, then, that one or another form of insanity defense or special provision for dealing with the gravely mentally disturbed is a fixture in legal history.[29] Of the powers presupposed by the rule of law, there are two that are taken to be the anchoring points for the rest: the power of deliberative, self-reflecting thought, and the power to conform one's behavior to results of just such deliberation.

In the common vernacular, which the settled law must be able to address if it is to be intelligible to those whose fidelity it depends upon, the first of these powers is expressed as *knowing what one is doing and why one is doing it.* Those in the thrall of pathological delusions or hallucinations are regarded as not fully responsible, for responsibility presupposes adequate powers of deliberated comprehension. It is not just a matter of comprehension, for one who believes herself to be Helen of Troy will fully comprehend that it is only a matter of time before the Achaians will set sail to restore her to Menelaos. There must be the power of *deliberated* comprehension such that one's beliefs can be tested against the background of evident facts. The second of these powers addresses what is commonly referred to as self-control. Where conduct is not properly controlled, the relevant question of legal *fact* is whether the actor lacked the power, or had the power vitiated by coercion or duress, or simply failed to make use of it. The power here is *conative.* When expressed, it reveals the intentions and desires of the actor. When expressed after due deliberation, it expresses not merely a choice but a choice for which the law will hold the actor accountable.

Standard texts are clear on the standards to be applied when allegedly mitigating conditions are at issue. Consider how juries are to take into account intense emotions when called upon to distinguish between murder and manslaughter. In *Federal Jury Practice and Instructions*, Mathes and Devitt summarize the law's understanding:

> The law does not permit a person to set up his own standard of conduct, or to justify or excuse himself, merely because his passions were aroused, unless the circumstances in which he was placed, and the facts with which he was confronted, were such as would have aroused the passion of the ordinary reasonable person, similarly situated. So, the test to be applied in determining whether a killing was in the heat of passion which will reduce murder to manslaughter, is whether or not, at the time of the killing, the reason of the accused was obscured or disturbed by passion to such an extent as would cause the ordinary reasonable person to act rashly and without deliberation and reflection, and from such passion, rather than from judgment.[30]

Later revisions in the Model Penal Code, shifting from this "objective" standard to the more subjective one that would have jurors project themselves into the defendant's state of mind in the circumstance, are largely beside the point at issue here. Jurors under either set of instructions presume that defendants have rational powers of deliberation and choice, of judgment and self-control. On the vexing question of just how much of a given power must be possessed for one to be subject to the judgments and penalties of law, there is really only one standard the law reasonably could adopt. It is the standard ordinary rational beings bring to bear on the situations life presents when they exercise their own powers of deliberation and express their own aims and longings. If deliberation and desire were mechanically programmed into persons, such as to strip judgments, desires, and beliefs of their authenticity, the actions arising from them would actually be *reactions*, of a sort one might obtain hypnotically. It is because rational and autonomous beings know in their own experience the difference between intentional and elicited movements, between reasonable fears and rank superstitions, between veridical perceptions and tricks of the imagination, that they are able to judge the actions of others along such lines. Indeed, jurors systematically and carefully instructed as to standards of capacity and responsibility nonetheless bring their own rich experiences to bear in interpreting the standards and applying them to the case at hand.[31]

To suggest, on the basis of a powerful but abstract philosophical thesis, that the entire enterprise is freighted with the products of brainwashing, socialization, Pavlovian conditioning, genetically induced feelings, ironically casts one's interlocutor as an entity whose agreements or objections would be irrelevant. The very basis on which such a thesis recommends itself includes the auditor's powers of deliberation and desire; the power to weigh alternatives and to commit oneself to those that have survived relevant and even relentless critical assessment.

Deliberative and conative powers subject one to sanctions not only when wrongly deployed but when unjustifiably withheld. To be negligent is, in the language of law, to display *a want of proper care*, which indicates an insufficient desire to respect the rights of others. To be reckless is to yield to desires in such a way as to imperil oneself or others. It is to act either on desires that are themselves blameworthy or to act on what is the wrong desire in the context. In the latter case, the failure is one of deliberative self-reflection. What is heroic in combat may be reckless in times of peace. One's desires to achieve a worthy outcome by force of arms are subject to praise or blame depending on the context and on one's proper functions within that context.

There is, of course, much more to these provisions and understandings of law, but this summary of the basic assumptions offers means by which to assess the place of nurturance-luck in the overall moral scheme of things.

Law itself is predicated not only on assumptions regarding the powers of those fit for the rule of law, but also on assumptions about how "human nature" and its surrounding conditions dispose persons to exercise those powers. The law cannot without inviting contradiction command one to violate the laws of physics. The law cannot without inviting ridicule command one to do what inevitably and eagerly and regularly nearly everyone does or tries to do; to sleep well, to enjoy the company of good friends, to engage in interesting projects. The commands of law are directed at actions that one may be inclined and even strongly inclined to perform, but actions that are nonetheless hurtful without justification.

The sources of these inclinations are many, various, both stable and episodic, of different intensity, subject to multiform varieties of gratification, contextually sensitive, tied to one's situation in life, one's background, one's temperament. The sources are, alas, *the human condition* itself. Legal enactments are not indifferent to, indeed arise from, the realities of the human condition. Were there nothing to tempt us, no irrational appetites or desires, no vices or hurtful vicissitudes, no temporal variation in moods and manners, there would be nothing to legislate. Between sainthood and mere machinery there are reasonable beings capable of sufficient thought and self-control to enter into a civic form of life, the contours and bounties of which are set by the requirements of law.

To have good or bad nurturance-luck is, on this understanding, not to gain or lose one's fitness for the rule of law. Instead, it is to come under the protections and promises of this very rule, equipped or burdened by any number of innate or acquired dispositions that must be lawfully exercised. There is room in all of this for the hard determinist to establish that some candidates for the protections and promises of law actually fail to gain membership owing to a total or significant loss of the requisite powers: a loss caused by hereditary or traumatic factors. There is room for the hard determinist to establish that, for purposes of law, a given actor is incompetent, having no power (*non compos*) of the relevant sort. Nor does the thesis of incompatibilist–free will rule out gradations or degrees of loss. One may have the requisite powers but not to the degree necessary for full legal (or moral) responsibility. The law is not aloof to species of "degree determinism." What adjudication seeks is justice, this calling for judgment rather than arithmetic computations.

There is another property of juridical appraisals that informs the issue. Juridical appraisals are generic in their categories but individuated in their judgments. The category of "theft" or "libel" or "treason" is one under which indefinitely large numbers of topographically distinct actions can be subsumed. The offenses may take the form of words, symbols, drawings, mechanical devices, even facial expressions or vocal intonations. Murder can be achieved in countless ways. By establishing reasonable linkage between intentions and likely or actual outcomes, the adjudicative process is able to identify an action as "libelous" or "treasonous," and so forth. Yet this very linkage requires attention to the instant case, for it is *this* defendant whose intentions and actions are the subject of the cause and not "the average liar" or "traitors in general." The process itself, which has been remarkably consistent over a period of perhaps three millennia, has derived benefits from advances in science and technology in garnering those facts that may be taken in evidence, but neither scientific nor technological progress has any bearing on the need for, and the nature of, the linkages and their individuated character. All libels are alike in being libelous, though no two libelous utterances need to have a word in common. All libelers are alike in committing libel, but no two of them need to have an identical motive, save that of causing harm or garnering undeserved advantages.

The pliant capacities of each genre of offense or infraction, combined with the individuation of tests of guilt, offer abundant evidence of the difference between causality in the law and causality as understood by the hard determinist.[32] In these respects, they also match the cognitive and conative powers of the individual person. By way of cognitive power, the actor is able to recognize a great diversity of actions as nonetheless being instances of "theft." By way of this same power the actor can recognize certain motives and desires as unreasonable, exaggerated, or wrongly targeted. By way of conative powers, the actor is able to retain the force of desire but train it on worthy targets, and to a degree that is right in the circumstance. Each actor in this way is something of a jurist, prosecutor, defendant, and legislator on behalf of a private and public life capable of realizing praiseworthy or blameworthy ends.

The cognitive powers by which one recognizes an action as a species of theft are not "socialized," for socialization itself depends on these same powers. Rewards and exhortations, to be effective, must be directed at one capable of desiring and capable, also, of understanding what is expected of him or her. There may be such horridly bad nurturance-luck, such profound and prolonged deprivation, that native cognitive powers undergo atrophy. There may be so unfortunate a toss of the genetic dice or so devastating an assault on one's biological systems as to deprive the actor of the very capacity for deliberative self-reflection. In these cases praise and blame have no place, any more than the legal concepts of guilt and innocence. But in the absence of such tragic limitations, persons are assumed to have as much as it takes to live under the rule of law and be held responsible to its terms. "As much as it takes" refers here to just those psychological and moral resources that make socialization itself possible.

Considerations of nurturance-luck are also central to issues of compensation and distribution within society. If it is the case that one's early nurturance has placed one under social and economic handicaps, then not only are these immune to blame, but they call for remedies. It is widely held that, in a just and fair polity, the graver consequences of bad nurturance-luck should be ameliorated by compensatory schemes of resource-allocation. Egalitarian remedies have in common proposals for correcting, as it were, outcomes readily traced to nurturance-luck. In the more radical form, egalitarian remedies are predicated on the twin assumption that those worst off have been made so by bad nurturance-luck, and the best off by good nurturance-luck. The latter, therefore, have no special moral claim to their good fortune and thus no basis on which to resist distributive measures aiming to achieve relevant equality.

There have been interesting assessments of the luck-neutralizing rationale of egalitarianism. Susan Hurley, for example, proposes a decision-model based on aversion to uncertainty as a better rationale for distributive justice than that based on assumptions about good and bad luck.[33] She examines egalitarian precepts in relation to the "Regression Principle," according to which one is responsible for x to the extent that one is responsible for the *causes of x*. It is useful to stay with this Regression Principle (RP), for it exposes another feature of the concept of nurturance-luck. Children, of course, are not responsible for the conditions that might have causal influences on their own development. It is in this patent respect that such developmental consequences cannot serve as warrants for blaming the adults whose childhood nurturance was severely defective. Yet, unless radical determinism is accepted, it must be assumed that *at some point* the victim comes to possess powers of discernment and choice, powers by which to recognize one's situation, compare it with alternatives, recognize different possibilities. Granting the moral force of RP, then, the question that arises is whether there actually is a point or stage in development at which the appearance of relevant powers now casts the person as the "cause" of conditions and events brought about by that person's deliberated choices. It is a precept of incompatibilist-libertarianism that such a point or stage is reached in all but the pathologically retarded; that, no matter how deficient and defective early nurturance may have been, persons come to have active powers, including powers of discernment, comparison, evaluation, and choice. They are the powers that confer responsibility and, therefore, the potential for warranted praise and blame. There is, to be sure, bad nurturance-luck, but what is rejected is the conclusion that by itself it strips one of the powers or relieves one of the burdens of choice.

Event-Luck and Pure Chance: A Word about
Gauguin and Anna Karenina

Events, including those that one strives diligently to bring about, often are subject to conditions unforeseen or otherwise beyond the control of the participants. It is perhaps a veiled expression of ignorance to refer to unsuspected events as the gift of "chance," but there is no reason to think that knowledge will ever be so complete as to allow accurate predictions of all events in the world at large. Cliches capture this when noticing that, "there's many a slip 'tween the cup and the lip." In most realistic contexts, any number of factors crop up to give an outcome a different and sometimes radically different character from the one intended.

Examples are easily multiplied: the odd bounce of the ball, the sneeze that arouses one who might have just fallen asleep at the wheel, the weapon that misfires, the romance that begins with a mistaken identity. Noted already is the moral standing of one who intends a killing but misses the intended target; or the moral standing of one who means only to fire at an inanimate target but accidentally causes a death. Many philosophers have found nothing of moral consequence in such instances, for the moral standing of the actor is established by intentions and the actions they precipitate, whatever the actual outcome.[34] To intend harm and proceed to a course of action fully expressive of this intent qualifies the act as morally blameworthy, even when, for any reason, the intention is unrequited. Thus, just in case the actual outcome is best explained as the result of "chance" factors, the moral judgment would be the same. In law, too, though a lesser punishment is reserved to failure in such attempts, the attempts themselves count as felonies and are severely punished.

Yet, what of "chance" events that result in unintended, unforeseen but significant outcomes? The problem is often framed as a thought experiment: take two persons, genetically identical and having identical personal histories. Each now arrives at a choice-point where one option is, for example, truth-telling but at great personal cost and the other is, again for example, deceiving but for great personal gain. It is conceivable that the actors make different choices. Alfred Mele summarizes a widely shared conclusion:

If there is nothing about the agents' powers, capacities, states of mind, moral character . . . that explains this difference in outcome . . . the difference is just a matter of luck.[35]

The force of such examples is in their apparent generalizability to settings in which chance again may be decisive but less transparently so. The weakness, however, is greater than the force, for all such instances make room for luck by erasing differences in powers, capacities, states of mind, moral character, and so on. The defender of indeterminist–free will rejects any theory that allows radically different choices where powers, capacities, states of mind and moral character are the same. True, there may be radically different outcomes, for one's chosen outcome might be contravened by other events and conditions. This is different, however, from radically different *choices* that, on the libertarian theory, express nothing but the character and powers of the agent. For the libertarian, therefore, different choices at morally significant choice-points can only point to differences in the powers, capacities, and moral characters of those making the different choices; or, less controversially, in those ambiguities of the case that allow reasonable and morally competent persons to reach different conclusions as to which is the better course of action.

It is useful in this connection to recall the distinction Frankfurt made between the surface desires that might impel undeliberated actions and those "second-order" desires that reach the level of self-appraisal.[36] The morally self-aware person is able to take a critical position on desire itself, raising questions about which desires one should actually harbor. The object of this criticism is the strengthening of worthy inclinations and the weakening of those that compromise one's integrity. At a choice-point of the sort envisaged in the thought-experiment, persons with very similar (if not identical) nurturing backgrounds and general powers are not restricted to what is on offer in the external world, for they have been able (it is argued) in the course of a lifetime to develop any number of second-order desires. Herbert Fingarette has addressed this feature of moral life in these terms:

> I should emphasize that as I use the term "will" here, it does not refer to some supposed unitary agency or mental faculty. . . . I use it in the spirit suggested by the concept of suffering. It is the rubric, broad and admittedly vague, for the ways in which we are actively biased with respect to the possible actualization of some condition conceived as not actual. Among the manifestations I include under will are, for example, such different (and not infrequently conflicting) biases as are called desires, wishes, hopes, appetites, purposes, intentions, motives. I propose, then, that we view conscience as a form of will, the will to impose a requirement on our own conduct.[37]

What the "cloned" pair at the choice-point arrive with are not simple desires alone, not even the secondary-desires as additions. They arrive also with a conscience, formed and self-formed such as to confer some degree of judgment and judicial detachment in the face of what otherwise makes the world attractive or repulsive.

To introduce conscience into the analysis is to reconsider the different "lucky" scenarios that might have been lived out by Bernard Williams's Gauguin and Anna Karenina. Here "lucky" covers both the good and bad versions. Beginning with Gauguin, we have been presented with that breed of true artist prepared to abandon everything in response to his vocation. One of Freud's letters quotes Schiller's description of one who has a Mephistophelian compulsion in whose service he knows no limits. This is a revealing way of stating the case, for it suggests an actual incapacitation of sorts, though the extent to which it has been self-inflicted remains to be settled. How should it be settled if praise and blame are to be deployed fairly?

On the understanding defended by Aristotle, a case such as this may be relevantly like one in which damage is inadvertently caused by someone in a drunken state. The laws of Athens would assess a doubled penalty: one part for the damage done and the other for putting oneself in a state rendering such outcomes more likely.[38] Just in case the drunkenness is habitual, qualifying an actor as "alcoholic" in the sense of "addicted," the reasoning behind the defense of blame would be unaffected. At some point in the chain of indulgent acts there is the power necessary to recognize the course one has entered on and the power to abandon it for a safer one. Granting that toxins may diminish these powers and become principles or sources of action in their own right, what Aristotle calls the "primary principle" was misused in such a way as to allow these secondary ones to grow in strength. Early in the course of drinking one is supposed to recognize a mounting *risk*. It is the discounting of the risk that then lays the foundation for valid ascriptions of blame.

Williams's Gauguin is a veritable repository of lucky charms, some constitutive, some antecedent, some examples of event-luck. The luck of native ability was considered in the previous chapter, and nurturance-luck in the preceding sections of this chapter. What remains to be examined are several of the *events*, over which Gauguin has no control, which nonetheless will dispose others to praise or blame. The event of marriage and the lottery that determined there would in fact be dependent offspring resulted in duties that would not have arisen had Gauguin remained celibate and a bachelor. Surely neither of these "events" can count as simple "luck," for each was the product of actions over which Gauguin had the power of self-control, and each carried with it well-recognized possible and even likely duties. The concept of "risk" is not univocal. It includes not only potentialities for danger but also for the forfeiture of otherwise desirable options and assets. Reckless driving exemplifies risk in the first sense; committing oneself to a lifelong relationship exemplifies risk in the second sense.

There are other ostensibly lucky events that Gauguin might invoke later in life when attempting to justify (rather than simply explain) his chosen course of action. He may point to the fact that his paintings soon attracted the praise of a few persons whose aesthetic judgments mattered to him, though he had no way at the outset of knowing that he would even meet these people. He may say that he had enough money for a one-way ticket to Tahiti and initially planned to go there solely to be beyond the reach of the domestic courts that had charged him with abandonment. How could he know that Tahiti was to provide the ideal subjects for his genius? He could add to all this the event-luck (here *bad* luck) of falling victim to a tropical disease that cost him much of his color-vision but then (here is the *good* luck) learning the art of charcoal drawing from a local native.

It should be obvious by now that the life of the fictional Gauguin is porous to any number of lucky occurrences, just as is the life of actual persons. But he, as they, still retains the power of choice and still stands as a target of just praise or blame depending on the choices made. In the circumstances that count, choice is not exemplified by flipping a coin, for that approach, if it is ever warranted, indicates that no degree of further deliberation will yield decisively good reasons for acting. In the circumstances that count, choice arises from deliberation, and the process of deliberation includes centrally considerations of risk. It is not just actions that are reckless. There are reckless choices; negligent choices, choices that put others at risk. Gauguin has no more of a defense in pointing to his muse than does a drug-addict pointing to a vile of cocaine. The "muse" is but the summons of intense desire, and part of Gauguin's standing as a moral being depends on his stepping away from this desire long enough and at a sufficient distance to determine whether and to what extent it is to be gratified.

In his defense, Gauguin might insist that the account of relevant events here is too thin. He might contend that many persons would do as he did were it not for the fact that they were not lucky enough to be born in his country, in an era of artistic originality and freedom, in a local world such as Gauguin's, which included some of the best specimens of artistic genius and integrity. He might then go on to say, in a surprisingly academic way, that he certainly weighed the consequences of the action he was about to take, but that conduct (his and everyone else's) is based not on beliefs about consequences but on *desires*. With Hume and many others, he would insist that beliefs and reasons are feckless at the level of behavior, unless absorbed into the processes associated with desire. His defense here is what Robert Noggle calls "radical conativism," declaring it to be "just false, at least for human beings."[39] What is false about it, according to Noggle, is that it denies that beliefs can affect motives. As discussed in the previous chapter, the theory of motivation that would have to be accommodated by the critic of radical "conativism" is a mechanistic, causal theory that is woefully defective in its own right. Thus, for Gauguin to defend his actions by noting that they were in response to belief-defeating or deliberation-defeating desires is for him merely to restate the basis of his blameworthiness.

To this, Gauguin might (again with surprising philosophical acumen) insist that those who would blame him have adopted a version of cognitivism that requires of beliefs that they have motive powers; that to *believe x* to be a worthy outcome is sufficient for one to be *moved* to bring it about. At this point, Gauguin (or, more plausibly, his defender) has rehearsed precisely the standard by which actions are to be judged. Robert Noggle has again summarized the thesis with commendable economy and clarity:

If cognitivism is to be plausible, it will have to claim that certain motivating beliefs—what we might call practical axioms—are *basic* in the
sense that they are not derived logically from or produced causally by
any other motivating beliefs. The content of these basic motivating beliefs (and in particular their moral content, if any) is an empirical matter left open by cognitivism.[40]

The cognitivist's reply to Gauguin is that belief about risks and duties
constitutes a basic reason for acting in a certain way, when the belief is
based on those rational and deliberative undertakings designed to test the
credibility of beliefs. It is because of the power of belief that we are under
an obligation to weigh our own according to standards of rationality and
relevant evidence. It would, after all, be as idle for Gauguin to defend his
actions as being *caused* by belief as being caused by his muse. Richard Swinburne notes that "the free agent is one who *chooses* whether to be rational
and is not necessitated to be determined by reasons."[41]

Doxastic incontinence is an especially dangerous form of the general mal-
ady. Far from grounding a worthy defense, it adds to the blameworthiness
of actions guided by it. The cognitivist also would want to qualify, but not
reject, Noggle's classification of *basic* motivating beliefs as having a content
to be settled empirically. Gauguin, after all, could truthfully claim that his
calling was authentic and that there are surely no more basic reasons for
action than the belief that one's very vocation requires it. But the most basic
reasons for action are not subject to plebescitic review or national polling.
A population gone mad cannot be a warrant for replacing sound beliefs with
delusional ones. The sense in which the content of basic action-guiding beliefs is "empirical," then, must be that of a defensible conception of the essential nature of human nature itself; the sense in which the Thomist would
note that, were our natures different, our duties would be different. But "natures" here covers much more territory than occurrent desires and episodic
needs. As discussed in the previous chapters, there is nothing fallacious
about the so-called naturalistic fallacy, unless human nature itself it taken to
be no more than a set of merely contingent, "situated," shifting facts.

On such a reading, there might be a temptation to say that, yes, certain
principles are right and obligatory *for us*, but not, say, for butterflies or her-
ons or, for that matter, for Neanderthal man, or for some future Homo sapi-
ens radically unlike us in basic desires and social life. On such a reading,
then, Gauguin is just evidence of what some other *kind* of human being is
like; that is, one obsessed with art and prepared to jettison the conventional
morality of the uninspired. But there aren't other *kinds* of human beings, for
human beings are *natural* kinds. There are, to be sure, great differences in
how this kind of life expresses itself. Integral to that form of life that is a
basic property of the kind, however, is sufficient rational power such that

the actions arising from that life are grounded in reasons. There is no basis whatever for assuming that, alone among the facts of the world, all reasons are good reasons. What is clearly a bad reason for action is one that strips the actor of reason itself. That there are other kinds of entities whose actions are not reason-based is not an argument for the relativity of good reasons, any more than the climate of the desert is an argument for the relative nature of rain.

There is something amiss in any thesis that rests on the proposition that we would be different if we were different; or in any thesis that would have the way we are merely contingently the way we are. Smith could have become a different person, but he is not who he is *contingently*, even if contingencies participated in the formation of his desires, habits, sentiments, and aspirations. Some, even all, of these contingencies might be taken as strokes of good or bad luck, but they are precisely the contingencies that face any life competent enough to be judged. It is in having rational power, the power of deliberated choice, that one becomes fit for judgment; and it is the possession of this same power by those who would make the judgment that the basis of mitigation, praise, blame, forgiveness, and (commonly) confusion is established. It is true but trivial that Gauguin would have been different had his early life been significantly different from what it was. But different from whom? There is no other Gauguin in place for purposes of comparison. It is true but trivial that human nature would have been different if the overall environment of planet earth had afforded possibilities and imposed challenges radically different from those that have obtained since a time beyond memory. Yet there is no other human nature in place for purposes of comparison. Yes, Gauguin's duties would have been different if his nature had been different; so different as to remove him from the set of entities fit for moral assessment.

It is not necessary for the cognitivist to argue against the possibility that Gauguin's course of action was influenced to some extent by what we call "lucky" events. It is sufficient to note that every sober deliberation, called for by choices that really matter, must always make provision for the appearance of the unexpected; not that the deliberation has any way of including specific events, but that it is able to leave reasonable room, *just in case*. One is to drive through a residential neighborhood in a certain way, just in case a child might suddenly appear in the street. Gauguin is to approach the very question of getting married in a certain way, just in case his obsession with painting might prove lethal to the vows that marriage entails. Violating these vows on the grounds of an obsession would be no more (and much less) defensible than violating the terms of a loan agreement on the same grounds. It is, therefore, arguable whether, in the examples given by Bernard Williams, luck even enters at the key points.

These same considerations apply in much the same way to the revised Anna Karenina; the one whose Vronsky dies before they ever meet, or who suffers from an influenza that robs her of rational powers, or whose family moves to Cincinnati when she is born, and so forth. Clearly, the life of Anna Karenina, as scripted by Tolstoy, would have been entirely different if any of these lucky or unlucky events had occurred. Omitting cases of debilitating pathology, however, we discover that, from a moral point of view, nothing much would change. Anna, growing up in Cincinnati, would face her own moral dilemmas and would come to be answerable for the choices she made. Yes, if Vronsky died before they met then, indeed, their affair would not have taken place, nor would the deep sadness that moved her toward suicide. So events of such a sort proved to be decisive in her life, yet she was not personally responsible for Vronsky not having died before they met, and so on.

There is a fundamental difference, however, between responsibility *for* luck and responsibility *with* luck. Anna is not responsible for there actually being a Vronsky now able to enter into her life and feelings. But she is responsible for what she does with this lucky (unlucky) event, once it has taken place. She is not the only woman ever to meet Vronsky. Presumably, she is not the only one to find him appealing. One might guess that the Count's wife also is or was attracted to him. It may well be that the Count's roving eye has paused in the past, only to elicit the chastening glance of a woman not pleased by impertinent advances. There are, as it happens, a number of "scripts" concurrently realized in life, each with its own share of the adventitious. The maxim that requires one to "play with the hand that has been dealt" is broadly applicable. Event-luck dictates the cards as dealt. Whatever the hand, one does not have a licence to cheat, to risk irreplaceable treasure, to imperil others dependent on one's own conduct.

Both in law and in "folk psychology" distinctions are made between what ought to be regarded as reasonably foreseeable. Experimental studies indicate that persons have little difficulty in withholding blame and mitigating guilt for the unforeseeable consequences of actions otherwise blameworthy.[42] Just as one is not held responsible for what was not reasonably foreseeable as a consequence of a wrongful act, so one is responsible for events that one did not *cause*, but could have prevented by foresight. Liability in the law of torts covers such instances. Thus,

> when the railroad is held liable for the rape of its passenger, it is not Liable because it caused the rape by a third party; rather, it failed to prevent the rape when it could so easily have done so by carrying the passenger to a place of safety.[43]

In assessments of the mitigating weight of event-luck, both law and folk psychology are, or should be, governed by considerations of probability and warranted confidence. In the given situation, there is the temptation to fall victim to one or another version the "lottery paradox":

a. Someone will definitely win the lottery.
b. It is extremely unlikely that mine is the winning number.
c. It is just as unlikely that yours is the winning number.
d. It is just as unlikely that *anyone's* is the winning number.
e. It is extremely unlikely that anyone will win the lottery.[44]

The paradox is based on the mistake, of course, in not summing the negligible probabilities. If Smith has one chance in one million of holding the winning number, and if there are exactly one million lottery tickets in circulation, the *set* of all ticket holders has one million (one millionth multiplied by one million) chances in one million of containing the winning ticket. In everyday life, the paradox often and reasonably leads to the confident conclusion that "it surely won't happen to *me*," as one buys an airliner ticket. It is a near certainty that a commercial airliner will crash at some time in the future. It is not impossible that the one that will crash is the one on which we have just booked a flight. The reasonable risk-benefit calculation nonetheless leads to the purchase, for there are some "chances" one simply must take as a condition of living in the real world. Accordingly, it is not just the gravity of the risk that enters into the calculation, but also the likelihood. The trade-off is between risk and probability; the lower the latter, the more of the former might be justified. Lucky or "chance" events are part of life, and summon persons to the burdens of thoughtful, careful deliberation. Their powers here are indirectly established by the fairly consistent grounds on which they hold others responsible for insufficient or inept exercise of this very power.

The lottery paradox is a useful way of drawing attention to the difference between lucky and exceptional events, where the latter arise from powers within the actor's control. First-person versions of the paradox are seen to be nonsensical, even where the third-person account is plausible. Thus:

Third person:
1. That there is a distinct probability that someone is going to drive past a stop sign without stopping was inevitable
2. Smith is a member of the set of all who are *someone*.
3. There is a distinct probability that Smith will drive past a stop sign without stopping.
4. Smith's driving through a stop sign without stopping, if it takes place, was to some extent fated.

First Person:
1. There is a distinct probability that someone is going to drive past a stop sign without stopping.
2. I am the member of the set that includes all who are *someone*.
3. There is a distinct probability that I am going to drive past a stop sign without stopping.
4. My driving past a stop sign without stopping was to some extent fated.

The difference between the two voices here does not rule out that one or the other driver will commit the infraction. Rather, it points to the difference between the *external* view that is more or less hostage to calculations of probability and thus to notions of luck and chance, and the *internal* view that calls for no calculation at all. If I *do* drive through a stop sign it will not be because of a priori probabilities, but for reasons I have and can offer. Stated another way, the external view cannot distinguish between infractions arising from "chance" (for example, a distracting event, a sudden cramp, poor night vision) and those arising from the driver's decision to ignore the sign. The internal view is under no such limitation. Accordingly, the fact (when it is a fact) that the best explanation of an action from the external view is framed in terms of luck often says more about the limitations of the view than about the sources of the action itself.

The Relativity of Moral Luck

One is not only the recipient of lucky or chance events but, from the perspective of others, is often the source of the same. To describe one's early life as having been blessed by good parents or cursed by bad ones may refer to good or bad luck for the recipient, but not with regard to the parents' actions. Williams's Gauguin and Anna Karenina act in ways that were not anticipated by those intimately associated with, and thus standing as potential victims of, their wanton or selfish or tragic actions. Were Williams's Gauguin to be part of a family rendered destitute by the artist's departure for Tahiti, we would take it as a cynical and contemptible remark were he to refer to their "bad luck." In such instances, there is something of a conservationist principle at work, the pleasures won in the name of self-indulgence being more or less matched to the pain suffered by those neglected. Luck has nothing to do with any of this.

The Gauguin of Williams's example is what Thomas Nagel called the "practical solipsist.[45] A sketch of Nagel's argument will help to establish the moral standing of the allegedly "lucky" in the sorts of examples treated in this chapter. What Nagel requires is the ability of the actor with first-person knowledge of his own interests, properties, and states to project the same or comparable interests on to entities relevantly like himself. Where the properties are patently objective the movement from first-person to third-person ascriptions is unproblematic: "I am six feet tall" projected correctly on to one's neighbor, as in, "He is six feet tall," is a factual statement the validity of which is independent of voice. In both statements, the content is the same.

What, now, about one's first-person knowledge of a desire or aim? What about statements of the sort "I have a good reason to do x?" Just in case the best explanation of the behavior of another is that "He has a good reason to do x," the change in voice has no effect on what is now the "motivational content" of the statements. It would on this account be a species of solipsism to insist that, although one can explain one's own behavior on the basis of motives and reasons, there are no comparable and reasonably ascribable motives and reasons available to anyone else. Understood this way, there are objective grounds, not to mention grounds of conceptual coherence, on which to defend moral ascriptions. Gauguin cannot coherently explain and justify his course of action on the grounds of authentic and significant motives without considering the authentic and significant motives of others likely to be pained and thwarted by this very course of action. To regard only his own motives as "real" would be akin to regarding only his own height as real. This is not to say that one cannot coherently and objectively weigh one's own motives as worthier than those in conflict with them. But this process of weighing and comparing presupposes the reality and importance of the conflicting motives. It is a process that takes the interests of others seriously. To do less is to earn blame: blame for negligence, for reckless disregard, for an obtuse comprehension of rights and responsibilities.

It may be argued, however, that Nagel's "motivation content" is fully unlike inches and feet. The sense in which Smith and Jones are both six feet tall surely does not match up with the sense in which Smith and Jones both have compelling desires and interests. Gauguin may be fully aware that his escape to Tahiti will leave his family impoverished but may consistently believe that this is a price worth paying for his potentially great artistic gift to the world. Needless to say, Mrs. Gauguin and the children have calculated the utilities differently and thus believe he should remain home with them as provider and loving husband and father. What counts as good or bad luck in the context depends on whose calculations prevail. Gauguin listens patiently and then buys his ticket to Tahiti; not owing to solipsism or indifference or selfishness, but owing to a different ordering of moral imperatives, with art trumping all the rest.

Gilbert Harman has offered a vigorous defense of moral relativism that, though fully respectful of the significance of the moral canons by which one hopes to live, confers trumping power on one set of moral imperatives over all the rest.[46] Mary bets on a horse who runs well on dry turf, Tom on the horse who runs well in the rain. A rainy day at the track is good for Tom and bad for Mary. This, on Harman's understanding, is precisely the framework of conflicting moral outlooks:

> Something that is good for some people is bad for others, indifferent to yet others. Moral relativism says that the same is true of moral values and moral norms. According to moral relativism whether something is morally good, right or just is always relative to . . . a certain moral point of view.[47]

The force and subtlety of Harman's defense of moral relativism are most in evidence where he separates his position from those whose defense of relativism is limited to the fact of diversity in moral appraisals. The relativity of morals for Harman is distinct from the fact that persons happen to hold different views as to what is right and wrong. By itself, different views certainly do not *entail* moral relativism. A world of mathematical incompetents might firmly believe that there is no right answer to the equation, $4 + 7 =$, but this does not entail that there is no right answer. Rather, "we have to consider what differences there are or could be and why this might be so."[48]

It would be churlish and perhaps unfair to ask why, absent a stable and universal moral framework, we are under some obligation to consider the nature and sources of these differences. If, at the end of the day, the only prescriptivity contained in moral maxims is that which the actor has already adopted as part of *his* morality, then Harman's position might simply be refused a hearing; or it might simply be installed as final and official. What is not churlish but at the core of the dispute is the universal expectation that theories be consistent with known facts, be developed in a coherent manner, and otherwise supply good reasons for their acceptance. Implicit in the expectation is that the theorist is not perpetrating a fraud, has not misrepresented the facts, and has not framed alternative theories in so prejudiced a fashion as to prevent valid comparisons. The very project of seeking the best explanation for, to take one example, differences in controlling moral maxims, is itself a morally guided project that cannot be regarded as worthy except in so far as it is scrupulously prosecuted.

Nor is it idle or argumentative to raise questions about just why anyone should want to know the answer to the question posed by Harman; the right answer to any question pertaining to how one should behave and live one's life and relate to others; why anyone would expect others to tolerate or even celebrate diversity in the opinions and values of others, or labor to preserve the freedom of others to embrace values different from one's own. The point here is that some measure of moral absolutism is required just to get the project of moral relativism started and to keep it on a path toward completion.

Willing and Achieving: The Limits of Voluntarism

Gauguin and Anna, having read the foregoing passages, might confer with one another and issue the following position paper:

1. We agree that we acted rashly and selfishly, disregarding the legitimate interests of others as we pursued what we took to be essential to our happiness.

2. It would have been better (more "moral") had we desired something other than what we actually desired. Each of us, in fact, tried to do just this. We tried, through our respective *will power*, to desire something else, but we failed abysmally. One of us *willed* not to allow art total control of life, and the other *willed* not to be in love with Count Vronsky.

3. If our lives are representative of the human condition, we are prepared to assert as a truth that *one's desires are not willfully brought about*.

4. If moral fault is a fault of the will, then the desires that moved us could not be morally faulty, since they were not expressions of our will.

5. If the desires that moved us were inextricably bound up with conditions in our little patch of the world—conditions we would not have confronted had we been born elsewhere, even ten miles away—then the desires themselves were not the result of personal initiative or causation.

6. We're sorry for hurting others, but it wasn't our fault, because *it's nobody's fault*.

If this position paper would benefit from footnotes and related scholarly apparatus, one might expect to find reference to, for example, William Alston's *Epistemic Justification*, citing the pages that include the lines, "Can you, at this moment, start to believe that the United States is still a colony of Great Britain, just by deciding to do so?"[49]

One's beliefs are not readily brought about merely by *deciding to believe*, though this is not the same as exempting them from the rather different disposition that is the *will to believe*. The *decision* to believe what is patently false would be a sign of serious mental disorder. But the *will* to believe that one of two plausible, but conflicting, theories is true is not only possible but common.

William James reflected on this in "The Will to Believe," in which he differentiated three genres of belief; those that are either living or dead; those that are either forced or avoidable; and those that are either momentous or trivial.[50] For James, beliefs that present us with what he calls "genuine options" are those that are "living," "forced," and "momentous." The alternative candidate-beliefs, "I am going to grow feathers on my body" and "I am going to grow scales on my body," form a dead pair, neither a plausible option. Similarly, "Regard my theory as true or regard it as false" fails, too, as a genuine option, for it excludes the possibility of taking no position on the matter at all. That is, nothing in the pair requires or forces the commitment of belief. What if, however, I say, "Either accept this truth or go without it"? Then, as William James says, "I put on you a forced option, for there is no standing place outside of the alternative."[51]

Where the options that might constitute the contents of our beliefs are alive with possibility; where they are such that to choose one is to lose the other; and where the choices generate momentously different ways of living our lives; in these cases, there is likely to be so strong a will to believe as to both adopt the belief and elevate it to the status of an object of desire. There is a good reason why we are unable to *decide* to believe that the United States is a colony. The reason is that "decision making" is a deliberative process "at a choice-point," weighing relevant and available facts by which to justify

CHAPTER 3

the decision. Where the facts are indisputable and all on one side of the matter, there is simply nothing to decide. Gauguin and Anna may be said to have confronted choice-points rife with relevant facts which they *chose* to ignore. The choice here was to forego deliberation and to act on desire, and this is what exposes them to censure. The Jamesian "truth" they were expected to bring to bear on their choices was of the form "I must not gratify my desires in such a way as to cause avoidable harm and suffering to innocent others."

To say that one cannot "desire to believe" is to say one is incorrigible. There are, after all, any number of candidate-beliefs as to what should govern our conduct. Though radically different, the main ones have at least something recommending them to rational beings capable of deliberation and judgment. One such belief is that whatever causes pain is evil and is to be shunned. This would rule out life-saving surgery, not to mention competitive sports or even the writing (and reading!) of philosophical treatises. So we decide *not* to believe this to be a controlling maxim, owing to its exclusion of what reason recognizes as worthy. Another candidate-belief is that it is never permissible knowingly and intentionally to cause harm to non-threatening others. The strong inclination (read "desire") to conduct oneself according to this teaching may be tempered by various treatises regarding the "just war." In all, then, there are many instances in which the desire to achieve something of value, to the extent that it depends on believing something to be valid or true or plausible, carries with it the desire to believe this very something.

There is no assurance that even a very strong desire to believe something to be true will succeed in establishing the belief as authentic. It is said that Heisenberg desired intensely to continue to believe in the certainty of physical laws undermined by his own principle. For a time, his desire to believe that the uncertainty principle was invalid succeeded, and he therefore believed it was invalid. But continuing deliberation, fortified by experimental findings and by the coherence requirements of scientific theory, brought him around to the conflicting belief that, at the level of subatomic particles, all interactions involve uncertainty relations.

The inability to believe—through the mere desire to believe—that the United States is a colony, establishes not the independence of belief in relation to desire, but the superior force of knowledge over desire in the formation of beliefs. The belief—through the mere desire to believe—that all allegedly mental events are in fact solely physical events in the brain establishes the superiority of desire in the formation of beliefs where knowledge is insufficient to affirm or refute the belief. Some beliefs are formed out of little more than the resources of desire, which is what childhood fantasies are all about. Say what one will of these fantasies, but they make abundantly clear that, at least in childhood, desire alone can render the impossible credible.

Gauguin and Anna so strongly desired to possess the objects of their obsessions that they came to see only one course of action, sight here reduced to tunnel vision. Here, then, is but another form of reckless driving, another type of negligence, just waiting for a ball to roll into the road. At decisive points in the arc of their narratives, they had choices to make and the resources needed to make justifiable choices. Taking the first drink is not a matter of luck, even if one was merely lucky to find that it was available. Taking the second drink is also not a matter of luck, and so becoming senselessly drunk is not a matter of being unlucky. Good and bad luck had nothing to do with any of this. It never does.

Tout Est Bien

Voltaire's *Candide* is better known than his *Poem about the Lisbon Disaster*, but it, too, reduced to the ridiculous Leibniz's famous insistence that this is the best of all possible worlds. Not only did Leibniz argue for this in his *Theodicy* (1710), but Rousseau defends the same "optimism" in *Emile*, as does Alexander Pope in his *Essay on Man*, concluding that "whatever is, is right." The essence of the *Theodicy* is found in Leibniz's "Essays on the justice of God and the freedom of man in the origin of evil." In sections 8–10 the argument of the essays reaches the conclusion that the world as it is can only be the best possible, "since God has chosen this world as it is."[52]

It is not necessary to invent a different Gauguin or Anna Karenina in order to illustrate how innocent lives are transformed or ended by sheer, unrelieved, unpredicted bad luck for which no one is in any sense responsible. Nor is it necessary to remind ourselves of the all-to-general inclination, noted in chapter 1, to attribute fault to victims. The Old Testament is filled with instances in which what seem to be natural calamities are understood as punishments inflicted on the corrupt and the faithless. In its unsteady evolution under one or another veil of ignorance, the law itself has been used to cast blame on the victim. In A.D. 636, Rothair, the Duke of Brescia, issued his 338 *Edicts*, number 180 making provision for dissolving oaths of betrothal in the event of blindness or leprosy:

> Concerning the girl who becomes a leper after her betrothal. If it happens that after a girl or woman has been betrothed she becomes leprous or mad or blind in both eyes, then her betrothed husband shall receive back his property and he shall not be required to take her to wife against his will. And he shall not be guilty in this event because it did not occur on account of his neglect but on account of her weighty sins and resulting illness.[53]

If in the time of Rothair wise counsel was nonetheless convinced that blindness and leprosy are inflicted on one owing to weighty sins, why is it not reasonable to assume that our contemporary wisdom assigns praise and blame on grounds that will ultimately be understood as physical rather than moral? The victims of the Lisbon earthquake would not have agreed with Leibniz that an omniscient and providential God had sufficient reason for constituting the material world in a way that causes death and disaster for the innocent. The parents of infants with cancerous brains are likely to resist Pope's confident appraisal of reality, that "whatever is, *is right*" (italics added).

This much acknowledged, the aims of the present chapter do not require a defense of one or another "theodicy" by which to show that innocent victims are somehow necessary if reality is to contain the maximum possible good. Less is it necessary to deny that our own era or moral thinking is plagued by an ignorance that only later scientific and conceptual developments will correct. Rather, it is sufficient to indicate what conceptual analysis not only establishes, but indeed does so with such coherence as to guarantee continuing validity. To wit: *Where events are unprompted by or indifferent to the realization of a moral precept, the events are nonmoral*. It is simply part of the very concept of "praise" and "blame" that they are validly ascribed to *agents* and not to accidents; that they reach their target, which is the presumed *will* of the agent, if only by way of the observable effects of that will. None of this is at the expense of Leibniz's or Pope's optimism. If it is actually the case that, for God to create a world optimized for goodness, some number of morally innocent beings must suffer disease or disaster, then neither they nor God would be subject to moral disapproval. It is something of a maxim in law, and implicit in moral evaluations, that *one does all that one must when one does all that one can*. God's omnipotence has no trumping power over logic. If it is just in the very nature of the natural world—a world taken to be *good as such*—that it must be a place in which suffering, death and disaster also occur, then their occurrence cannot count as a *fault*, but as the inevitable results of the achieving of the greatest good. It is not necessary to defend Leibniz's conviction that this is, in fact, the best world possible in order to understand that such an argument is not defeated by the mere fact of disastrous bad luck.

As for veils of ignorance, they have no bearing on the coherence or validity of the maxim, only on whether, in the given instance, we are correct in judging that observed events *are unprompted by or indifferent to the realization of a moral precept*. The leprous or blind women reached by Rothair's 180th Edict would now be recognized as victims of disease rather than divine retribution. This gain in knowledge would portend the elimination of all moral ascriptions in time only on the further assumption that radical determinism is correct. As the arguments for radical determinism have been shown in previous chapters to be unsuccessful, there is no good reason to assume that the lifting of successive veils of ignorance will leave as evident only the bare physical facts of mindless matter.

Does luck, then, have no place whatever in moral appraisals? The answer to this question calls for a more granular classification of those deliberations, choices, actions, and consequences that warrant moral appraisal. The pistol that by chance misfires, thus saving the life of the intended victim and also startling a driver who otherwise would have fallen asleep at the wheel presents results largely useless to a proper assessment of the character of the one who fired. We can agree that both the intended victim and the startled driver were lucky. Might we not also say that the assailant was *unlucky*, in that some other event that would have moved him to a different action just failed to take place?

Alas, might we not offer a quasi-Leibnizian calculation to show that the Lisbon earthquake actually interfered with and prevented so large a number of contemporary and future criminal and immoral acts that, had it not occurred, the net evil in the world actually would be greater? Along these lines, Scott Davison, adapting an illustration from St. Augustine, introduces Successful Jim and Unsuccessful Tim, each keenly attracted to a neighbor's lovely pears, each committed to stealing one. Successful Jim does just that but Unsuccessful Tim, just as he enters the neighbor's yard, is struck by a bolt of lightning. Only luck prevented Tim from succeeding. Thus, from a moral point of view, the two are equally bad with respect to their moral character. So, "There is no difference between (them) with respect to moral character, but there is a difference between them with respect to moral responsibility."[54]

Even in this, however, Davison correctly identifies comparable moral responsibility, too, for both Jim and Tim did both form the intention to steal, and one is responsible for forming intentions. Subtle differences aside (including the precise point in time at which the lightning struck Tim and where, at that point, he was in the forming of his intentions), there is a fundamental distinction to be drawn between appraisals of character and appraisals of responsibility. As Davison says, "One can be responsible for performing an action only if one actually performed it."[55] The maxim according to which events are nonmoral just in case they are unprompted by or indifferent to the realization of a moral precept is applicable to both Jim and Tim. Both undertook (even if only one completed) an action violative of a moral precept and both were therefore morally blameworthy. As only one achieved the immoral objective, only one is responsible *for the outcome*. Both, however, are responsible for the initial *event* of willfulness toward wrongdoing.

To consider Jim and Tim in passive terms, the one luckily avoiding death by lightning and the other thwarted by the occurrence of a rare event, is not to raise doubts about the reality of moral space but to point to other significant spaces in which much of life proceeds. There is a distinction to be kept in mind between moral blame and legal guilt. The law is engaged either by the accomplished act or by actions that constitute so clear and imminent a danger as to warrant prior restraint. One's motives and intentions are considered within the adjudicative context as part of the process leading to conviction or acquittal, or leading to judgments of reduced liability. One might spend one's entire lifetime contriving a "perfect crime," and even intending to commit it, but without ever giving that degree of publicity to the intentions and plans sufficient to come under the law's regard. The *moral* appraisal, however, requires no such publicity; it is enough to know what the actor would achieve were constraints relaxed. Williams's Gauguin, having thought the matter through and having concluded that his duty to art counted more than all the needs and interests of others, including those hopelessly dependent on him, would have earned a negative appraisal of moral *character* even if he never did take the steamer to Tahiti. But in that case he would not bear the added burden of failing in his moral *responsibility*. So, too, just in case he was struck by lightning as he walked toward the ticket counter, ready to book passage to Tahiti, and this even if his resulting death left his wife and children prosperous from the insurance settlement.

Implicitly exempted from this analysis are the compulsions arising from actual pathological or toxic states, such as those caused by tumors, drugs, lesions of one sort or another, as well as those elicited by threats or torture. It would be at least plausible to say that Williams's Gauguin "unluckily" developed a reason-defeating neuropathy. It is not plausible, at least not plausible in the same sense, to say that he "unluckily" developed a plan to abandon his responsibilities to others as he pursued his artistic calling. There is all the difference between an unlucky plan and the act of planning "unluckily." No philosophical analysis is needed for us to know the parts of our moral lives that have been aided or thwarted by unforeseen events. In the quiet moments, when the light of conscience illuminates more fully the motives and desires that have pushed us toward or away from candidate-actions, we claim competence in subtracting the merely lucky elements from the scorecard of our moral worthiness.

What if, however, all the soul-searching and ostensibly judicious self-appraisal is hopelessly superficial and even somewhat delusional? Might it not be the case that the correct account of significant action is to be found somewhere between radical incompatibilist freedom and radical determinism? Perhaps what can be learned from the reason-defeating power of disease is that any number of processes taking place beyond the range of conscious awareness can have comparably powerful influences over behavior and perception, but in ways that are not as easily discovered as are space-occupying lesions. There remains, then, that especially intriguing specimen of nurturance-luck, thought by many to interact with event-luck and constitutive luck to reduce theories of incompatibilist freedom to the status of a venerable superstition. It is the psychoanalytic version, with its emphasis on "unconscious" motivation, early traumatizing events, ego-defenses that warp reality, and a biological pedigree guaranteeing a lifelong conflict between the demands of the pleasure principle and the demands of social reality. So pervasive has been its influence that much of the next chapter is devoted to it.

4.

IGNORANCE, UNCONSCIOUSNESS, AND RESPONSIBILITY

As is known, many persons argue against
the assumption of an absolute psychic determinism by
referring to an intense feeling of conviction that there is a free
will. This feeling of conviction exists, but is not incompatible with
the belief in determinism. Like all normal feelings, it must be
justified by something. But, so far as I can observe, it does not manifest
itself in weighty and important decisions; on these occasions
one has much more the feeling of psychic compulsion,
and gladly falls back upon it.
—SIGMUND FREUD, *THE PSYCHOPATHOLOGY OF EVERYDAY LIFE*

A healthy person's beliefs are not incorrigible. —KARL POPPER,
THE MYTH OF THE FRAMEWORK

IN DIFFERENT WAYS the constitutive-luck and the moral luck arguments against incompatibilist freedom miss something important about moral experience. Constitutive luck focuses on the "givens" in our biogenetic resources and thus can only awkwardly accommodate the radical changes in perspective, conduct, motivation, desire, and emotionality taking place over the course of a lifetime and in response to the experiences of a lifetime. The sense in which being seven feet tall is "constitutively" lucky must be different from the sense in which one was not highly motivated to study medieval iconography until one heard a great lecture on the subject. The problem with constitutive luck as a significant feature of moral life is that the latter is subject to dynamic variations incompatible with what is constitutively set. Moral luck, on the other hand, suffers from a lack of individuation. Granting that strange and unpredictable events crop up, they are dealt with differently by different persons and even by the same person under different conditions. If the successful theatrical career often hinges on the "lucky break," it also depends centrally on the talents that "break" thereupon reveals.

In a much more similar way, both constitutive and moral luck, as ingredients in a credible account of moral experience, have a property that many would take to be a deficiency rather than a strength; namely, the property of being *evident*. Having a favorable or defective constitution is something that can be measured and classified; so, too, with a good or bad run of luck. What many find lacking here is any room for those hidden, unconscious impulses and desires that are the staple of depth psychologies and that, according to theory, are the wellsprings of mental life's defining features. Those who have been the beneficiaries or victims of either kind of luck are able to justify or account for their successes or failures by referring to the lucky elements. They might go so far as to acknowledge that the luck was good or bad only in light of prevailing social values and that at other times or in other places the same endowment or set of events would have conferred no advantage or imposed no disadvantage. In these respects, "luck" of both sorts is public and thus can be used to add or subtract from praise and blame.

"Prevailing social values," however, is a phrase that cannot explain anything until it, too, is explained. At a philosophical level, it might be sufficient to invoke "luck" and "chance" as code words for all of the conditions and events that somehow create or remove moral responsibility. For the determinist, "luck" is simply a term of ignorance, to be replaced by the delineation of actual causal links in the chain culminating in the event to be explained. One who becomes devoted to the subject of iconography after hearing a lecture on the subject is thus not just "lucky," but is, as it were, a datum that scientific psychology must be able to explain. So, also, with "prevailing social values," being "moved" by "faith," and so forth. From a scientific perspective, which must be the determinist's perspective, "luck" is what is eliminated once one discovers what is actually going on. If, however, neither introspective nor public account is able to reveal the causal mechanisms, then scientific inquiry must press on to levels of observation and analysis more granular and systematic. Enter Hobbes (again).

Hobbes and the "State of Nature"

The philosophical tradition that gives pride of place to rank ignorance and self-deception in accounts of human activity has a long pedigree, extending back even before Socrates. With Hobbes's *Leviathan*, however, metaphor and allegory are replaced by a theory regarding real conditions and their causal part in the production of social and historical institutions. Hobbes anticipates any number of contemporary and influential accounts now featured in the literature of social constructionism, behaviorism, evolutionary psychology, and sociobiology. The anticipation is not merely in one or another particular, but in the perspectival shift from first-person accounts of motivation to something of the natural history of socialization. The account is a narrative, featuring hypothesized conditions that are no longer evident but which actually and even mechanically *necessitated* what we innocently assume to have been the result of conscious, rational initiatives. The orderly, law-governed, political and civilized world that seems so "natural" to those who live in it, and are nurtured in such a way as to preserve it, is in fact an artificially constructed space arising from natural conditions that neither

history nor personal memory can reach. Humanity itself arose from a funda-
ment or primordium that can now only be inferred on the basis of its effects.
Whence, then, the source of morals, rights, duties, justice, law? The source
is that "state of nature" in which beings of comparable powers and desires
would otherwise constitute so menacing a daily threat to each other that
only a reluctant investment of police power in a sovereign might spare one
a violent death. This is not an account accessible to consciousness or the
arts of introspection, nor is it recovered by any superficial examination of
statutes or political history. It is unraveled by way of that reductive "resolutive" method of the Paduan school, capable of unearthing the basic principles on which even the most complex mechanical operations depend. Those
institutions and juridical precepts long attributed to a providential god are
in fact the outcome of avarice, fear, competition, danger. Centuries before
Darwin and Freud, *Leviathan* staged the macabre encounter between the
"pleasure principle" and reality.

As noted in chapter 2, of the numerous criticisms aroused by *Leviathan*
among the providentialist Christians, perhaps the most detailed, influential,
and insightful were Samuel Clarke's, delivered in his Boyle Lectures.[1] These
went through eight editions in less than thirty years, and would be a staple
in religious defenses of the Christian conception of moral freedom. Now
three centuries in the past, Clarke's analysis is easily but unwisely dismissed
as dated. It remains, however, as worthy of attention as are contemporary
versions of those "state of nature" or "original position" theories Clarke
brought under close scrutiny. Whether explicitly Hobbesian or even explicitly contrary to those of Hobbes, these theories share this much with the
original: some sort of compact or agreement, based on notions of utility and
self-interest, is made either imperative or "reasonable," given what the parties to the agreement do or can know about their powers and deficiencies.
Clarke's evaluation of these foundational assumptions continues to inform
this part of the "long debate" and repay examination. The most economical
way to do this is to paraphrase the Hobbesian principle and then summarize
Clarke's rebuttal:

HOBBES: The most basic of the assumptions about the "state of nature" or the
   "original position" is the essential equality of powers and desires of those
   finding themselves in this state.[2] Absent a ruling authority, there is simply
   no basis on which either can claim a sole right to what another desires.
   Thus is a state of war established in principle, whether or not it is realized
   at any given moment.
CLARKE: It is simply contradictory to affirm that *both* parties have a full right
   to the same thing, for this, "is saying that two *Rights* may be contradictory
   to each other; that is, that a thing may be *Right*, at the same time that 'tis
   confessed to be Wrong."[3]

Clarke here assumes that the possession of a full right to something logically entails that others do *not* have a right to it if, in the exercise of that right, they prevent the holder from equal exercise. We may say that everyone has an equal right to breathable air, but in this there is no contradiction, for the exercise of the right by one person does not in any way infringe the right of the other. Hobbes, however, is speaking of limited and not limitless resources, such that what one desirous party takes is no longer available to another. If this is so, says Clarke, then it is absurd to say that either, let alone both, has *full right* to the thing in question.

Hobbes's thesis, therefore, must be modified to include only what is vital to each person's survival. It cannot be a theory about sundry and expendable resources, for in that case there would be nothing but contradiction in maintaining that each person has an equal right to such items and that, in the state of nature, would have no reason to honor any other claim on it. What one has a full right to in the state of nature, therefore, must be a fundamental ingredient in life itself. To wit:

HOBBES: As everyone has a right to protect his life, everyone *in the state of nature* has a right to those things necessary to the preservation of life. And, given the perpetual jealousies and suspicions obtaining in our association with others, self-preservation confers on each man the right *to oppress and destroy* the competitor.

CLARKE: But if the primary impulse behind our actions is self-preservation, ". . . what can be more ridiculous, than to imagin a *War of All Men against All*, the directest and certainest Means of the *Preservation* of all?"[4] If Hobbes is contending that, as a matter of deliberated choice and rational initiative, one actually sets out to preserve one's life, then it would be absurd to participate in any scheme that creates or sustains a *War of All Men against All*. Rather, the obvious strategy would be one of pacifism and accommodation.

HOBBES: Whatever the strategy, it is necessary that those whose interests are vitally at stake reach some agreement, some covenant or compact, binding them to a mutually agreed upon course of action and interaction.

CLARKE: But whatever it is about a compact that *binds* must be grounded in some "antecedent *Law of Nature* which obliges Men to *Fidelity*."[5] If such a law can regulate conduct after the compact is formed, it surely could do so beforehand, owing to a sense of duty common to human beings. That sense of duty or fidelity on which all such agreements depend not only gives force and efficacy to compacts but undermines Hobbes's basic assumptions about avarice, selfishness, and destructive jealousies.

HOBBES: In the state of nature the only law is each man's will, the natural exercise of which cannot be "unjust." Justice, after all, arises not in the state of nature but in the political state. Accordingly, one who is victimized by the will of another can have no *just* reason to complain of wrong. Justice and injustice are creations of civil society, based on the commands of the sovereign and issued as positive law. In the absence of this, notions of right and wrong are unintelligible. In response to these realities, they are by the very nature of things obliged to seek peace. They cannot live, as ants and bees do, in cooperative society without benefit of laws, for men by nature seek "Honour and Dignity," leading to vicious envy, pride, and domination.[6]

CLARKE: To be required in one's conduct by the very nature of things is, in the end, to have deliberated rationally on a course of action, a course of life that is itself reasonable, proportionate, subject to moral scrutiny. Hobbes's *state of nature* is a state of corrupted human nature wherein reason is replaced by passionate and immoderate quests for power at any price.

The point of these comparisons is merely to show how two radically different narratives are able to address the complex and various facts of social life. There is sufficient good and evil in the world of human affairs to support Hobbes or Clarke. For Hobbes, the will of God is to be obeyed owing to the power of punishment held by God. For Clarke, the very goodness of the Creator is sufficient to summon obedience, love, and gratitude. The region of agreement between Clarke and Hobbes is not negligible, however. If the search for peace and common cause is the mark of universal brotherhood for one, or a defense against the prospect of violent death for the other, both can still concur that civil society and the rule of law are the *reasonable* consequence. Both eschew what their times would classify as absurdities; complex social actions for which none of the participants could offer a reason; cherished states of affairs that, in fact, were outgrowths of ingrained desires nonetheless unfelt by and unknown to the actor himself.

In this connection, however, it is useful to recall Bernard Mandeville's *The Fable of the Bees.*[7] It was one of the influential pre-Darwinian expositions seeking to explain the moral dimensions of life in terms of natural inclinations coming to terms with social realities; coming to terms, however, not as an expression of rational deliberation but through unconscious, instinctual forces. In his introduction to the subject of moral virtue, Mandeville warns his readers that, unlike those who prate on about how persons *ought* to be, he will tell them "*what they really are,*" and this turns out to be "*a compound of various Passions, that all of them, as they are provoked and come uppermost, govern him by turns, whether he will or no.*"[8]

Mandeville argues throughout that human nature is especially unfit for social life owing to these passions, and that it is only through the discipline of moral education and the rule of law that he becomes "sociable." Thus,

Whoever would civilize Men, and establish them into a Body Politick, must be thoroughly acquainted with all the Passions and Appetites,

Strength and Weaknesses of their Frame, and understand how to turn their greatest Frailties to the Advantage of the Publick.[9]

The process of socialization envisaged by Mandeville (and in this he is but an early and a more famous representative of an entire school of eighteenth-century thought) is one in which the product is just that; a *product* made to believe that self-sacrifice and courage in the face of mortal danger are natural.[10] Mandeville grants there are, to be sure, such natural qualities as friendship and kindly feelings. Neither these, however, nor

the real Virtues he is capable of acquiring by Reason and Self-Denial are the Foundation of Society; but that what we call Evil in this World, Moral as well as Natural, is the grand Principle that makes us sociable Creatures, the solid Baisis, the Life and Support of all Trades and Employments without Exception: That there we must look for the true Origin of all Arts and Sciences, and that the Moment Evil ceases, the Society must be spoiled, if not totally dissolved.[11]

Featured here is design without a conscious designer. It is in the very nature of human nature and in the possibilities afforded by the natural conditions of life that certain "moral" outcomes are more or less inevitable. The actor by nature is a self-protecting, vain, and avaricious being, but also one naturally inclined to fellowship and to kindly feelings. These are not the only sentiments, of course, for human passion runs the gamut from sympathy to destructive rage. Out of these resources the needs and powers of the social world begin to forge a character less dangerous, more helpful and agreeable, and one who must be made to think that what is expected of him is actually what he authentically would proffer. The analysis leads to what seems at first to be absurd, even oxymoronic: the notion that, of all the motives inclining persons and whole societies toward significant ends, the most powerful are unconscious! Enter Freud.

Responsibility and the Psychoanalytic Project

The expansive role Freudian thought has had obscures the rather modest and specific problem its famous creator was attempting to solve.[12] As a practicing neurologist, Freud saw patients complaining of symptoms that still found their way into the neurology clinic but were not referable to known or even possible neurological causes. "Glove anesthesia" is the textbook example: The patient has lost all sensitivity only in the hand, and only over an area that would be covered by a glove. But the distribution of sensory nerves in the hand is such that *that* loss of sensitivity could not be the result of a specific neurological lesion. The same is true of a number of sensory and motor deficits, some of them highly complex.

In Freud's time, techniques for distinguishing neurological and "psychogenic" factors were limited to careful clinical examination. It was a cause for some excitement, then, when the celebrated Pierre Charcot demonstrated the value of hypnosis in differential diagnosis. In the hypnotized patient, sensory and motor symptoms can be produced, temporarily eliminated, or even moved from one part of the body to another, something that cannot be achieved with bona fide neurological deficits. Freud spent 1885–1886 in Paris at Charcot's clinic, returning to Vienna equipped with hypnotic techniques he would soon abandon. Their success with hysterias was transient, not all patients could be hypnotized, and the entire process struck Freud as rather mysterious. What was clear to Freud, however, from the very success of hypnosis, was that hysterical symptoms are part of a dynamic psychic process that can be accessed by a therapist but not by the patient.

With less than credible modesty, Freud himself habitually referred to philosophers who came before him and saw as deeply into the heart of things. In the 1909 lectures at Clark University, in reviewing the history of the psychoanalytic "movement," he cited Schopenhauer and Nietzsche as forerunners, Freud himself willing

> gladly to renounce all claim to priority in those many cases in which the laborious psychoanalytic investigations can only confirm the insights intuitively won by the philosophers.[13]

What is interesting and revealing in this quoted passage is the contrast Freud offers between psychoanalytic investigation and what he calls the "intuitively" won insights of philosophers. The plain truth is that the psychoanalytic investigation so-called is guided, marked, and validated, from beginning to end, by what can only be classified as intuitive processes. The passage is interesting in that it expresses yet again Freud's eagerness to establish psychoanalysis as a scientifically respected form of investigation; one based on facts and integrated into a theory ultimately validated by the basic science of neurophysiology. This expectation will be considered in greater length. Staying with the first of the Clark University lectures, it is notable that Schopenhauer's *The World as Will and Idea* is cited along with Nietzsche, for Schopenhauer draws attention to the total *embodiment* of the most basic psychic processes. Passages to this effect abound; one is sufficient to convey the importance Schopenhauer attaches to the relationship:

> Every true, genuine, immediate act of the will is also at once and directly a manifest act of the body; and correspondingly, on the other hand, every impression on the body is also at once and directly an impression on the will. As such it is called pain when it is contrary to the will, and gratification or pleasure when in accordance with the will.[14]

Schopenhauer's thesis on this central point is not "philosophical" but scientific: The will is imbedded in a *psychophysical* nexus necessitated by our very embodiment. Pleasure and pain are not "representations" in the manner of percepts, but "immediate affections of the will" that summon us to action.[15] The very character of emotional life is also embodied, for every passion or deeply felt pain or pleasure works on and through the body, revealing itself in the actions of the body. What Freud could find in Schopenhauer, then, was not the happy coincidence of philosophical intuition matching up with a later and rigorously produced body of medical evidence. What was in Schopenhauer's theory just *is* Freudian theory, one no less intuitive than the other.

The same may be said of the debts to evolutionary theory. Darwin's *Descent of Man* (1871) and *The Expression of the Emotions in Man and Animals* (1872) made out the strongest case for the psychological functions of the animal kingdom being arrayed along a continuum of complexity.[16] Chapter 3 of *Descent* is titled "Comparison of the mental powers of man and lower animals," and chapter 5, "On the development of the intellectual and moral faculties during primeval and civilised times." For all the superficial differences, evolved species and various types within a species have in common the achievement of successful adaptation in the struggle for survival. Darwin's shift in emphasis from *natural* selection to *sexual* selection was prompted by his observation of mating patterns and in order to complete the account of the variables that govern the survival and perpetuation of species. The theory as a whole finds complex social behavior accounted for in terms of organisms acting *for* a purpose without necessarily acting *with* a purpose. Understood in this light, evolutionary theory contains the seeds of a theory of unconscious motivation in that it includes the motive force of desires that actually serve ends beyond the immediate aims of the participants.[17] Then, too, it is a theory in which pleasure and pain are the essential psychic guides to successful adaptation. The direct application of the theory to the widest range of psychological processes was widely recognized within psychology and was the subject of any number of detailed and influential texts before and just after Freud's medical schooling and at the time psychoanalytic theory was being formulated.[18]

One can, of course, cavil over questions of priority and anticipation in the matter of Freudian theory. There was, however, no one before Freud who incorporated unconscious processes so fully and coherently within the framework of medical diagnosis and treatment. They are the linchpin of the theory, for they serve as the mechanism for that theory of *repression* on which the entire theory depends or, as Freud put it, "the pillar upon which the edifice of psychoanalysis rests . . . really the most essential part of it."[19] Repression is not simple forgetting, nor is it innocent ignorance. It is an active process that serves the most vital interests of the person, though in a way that of necessity cannot be known and volitionally employed. The thoughts and actions arising from repressed material cannot, therefore, be fully free, for the actor cannot be said to be acting on the basis of a rational deliberation of means and ends. What has been repressed and is no longer available to consciousness continues to influence thought, but does so in ways beyond the cognitive powers of the thinker. The usual means by which one selects themes and issues for consideration are to no avail for, as Freud says,

> we are able to reject only those directing ideas which are known to us, and . . . with the cessation of these the unknown—or, as we inexactly say, unconscious—directing ideas immediately exert their influence, and henceforth determine the flow of the involuntary ideas. Thinking without directing ideas cannot be ensured by any influence we ourselves exert on our own psychic life."[20]

If it is actually the case that significant undertakings are impelled by motives different from those to which one has conscious access, then in what sense are the resulting actions validly praiseworthy or blameworthy? Psychoanalytic theory is a developmental theory according to which the seeds of neurotic conflicts are sewn early in life. The conflicts themselves are the inevitable result of a core of biogenetic evolutionary predispositions confronting the discipline of socialization. Each natural stage of psychosexual development, so gratifying in itself, must give way to the next, with normal development culminating in procreative heterosexuality. At each stage, there are opportunities for traumatic experiences, frustrations, punishments. The sexual maturation of the person leads to incestuous impulses and other taboos socially constructed to serve the general interests of the species. The very taboos and other means by which offspring are educated into standard roles are not consciously adopted by the community. Instead, they are overlaid with religious or moral justifications, themselves the result of repressive forces working to conceal the authentic erotic and self-gratifying creature of nature.

The Archimedean point from which the clinician can discover what is otherwise buried in the recesses of the unconscious is reached by way of dream interpretation that, according to Freud, is nothing less than the *via reggia* to all that is repressed. What is found in the dream are symbols and codes, ambiguous and transitory enough to keep the dreamer sleeping, if fitfully, but revealing enough for the skilled interpreter to unearth those wishes which can find safe fulfillment only in the dream.

Taking the theory as valid for purposes of argument, let us suppose that a person has written a will, the terms of which call for his entire fortune to be left to a distant aunt. It is a requirement of probate that a testator has a competent understanding of the nature of his possessions and the relationship in which he stands to those named as beneficiaries; further, that, at the time of authorizing the will, the testator was of sound mind, free of coercion, delusion, and other influences that would strip him of autonomy. In the hypothetical case, the testator—call him Mr. Sweet—has named his aunt (Mrs. Sauer) as sole beneficiary. Sweet goes so far as to state his reasons. The relevant passage reads as follows:

> Owing to the great love my aunt Vera Sauer has had for me all of my life, and owing to the fact that she forfeited much in my behalf, it pleases me to bequeath to her all of my worldly possessions.

As it happens, Sweet spent many years in psychoanalysis, and the Court of Probate has summoned the psychoanalyst, a Dr. Smith, to testify in response to a challenge from Sweet's son who was specifically excluded from the will. The son insists that his father utterly misrepresented the true nature of Mrs. Sauer; that she had no use whatever for the elder Sweet and, in point of fact, never gave up a farthing in his behalf. To believe the son is to judge the deceased to have been deluded as to the true nature of Mrs. Sauer and thus mentally disturbed, at least for purposes of probate. Dr. Smith, freed from the ethical constraints of confidentiality, summarizes his findings after years of treating the elder Sweet. The main points are these:

1. Sweet's mother was crippled in an accident when Sweet was thirteen. She was thereafter confined to a wheelchair.

2. Sweet suffered from an unresolved Oedipal complex, compounded by a sense of guilt that he had not shown his mother the care and compassion warranted by her condition.

3. His indifference, however, was the result of repressed oedipal desires that, through the mechanism of reaction formation, were translated into feelings of loathing and resentment.

4. Through the process of cathexis the erotic impulses were transferred to a distant aunt, not only related by blood to Sweet's mother, but resembling her physically.

5. As Mrs. Sauer displayed coolness and indifference toward Sweet, she served the vital function of "rebuffing" the unworthy lover. Sweet became obsessed with her "goodness," repeating often his earnest wish that he had "just a fraction of her goodness." This was clearly the sublimation of his desire to possess her in the biblical sense.

Taking all of this into account, should Sweet's will fail of probate? There is, after all, ample precedent for denying probate when psychiatric testimony convinces the court that a testator suffered from delusions, including a delusion as to the true feelings of one's offspring![21] Before answering the question, additional information is needed, this in the form of a second expert called by the court, this one a psychiatrist who has treated Mrs. Sauer for a number of years. His testimony runs as follows:

1. Vera Sauer had great love for her sister and became deeply depressed on the occasion of her death.

2. She knew that her sister's great fear was that, because of her illness, someone else would come to be a "mother" to her son, thereby replacing her.

3. To be sure nothing of the sort would happen, and against her own deep feelings of love for the elder Sweet, Mrs. Sauer feigned indifference and even hostility.

4. She indicated on a number of occasions that her nephew seemed to see all of this and could not be put off by her aloofness.

It should be obvious that there is no realistic limit to the number of narratives and refinements to each that might be composed, each of them more or less as credible as the rest. What all would have in common are two essential features: the first is that psychoanalytic statements are epistemic and, as such, may be right or wrong. The second is that, once the patient or client has successfully completed psychoanalysis, his own first-person reports will now be correct and will replace earlier self-reports distorted by the ego-defense mechanisms. Neither of these essential features warrants acceptance, however. It is doubtful in the extreme that Dr. Smith's statements in the above example are epistemic, for it is doubtful in the extreme that statements 2–5 could be evaluated by a form of public evidence. Even more telling, however, is the doubtful nature of the second feature that such accounts have in common; that is, the conviction or assertion that, just in case the client has a successful analysis, subsequent first-person reports will be in some sense "truer" or "true." The epistemic authority a percipient has in the matter of sensations and feelings does not extend to conceptual or theoretical explanations of those sensations and feelings. Sweet's word is the last word if the question is whether or not Sweet has a toothache or affection for Mrs. Sauer. But Sweet's accounts of just why he has a toothache or the basis of his feelings for Vera are subject to challenge. They are actually subject to unending challenges. Sweet's account of the cause of his toothache, even if it includes authoritative information about the firing pattern of the dental nerves, the activity in the mandibular branch, and so forth, not to mention poor hygienic practices, will always be subject to refinements and modifications: the local water supply was not fluoridated, the diet was poor in calcium, the whole family has bad teeth, Sweet has a rather low threshold for pain, ad infinitum. One might be satisfied with what is called an "inference to the best explanation" in such matters, but this just raises the question anew, for what is at issue is just what makes an explanation good, better, or best. Needless to say, when moving from Sweet's toothache to his affection for Vera Sauer, the burdens of explanation are massive.

At the level of psychoanalysis proper, there is nothing in the accounts that can claim epistemic authority or even greater credibility than competing plausible accounts. The elder Sweet may just have loved his old aunt and resented his son, pure and simple. If the psychoanalytic account is to gain pride of place amidst the welter of coherent narratives, it must do so (or so it has been insisted) by way of its kinship with a more basic science. Unlike the "folk" interpretations of the storyteller or the ordinary citizen, the psychoanalyst has (allegedly) the benefit of a primary science, on which the secondary science of psychoanalysis is based. There is at once a promise and a problem with this, to which Ernest Nagel gave general expression when considering the nature of reductive explanations in any discipline:

> A reduction is effected when the experimental laws of the secondary science . . . are shown to be the logical consequences of the theoretical assumptions of the primary science. . . . (But) if the laws of the secondary science contain terms that do not occur in the theoretical assumptions of the primary discipline . . . logical derivation of the former from the latter is prima facie impossible.[22]

Neurophysiology has no terms that could possibly match up with "repression," oedipal tensions, cathexis, sublimation, reaction-formation. Nor would hoped-for correlative research do anything toward the achievement of an authentic reduction. This is readily established by considering how such research would be conceived and what one would then have to make of the resulting data. As it is the theory of "repression" that the overall theory depends on, let us consider research that would ground repression in more basic neurophysiological processes. Assume there is no limit to the level of detail that can be attained in observing and quantifying events at the neurophysiological level. Assume further that one has limitless access to the thoughts and actions of the patient. Assume, finally, that at various times the patient rather innocently misplaces or forgets items, whereas at other times (according to the theory) the seemingly innocent forgetfulness is, indeed, the active process of repression. The salient objective of the research is to find some process, place or event within the nervous system by which to differentiate innocent forgetting and repression. Obviously, this objective can only be attained by taking some instances of forgetting as, in fact, the selective forgetting of repression. That is, unless the theoretical entity, "repression," is accepted, there is simply no basis for the correlative research in the first instance. Correlative research is just that, and it is possible only when there are at least *two* candidate-correlates. Thus, if psychoanalytic theoretical terms are to find some sort of validation at the level of neurophysiology, they will do so only by assuming their ontological standing ab initio, a patently illicit move.[23]

This much clarified, we can return to the question of unconscious sources of motivation and the general problem of self-deception in the matter of praiseworthy and blameworthy states and actions. It is not necessary to bar such sources stipulatively, but it is also not necessary to include them in their questionable Freudian form. Ariela Lazar has discussed irrational beliefs and desires, flights of imagination, and the harboring of fantasies as powerful forms of self-deception and thus as impediments to the exercise of practical reason.[24]

Nonetheless, the formation and sustaining of belief, as with the formation of one's very character, is an active process over which one may reasonably be expected to exercise control. When psychologists note that one does not "choose" one's character and conclude from this that it is in some sense created "for" the person, they simply miss the point.[25] Character is not a "thing" to be chosen or made, but an approach to life marked by aspirations. The aspirations that are self-improving and self-defeating are subject to the person's appraisals and control. It is not, therefore, one's character that one chooses, but one's choices, which forge character itself. Incontinence comes in various forms and the "doxastic" is one of them. The same may be said of what the clinician calls "ego defenses." Life could well become insufferable were one to eschew any and every face-saving stratagem, every embellishment by which to transform the prosaic into something a bit more affecting. In some instances, what is called "rationalization" is but an apology or excuse, if only to oneself. If, indeed, one is found lifting weights to "compensate" for a naturally weak body, the enterprise may well be laudable. To compensate for the same condition by adopting a threatening and aggressive attitude toward others is blameworthy.

One might contend that these are superficial expressions of the ego-defenses and that matters are far more complex with repressed desires that become expressed in self-destructive ways or in ways injurious to others. Not much imagination is needed to discover how the "ego" of the racist, the neo-Nazi, the bigot is served by having an assortment of scapegoats at the ready. From a moral point of view, however, whether or not such attitudes and conduct arise from unconscious motives or repressed desires or early psychic traumas is irrelevant *as long as the practices continue in the face of factually refuting evidence.* We can accept as a hypothesis that Mr. Sweet harbored sentiments toward his mother that he was unwilling to face. Perhaps in some sense these were "repressed" and in some way came to influence his behavior. But that behavior is subject to moral appraisal apart from any consideration of Sweet's unconscious or even conscious motives. To treat another unfairly is blameworthy and is no less so for the motive being obscure or "unconscious." Psychoanalytic theory may by certain lights "explain," but explanation is not exculpation.

In an even more basic way the psychoanalytic perspective misses what is essential in the functions of praise and blame. They are applied to intentions and actions as reflecting moral properties subject to moral appraisal. Praise and blame cannot be heaped on phantoms, on theory-terms, on what-ifs. It is sufficient to know why Mr. Sweet has decided to have his earthly possessions pass to Mrs. Sauer. If he makes the decision on the basis of her perceived merits, then it is clear that he seeks to reward merit, though he may be incorrect in assessing the merits of the case. Mr. Sweet would be properly blamed had his intentions been to reward what he took to be her wickedness or cruelty. If, however, Sweet labored under the weight of delusions so extreme as to be inexplicable under the light of ordinary perception, he would be judged incompetent owing to insanity. There is, then, a point beyond which differences of perception are no longer merely perspectival but evidence of pathology. This point is visible to all normal percipients and requires no trolling of the deeper waters of the unconscious.

Suppose, however, that Mr. Sweet as a unitary corporeal being nonetheless presented striking evidence of two distinct personalities: Mo Sweet and Les Sweet. Suppose further that witnesses to the signing of the will testify that it was Mo who dictated the terms and that, later the same day, Les looked at the document and promised to destroy it, preferring to burn all his assets so that no one would inherit anything. Who is "responsible" when there appears to be more than one *person* under the skin of one *body*? Enter Locke.

Multiple Personality and the Nature of "Self"

For all of the wasted humor inspired by Descartes's *cogito*, it was Locke's discussion of personal identity that gave impetus to the issue in modern times. The conclusion reached by Descartes was not in response to doubts about his existence but to a search for an epistemic certainty that would be immune to delusion, error, and deception. Looking for that one indubitable thing, Descartes found it in the very process of thought for, though one can be the victim of an evil spirit, a malicious deceiver, the undeniable reality of thinking is the necessary precondition even to be deceived. His analysis results in the certainty *that* he is and even *what* he is essentially; that is, a thinking thing (*res cogitans*), though it leaves unsettled and unaddressed just *who* he is.[26]

In *An Essay Concerning Human Understanding*, Locke caused something of a furor as a result of his discussion of personal identity.[27] If there is an unnamed target of Locke's criticism on this point it is not Descartes but an entire tradition of "substance" or essentialist theories of the "self." Included in the tradition would be Plato, the neoplatonists, most major Scholastic philosophers and, of course, his contemporaries among the Cambridge Platonists. At issue is whether the constitution of the mind requires sources that predate all experience, all consciousness: sources that comprise the true self, an immaterial "substance" (soul?) whose presence makes one just the person one is. The defense of so-called substance theories of the self typically rests on the lifelong continuity of one's personal identity, even in the face of radical changes in one's corporeality. Moment to moment, no state or condition of the body is static. The brain is in a constant flux of activity, each cell engaged in metabolic processes, whole aggregates ceasing to exist. The entire supply of taste buds is replaced often in a single year, even as the quality and familiarity of flavors remain nearly constant. In all, there is an apparent incompatibility between the dynamics of physical life and the continuity of self, indicating that there is some essential or substantial self over and against the body in which it resides.

The ancients were not unmindful of the issue. The annual sailing of the putative "ship of Theseus," celebrated from port to port by Athenians recalling the source of their treasured liberties, raised questions about the continuity of identity in the face of change. With each old and rotten plank replaced by new wood, the ship of Theseus was different from the original. At what point is it no longer that ship? And were all the old wood used to build another ship, would this one now be the original ship of Theseus? And how can an original go out of existence only to reappear *as the original*?

Locke's well-known solution to the problem reduces personal identity to the contents of consciousness. The answer to the question "Who am I?" is provided by the recollection of all of the experiences accessible to consciousness. Locke states his position directly:

> That with which the consciousness of this present thinking thing *can* join itself, makes the same person, and is one self with it, and with nothing else. . . . This may show us wherein personal identity consists: not in the identity of substance, but . . . in the identity of consciousness.[28]

Translating the ship of Theseus example to that of actual persons, one may ask whether the relocation of a collection of conscious elements from one mind to another is tantamount to the relocation of the *person* from one body to the other. Locke was satisfied that this is precisely what would take place and says as much in his thought-experiment with the prince and the cobbler. Suppose both fall asleep and, during the night, all that was in the consciousness of the prince is now transferred to that of the cobbler, the latter's then moved into the consciousness of the prince. On awakening each would be the same *man* who had retired the night before, but not the same *person*. Indeed, the cobbler would awaken to all of the responsibilities occasioned by the life of the prince. It is owing to the relationship between personal identity thus understood and responsibility that Locke regarded this sense of person as "forensic." It has been suggested that Locke speaks here for a defined cultural value, that of "enterprise," according to which who you are is more or less exhausted by considerations of responsibility, achievement, a role in the larger culture.[29]

If Locke was the voice of conventionalism, his thesis nonetheless elicited a spate of learned and also comic rebuttals from within that very culture. The wits who dubbed themselves the "Scriblerians," and who numbered both Swift and Pope in their ranks, had already decided that the pretensions and presumptions of natural philosophy had gone far enough. Just as Swift's Lilliput was a parody on the Royal Society, so were the playful pages of the

Scriblerians used against Locke. The murderer who, between his lethal assault and his trial, has sufficient time to stock his memory with fresh thoughts and experiences is now no longer the same person who committed the crime. Alas, the felon has simply disappeared![30] Berkeley's *Alciphron* and Reid's *Inquiry* present formal refutations, in each case Locke's theory understood as affirming an identity-relation between memory and personal identity. Thus understood, the theory is false. To wit:

1. Imagine a brave officer decorated for valor. Call him *B*.
2. *B* vividly recalls being the young boy once punished for stealing fruit from the orchard. Call the young boy *A*.
3. Imagine an aged General (call him *C*) who has a clear recollection of *B* but has completely lost all memories of *A*.

If Locke's is an identity-theory according to which "person" is identical to "memory," then: [*A=B*, *B=C*, but *A≠C*] and the identity fails Leibniz's "identity-of-indiscernibles" criterion.[31] Moreover, it is absurd to contend that a person's memory of having done something makes that person the one who did it. What Locke seems to be getting at is not what constitutes one's identity as a person, but the evidence available to one who, as it were, would know his own "self-identity." Much confusion on this point can be avoided if a different classification were made uniform; one that clarifies distinctions between and among the concepts of "self," "self-identity," and "personal identity." The amnesic person may be well-known to others who, therefore, can establish the patient's personal identity. The normal person among strangers is unknown to them (and cannot, therefore, be personally identified) but has no doubt about his self-identity. There may also be the total amnesic among strangers, now lacking both self- and personal identities; however, though he does not know who he is, and though others do not know who he is, he surely knows *that* he is.[32] The matter comes full-circle, returning to Descartes's *cogito* as the indubitable mark of that *res cogitans* distinguishable from its own embodiment and from any and every other *res extensa*.

However personal identity is to be understood, it is clear from the records of medical history and contemporary psychiatry that there are illnesses able to rob one of personal identity and able as well to establish multiple identities in the same body. The phenomena or disorders take on a variety of forms, all of which have caused difficulties, at once philosophical, religious, medical, and legal. Ian Hacking's *Rewriting the Soul* examines the issue in detail. One example discussed by Hacking involves the "sleepers" of the twelfth and thirteenth centuries who, in states of trance, would commit violent and criminal acts of which they were oblivious in their restored state of consciousness.[33] The "sleepers" exemplify one in a wide range of disturbances that include, but are not limited to, somnambulism, automatism, temporal lobe focal epilepsies, dissociative mental syndromes, and multiple personality disorder. What all have in common is either the loss of that expression of personhood to which responsibility is routinely assigned, or the presence of multiple "selves," each of which seems to be responsible in ways the others are not. As Hacking notes, the theological problem thus created is based on the Christian doctrine that reserves ensoulment to one body at a time. If it is ensoulment that stands at the foundation of rational and moral power and thus at the foundation of moral responsibility, then the presence of multiple souls in one "person" constitutes a most difficult challenge. Similarly, both legal and moral judgments require *personal* responsibility, and this presupposes an identifiable and continuing entity that just is *the person*.

For some, the problem has been exacerbated by a lingering metaphysics of substances, eager to preserve a special ontological niche for consciousness and the mental. Once the ghost is ejected from the machine, the "problem" of multiple selves becomes merely technical. Daniel Dennett, for example, understands the evolutionary process as having sufficient time and resources to try out all sorts of experiments, some of them gruesome. One body can host any number of "personalities" and, in instances of genetic clones, the same personality might find itself in two different bodies.[34] It has also been proposed that psychic traumas call for anesthetizing palliatives and that dissociation is just the remedy. Severe pain triggers the production and distribution of opiate-like substances in the brain; perhaps severe psychological pain triggers comparable but more complex defensive adjustments that lead to the appearance of a different self with different aims, memories, sentiments and attachments—a self with a different and more acceptable life.[35]

The relevance of these phenomena to the matters of praise and blame is easily misapprehended. If we choose to treat all such cases of multiple personality and dissociative disorders as instances of disease, causally brought about by neuropathological processes, then they simply are exempted from moral consideration. Diseases of this kind strip the sufferers of the very resources that render moral judgments plausible. The question of which personality is to blame never arises, for there has been no crime. There has been no crime because the defendant is judged as lacking the essential ingredient of mens rea, and this because the defendant is judged to be the victim of a "diseased" mind. The trigger that is pulled is a result of a muscular spasm induced by a brain tumor: No serious theory of moral responsibility has difficulty with instances like these. An action thus brought about is not an "action" within the ambit of the term's moral significance. What makes multiple personality and related conditions interesting from a moral point of view is an implication that some draw from them; namely, that what is regarded as personal responsibility in the usual case is comparably askew, for the usual case is itself an evolutionary outcome governed by the genetic hard-wiring and the software supplied by experience.

In his critical study of the history and theoretical interpretations of multiple personality, Ian Hacking reaches a position that is one of restrained skepticism. Apart from the possibility that at least some of the patients intentionally deceive, there is the distortion of fact introduced by the very vocabulary and foundationalist assumptions of psychiatry. Commenting on Morton Prince's most famous "multiple," he says,

> Prince knew exactly how to describe his patient so that she would be a multiple. Is it any wonder that scanning his interminable report we conclude that there are several persons in one body? This is not a test of how we use language in order to describe real people. It is a consequence of how the literary imagination has formed the language in which we speak of people—be they real, imagined, or, the most common case, of mixed origin.[36]

What patients present are accounts of their feelings and understanding, their sense of themselves and their position within what they perceive to be the context and framework of their lives. "Multiple personality" is a theoretical term adopted by those who judge some of these accounts as indicative of more than a single and unified "personality." But this is to employ one theoretical term in order to qualify another, for "personality" is also a theoretical term. Indeed, when examined finely, it is much like older substance-theory terms. Thus, there is Smith-the-person and then there is this "personality" of Smith's that is to explain why Smith-the-person reacts in characteristic ways, has identifying fingerprint-like preferences and aversions, and so on. Just in case Smith surprises us with two comparably settled but clearly distinguishable "personalities," we have before us *by definition* a "multiple personality."

Before the advent of professional psychology and its favored theories, there were equivalent modes of classification, for what are the ancient discussions of "character" or Elizabethan references to dominant "humours" or the physiognomists listing of "types" if not theories of personality. What has supported the various schemes is just the stability of one's reactions and approach to life's realities, one's way of dealing with events and persons, one's more or less dominant moods and motives. If the issue is to be settled by actual data, however, then the fuller account must make ample room for those who have turned over a new leaf, experienced a version of the Pauline vision, been transformed by grace, by trauma, by firm and relentless self-discipline, by new associations, even by learning to dance the tango! Once a theory of types is assumed to be valid, it is likely that tests of the theory will leave less than generous room for counterexamples or will simply exclude them as "outliers." It is a matter of the "psychologist's fallacy" all over again, which is what found William James fearful of the passion for the "controlled experiment."

Added to these reservations is one about the strategy of explaining the essential nature of things in terms of pathological deviations from the norm. There are, to be sure, those experiments of nature (metaphorically speaking); there are, to say it right, defective results included within the larger population of normally developing and developed specimens. But the phenomenon of color blindness does not serve as a warrant for doubting the normalcy of trichromatic vision. Rather, the normal process is what establishes dichromatic vision as "defective." To stay with this example, we would not say, having observed a sample of dichromats, that persons who refer to specific regions of the visible spectrum as "green" and "red" do so as a result of processes just like those leading to dichromatism. Rather, we say that the dichromat is lacking in an essential process and thus has defective vision. The fact that color vision varies in degrees of sensitivity does not render the state "normal color vision" relative; rather, it is owing to the established principles of color-sensing and color-coding in vision that all sighted persons can be graded in the matter of sensitivity to variations in wavelength.

Nearly any example would serve as well, including the one that has attracted so much attention in recent decades—the "split brain" patient.[37] The implications were not lost on philosophers or, for that matter, writers of science fiction. Detailed attention to these implications can be found in Derek Parfit's *Reasons and Persons*, with Parfit concluding from the clinical research that the case for the unity of consciousness has been overtaken by the data. The fact that surgical sectioning of the corpus callosum can result in a person at once affirming and denying the same proposition suggests a mode of neural organization admitting of all sorts of odd outcomes. Parfit's own thought-experiments along these lines lead him to conclude that a parallel set of different streams of consciousness in the wake of surgery presents not a unity of consciousness, but rather three distinct entities.

> And two of these entities cannot be claimed to be the kind of entity with which we are all familiar, a person. I am the only person involved, and two of the subjects of these experiences are *not* me.[38]

It was not necessary to await surgical advances, however, for the very presence of two symmetrical hemispheres joined by visible bands of fibers excited the imagination along similar lines in the middle of the nineteenth century. One of the leaders of thought then, in his most authoritative text, summarized the most ambitious speculations of the day:

> The opinions of Wigan ("Duality of Mind," London, 1844), who assumes a complete duality of mind in the two cerebral hemispheres; the conjectures of Holland ("On the Brain as a Double Organ," Chapters on Mental Physiology, 2nd ed., London, 1858, p. 179), that many mental disorders, especially the states of mental disunity and internal contradiction, depend upon a disharmony in the functions of both hemi-

spheres, and lastly, the recent attempt of Follet to refer mental aberrations to "disturbance in the equilibrium of the innervation of the two hemispheres," are wanting in sufficient proof.[39]

One might say such speculations still are. But it is unclear just how the thesis bears either on the "unity of consciousness" thesis, or on theories of personhood, or on conceptions of the self. Derek Parfit, for example, has recently argued for a "persons without selves" thesis on the grounds that no metaphysical advantage attaches to a self having a stream of experiences over and against that same stream occurring *here*, where the location is just the place occupied by a person.[40] On this view, nothing is gained by the addition of some shadowy "self" in which the experiences reside, contrasted with an account of the contents of the experiences taking place in a given and identifiable body. But there actually *is* a metaphysical difference in the two accounts. On one account, at least some of the experiences are of a nature that confers an epistemic incorrigibility on the first-person report that is utterly lacking in the third-person report. That is, "I have a toothache" has an epistemic standing different from, and more authoritative than "a toothache is being experienced *here*." Ownership matters in this regard, as does (to resurrect the old Russellian saw) the difference of knowledge by description and knowledge by acquaintance. There are, of course, no disembodied pains, but there are also no unowned pains. Ordinary language finds locutions of the sort "the self is having a pain," most odd and, if only in deference to ordinary language philosophers, one might recast such sentences. But there is nothing odd about saying in response to a suffering friend's report of toothache, "I know how you feel. Believe it or not, I'm having that pain *myself*." True, the reference is not to some entity, "myself," thought to be residing within my body. But neither is a reference to my *person* indicative of such a resident.

What, then, about the commissurotomized patient, steeped in contradictory claims, at once acknowledging and denying one or another object of perception? The answer, it would seem, is that a gross anatomical disruption of pathways involved in the integration of perceptual information not surprisingly produces pathological outcomes. That these patients are otherwise "normal" can be said of a great number and variety of victims of neurological diseases. Epileptics are normal between seizures. Schizophrenics, manic-depressive psychotics, somnambulists—all have periods of normalcy, sometimes only very rarely interrupted by tell-tale symptoms. In the face of this, there are only two practical hypotheses available when one is called upon to render moral judgments of persons and actions allegedly arising from profound medical or psychological disorders. One regards the offending action as the product of disease, the effect of antecedent conditions that the actor did not intentionally bring about and could not have controlled. The other is that the offending action expressed the intentions of the actor, and the intentions themselves were not the result of disease. For better or for worse, the presumption of law is that those fit for the law's judgments are and must be "sane." It is the defendant's burden to defeat the presumption. There are no compelling reasons for the moralist to adopt presuppositions different from those of the magistrate. Absent proof of a *morally* disabling condition, the warranted hypothesis is that the actor is responsible and qualifies for moral appraisal.

The "split-brain" patient, transformed by thought-experiments into two distinct "persons," must be judged in precisely these terms, and for reasons that apply in less dramatic cases. The most persistent criminal offender devotes the largest fraction of life to the combination of sleep, ordinary chores, lawful conduct, and acceptable behavior. The commission of crime is the rare event, often prompted by conditions that "bring out the worst." Defenses of the "I was not myself" variety are not always weak rationalizations. Let us suspend both science and credulity and grant the following scenario:

1. Jones as an infant undergoes a therapeutic sectioning of the commissures to prevent the spread of life-threatening epileptic seizures.

2. Jones's parents are both mad scientists, obsessed with testing a pet theory. Using state-of-the-art technology, they feed into Jones's left hemisphere the best of classical music, ancient philosophy, the lives of saints and heros, poetry of love and kindness, Stoic lessons of moderation. The right hemisphere is crowded with the opposite: the pleasures of self-gratification, ruthlessness, and aggression, the sheer value of defeating others by any means.

3. Jones is subjected to an operation at age 20, both hemispheres removed and transplanted respectively into two brain-dead recipients, Smith-1 and Smith-2. Smith-1 receives Jones's left hemisphere, Smith-2 the right one.

4. After full recovery, Smith-1 is found delivering medicine to impoverished settlements in South America. Smith-2 is operating a drug cartel in the same region.

What might be concluded from the published results of the research? Presumably, one would be inclined to think that Smith-1 and Smith-2 were the recipients of radically different nurturance-luck. But this is the same conclusion one would reach knowing nothing about brains and commissures and, at the same time, not doubting but that the functions of the brain were intimately associated with what Smith-1 and Smith-2 were doing. If, however, it is possible for persons, through their active powers and their capacity for rational deliberation, to overcome the effects of defective nurturance, then Smith-1 and Smith-2 pose no special problem. They are either robots owing to the surgery or they are not. Smith-2 might have the benefit of a merciful judgment that finds his offenses mitigated by the circumstances of his life (brain). Smith-1 might be the beneficiary of a somewhat attenuated praise owing to the great start he enjoyed as a result of the well-stocked cerebrum.

Whether or not Smith-2 is judged fit to stand trial might well depend on a more enlightened set of criteria than what now obtains. If it is the defendant's burden to prove a lack of fitness in matters of this kind, it is to be expected that the standards and criteria of such proof will change in light of scientific and medical discoveries. The same is true, however, in the matter of nearly any significant aspect of trial evidence. In medieval England, persons were regarded as mentally competent to stand trial if, among other abilities, they could calculate the correct change in a twenty-shilling transaction. Presumably we possess more precise and reliable measures of cognitive ability now and are certainly better in detecting subtle cognitive deficits. The functional MRI reveals lesions heretofore visible only on postmortem examination. The PET scan is twenty times more sensitive than the CAT scan, and one could go on. As new methods yield additional information, the moral and legal appraisals of ostensibly identical actions may change, yielding pardons where once there was confident condemnation.

All this pertains not to the rationale or justification or fixity of moral principles, but to the facts upon which these principles are brought to bear. It was ever thus. Clinical cases of automatism, somnambulism, multiple personality, and temporal lobe epilepsy are dramatic, even eerie, to the uninitiated. The inability to explain the symptoms poses no challenge to the moralist, however, for the same moral precepts are applicable no matter how the symptoms are ultimately understood. If the patient is discovered to be feigning illness, then the fault of fraud is added to the other offenses. If the patient is discovered to be stripped by disease of requisite cognitive or volitional power, then there is no event of moral standing to begin with and therefore nothing to judge. The fact that an earlier age comes to be seen as misguided or ignorant of facts that fall within the province of science should have a chastening effect on confidence regarding matters of *scientific* fact, but certainly not on the settled catalogue of *moral* facts. To learn that the "thief" was in fact fully controlled by electrodes implanted by a diabolical surgeon requires us to abandon the presumption of autonomy. It has no bearing at all, however, on the moral quality of theft. Whether or not the taking of property is a volitional act is a question that can be informed by scientific findings. Whether or not taking the property of others is "wrong" is a different question and one needing no scientific instruments to answer.

Medical Jurisprudence and the Emergence of the Experts

In his unsigned essay in the *Edinburgh Review* for June of 1829, Thomas Carlyle, reflecting on what he called "Signs of the Times," takes notice of the confident scientific materialism of the time. He pays special attention to the works of Pierre Cabanis, about whom he has this to say:

The metaphysical philosophy of this last inquirer is certainly no shadowy or unsubstantial one. He fairly lays open our moral structure with
his dissecting knives and real metal probes; and exhibits it to the inspection of mankind, by Leuwenhoek microscopes, and inflation with
the anatomical blowpipe. Thought, he is inclined to hold, is still se-
creted by the brain; but then Poetry and Religion (and it is really worth
knowing) are "a product of the smaller intestines"! We have the greatest
admiration for this learned doctor: with what scientific stoicism he
walks through the land of wonder unwondering.[41]

By Carlyle's time, the scientifically committed thinkers had long since
concluded that the moral side of life was to some extent a neurobiological
outcome, and unequivocally so in instances of moral depravity and criminality. The trust in science that was the hallmark of Enlightenment reformism
was apparent in the closing years of the eighteenth century when Gall's
Phrenology, Lavater's *Physiognomy*, and comparable grand "scientific" theories of the mind and human personality were claiming wide attention and
allegiance.

Developments in this department had a long and varied gestational period. As early as the European witch trials, reliance on "experts" was necessitated by the special and strange nature of mental disorders. In many instances, the illnesses and other untoward effects attributed to witches could
also be explained on the basis of natural processes. As a result, courts often
summoned persons thought to have specialized competence to determine
whether magic or nature was at the bottom of things. Not only was the
"witch pricker" relied on to locate the "devil's mark" (the bodily location
by which evil spirits were able to gain access and take possession), but specific tests were administered in the evidentiary phases of the trials: tests of
the defendant's capacity to form and shed tears, of the defendant's buoyancy
when suspended in water, and so forth. As the theory of witchery was defended and criticized, important treatises were composed by those identified
as physicians (including astrologers, herbalists, alchemists), even in this relatively primitive stage of medical science.[42] It is in the very nature of disorders of the mind that wholesale theorizing becomes more the rule than the
exception. For every theory, there will be an army of critics facing avid defenders. Added to this mix was the tumultuous climate of the Reformation
and Counter-Reformation, partisans on each side declaring opponents to be
awash in heretical superstitions.

It would not be an overstatement to attribute to the European witch trials
and executions a prominent role in the increasingly general acceptance of
science as the objective, if not the ultimate, arbiter of truth-claims. More
than one Renaissance "expert" on matters before courts of the Inquisition
would make clear that his own inquiries were prompted by an interest in

the purely natural phenomena of the world; that he neither had nor desired magical powers; that his field of inquiry was nature itself and not the occult. The excesses of the age were productive of a "rhetoric of objectivity" in this age before the dawn of objective science.

By 1800 not only were experts called in trials involving alleged insanity, but the expertise was now confined especially to a knowledge of the brain. In the celebrated trial of James Hadfield (1800), for example, the brilliant defense mounted by Thomas Erskine was given added force and credibility by expert comments regarding the defendant's brain injuries.[43] Advances in neuroanatomy, in the histopathology of the nervous system, and in clinical neurology had all added support to what was more or less taken for granted at the level of speculation throughout the second half of the eighteenth century; that is, that the moral, intellectual, and emotional aspects of life can be utterly transformed by disease of or damage to the brain. La Mettrie's *Man: A Machine* (1748) spoke for the leaders of Enlightenment thought when declaring that "man's preeminent advantage is his organism. In vain all writers of books on morals fail to regard as praiseworthy those qualities that come by nature."[44]

It was old philosophical wine in new quasi-scientific bottles. Hippocrates' school had reached the same conclusions; Galen had, as well, and based on actual surgical experiments; Gassendi advanced similar claims against Descartes's dualistic metaphysics. But in the century following the achievements of Newton, Boyle, Wren, Huygens, and Galileo—that legion of scientific savants—a La Mettrie could write with unchallenged confidence and finality. Again, by 1800 few among the learned would deny that at least mental *pathologies* were caused by brain defects, even if there was some hesitation toward a totally reductionistic account of normal social and moral life.

The nineteenth century actually made a *science* out of the speculative and optimistic materialisms of the Enlightenment. It was in the nineteenth century that Broca identified the diseased locus in the frontal cortex of the dominant hemisphere of his aphasic patient. Broca's "speech center"—*Broca's area*—seemed to locate that most defining of human powers, the capacity for linguistic expression. *Wernicke's area* and the comprehension of speech was added to the list of brain-based mental functions. Fritsch and Hitzig, with newly crafted electrodes, were able to elicit movement in (*unanesthetized!*) dogs by stimulating the cerebral cortex directly. The "motor cortex" proved to be topographically orderly and the results left no doubt but that *all* movements of the body, from the most gross to the finest, were explicable in terms of cortical functions. The widest range of cognitive, emotional, kinetic, and linguistic disturbances were systematically associated with specific brain regions, all of this accomplished through careful postmortem examinations and histopathological studies of diseased tissue.[45]

By an interesting twist of those fates that govern the popular enthusiasms, however, the very expertise that first brought science into the adjudicative arena—real or alleged expertise in the matter of brain function—came to be replaced by something radically different. The psychological and psychiatric testimony that has figured so prominently in trials and civil actions hinged to issues of competence makes only the most oblique contact with any settled method or body of knowledge claimed by the brain sciences. The historical sequence, though irregular and somewhat saltatory, begins with the aproned alchemist, moves uncertainly to the modest medical practitioner, thence to the practitioner with special insight into brain function, but then, oddly, to the *psychiatrist*! And, where Erskine's experts in 1800 were asked to reflect on James Hadfield's wartime brain injuries, the latter-day specialists have been queried on matters of early childhood traumas, unresolved sexual conflicts, repressed hostilities—none of these making any obvious connection with neuropathological states.

This is not the place to attempt to explain that chapter in intellectual and social history in which these shifting allegiances and enthusiasms are recorded. The rise of medical jurisprudence is a nineteenth-century phenomenon, and the lead in that century was taken by advocates of *brain* disease against the advocates of *moral* disease. The leading texts of the period are unequivocal on this score.[46] The bridge that had to be erected if authority was to shift from neurology to psychiatry was for psychiatry itself to claim the brain sciences as foundational. As noted above, however, this was never actually accomplished and still has not been accomplished. The argument developed above, if it is successful, goes further in establishing that it *cannot* be accomplished for, if it were, it would be at the expense of psychiatry itself and the very phenomena that give the subject *its subject*.

From Medical Jurisprudence to "Neuromorality"

The twentieth century featured the discovery and refinement of ever more precise modes of stimulation, recording, and visualization of different areas of the brain in health and disease, in the clinic and the laboratory, in human and nonhuman subjects. Added to the general findings compiled in the nineteenth century are now many thousands of studies marking out the boundaries within which surprisingly specific intellectual and emotional functions are organized. A small but growing library of books has incorporated these findings into what has become a new assortment of specialties including evolutionary psychology and "neurophilosophy." Why not, then, "neuromorality"? If there are unequivocal instances in which violent, criminal behavior arises from identifiable lesions in the nervous system, it would seem to be a defensible inference to conclude that lawful behavior arises from the normal functions of the nervous system.

But is this a warranted inference? It makes sense to say that, owing to the failure of the spark plugs in his car, Smith failed to attend the performance of *Macbeth*. It would be odd to say, however, that Smith attended *Macbeth* owing to the proper function of the spark plugs. It makes sense to say that Smith's hallucination caused him to be fearful of entering his garage. It would be odd to say that Smith is not fearful of entering his garage because he has not experienced frightful hallucinations there. Again, the descriptor is "odd," not "irrational" or "fallacious." One could insist that, of all the factors behind Smith contentedly entering the garage, one of them is that nothing untoward has taken place there. But this would not be Smith's explanation. Smith would say that entering the garage is the means by which to retrieve the car that will traverse the distance between home and theater, and that is how the family will get to see *Macbeth*.

The actions of persons, as explained in the first-person, are actions for which persons have good reasons or not such good reasons. Where there is no reason at all, persons are at a loss to explain what they've done. And when this is habitual, persons are likely to seek medical advice. There is no symmetry between pathology causing a specific range of deficits and (absent disease) the factors that give rise to a reasoned course of action in those who know what the reasons are and know also that they are acting on them. Thomas Nagel is surely on the right track when admitting that he is "inclined strongly to hope, and less strongly to believe, that the correct moral theory will always have the preponderance of reasons on its side."[47]

But he says more in this than perhaps he is wont to acknowledge. Among other admissions is that there is (a) a separation between desire (hope) and belief; (b) a means by which to establish that there are reasons for action; (c) nothing of moral consequence in behavior except insofar as it arises from reasons for action; and (d) an objective means by which to determine whether one or another alternative argument has the benefit of a preponderance of good reasons.

Attempting to translate this insightful fragment of Nagel into terms corresponding to neurological events is doomed, and it is doomed in much the way that Freud's desired "project" was doomed. One cannot obtain the requisite neural *correlates* of, for example, good reasons for acting, unless one already has the category *good reasons for acting*. Needless to say, having a lesion is not to have a *reason* for acting, but perhaps is being *caused* to act, even being *caused to have a reason*, as in running from a threatening (but hallucinated) menace. Exit neuromorality.

This has not prevented some from finding answers to the ageless moral questions at the tip of the electrode. What that tip penetrates is then understood as nothing but the utterly "natural" gift (curse) of evolutionary forces by which one combination of genes rather than another came to be present in this specific collection of cells.[48] The most recent two centuries have done nothing to diminish the confidence of the scientifically committed in the matter of the determinants of thought, feeling, and action. There is no need to rehearse here the arguments for and against psychobiological determinism assessed in chapter 2. It should be clear that the arguments against determinism, to the extent that they are compelling, remain so even as progress has continued in the brain sciences. It is a handy if imprecise measure of the nature of an issue that its weight and character are largely unaffected by technical progress and the sheer volume of fact compiled within what is alleged to be the foundational science. Yet, the laudable and brilliant scientific achievements of the past century leave the moral and juridical questions just where they have always been: One is responsible insofar as one has the power of rational deliberation, has not been made to act contrary to one's actual desire, and has not been the victim of relevantly disabling disease, coercion, deception, or duress. Inevitable scientific achievements can only be of great assistance in identifying conditions that defeat the presumption of autonomy, but surely cannot lead to the abandonment of the presumption itself. The success of a theory leading to such a conclusion would depend on the very rational acceptance that the theory regards as impossible.

Ignorance and Akrasia

"How is weakness of the will possible?" asked Donald Davidson in his frequently cited and discussed essay.[49] There is an apparent paradox. To say that Eugene greatly desires to quit smoking and knows that it is a foul and unhealthy habit is to say that Eugene has a good reason to quit and sincerely wants to quit. But Eugene is smoking. The warranted conclusion is that, in this case, the stronger of two desires prevailed. The conclusion in all such cases is that the actor's actual "doing" records the strongest occurrent desire and the decision to satisfy it.

What, then, of the ancient moral problem of *akrasia*? It is examined closely by Aristotle in the *Nicomachean Ethics* and has been a central issue in ethics ever since. It is in 1112a15—1113a10 that he fills out his conception of deliberated choice (*prohairesis*) and declares it is this that is most intimately related or naturally suited to (*oikeiotaton*) virtue.[50] In a most instructive and discerning analysis of Aristotle's treatment of the problem, David Wiggins sets the stage with the commonsense view:

> Almost anyone not under the influence of theory will say that, when a person is weak-willed, he intentionally chooses that which he knows or believes to be the worse course of action when he could choose the better course; and that, in acting in this way, the weak-willed man acts not for *no* reason at all—that would be strange and atypical—but irrationally."[51]

Thus understood, weakness of the will is not only possible, but lamentably one of the more common features of life. There is, then, a conflict between the understanding of certain philosophers and the understanding most non-theorists have about just what is involved when persons such as Eugene strike the match.

What makes "weakness of the will" particularly relevant in relation to praise and blame is that treatments of the problem (as Wiggins has shown) have been reductionistic and actuarial in ways that ignore the actual manner in which persons go about assigning values and making choices. As a question on a philosophy examination, the akrasia problem will probably be answered in a manner that does justice to Davidson's analysis. On accounts like this, choices are made between specific, quantifiable desire-states, the strongest desire "determines" the choice, and this then supplies the actor with the "reason for action," and so forth.

As a practical matter in real life, akrasia requires a treatment of the sort Aristotle himself supplied and Wiggins has enlarged and clarified. Eugene strikes the match even as he records his understanding of the health risk; even as he sincerely resolves to try to "kick the habit"; even as he acknowledges the overriding value of "health" in the abstract sense. It is not because of some corrupted axiology in terms of which smoking is "more desirable," "better," "based on good reasons," a practice that, though dangerous, has its "compensations." Wiggins recognizes in Aristotle's treatment a "slight tendency" toward the compensation thesis, but also that only a minor shift in focus will

> exempt his construction from this intolerable burden. In the definition of self-sufficiency, we need not take "lack in nothing" to mean "lacking in nothing at all that would be found valuable by anybody pursuing whatever course," only "lacking in nothing that a man who had chosen the great good of eudaimonia would regard as worth bothering with."[52]

It would be a conceptual truth that a person who had become unalterably committed to *eudaimonia* (in the full, Aristotelian sense of "flourishing") would obviously forego the transitory pleasure of tobacco if its use were to imperil the entire project. Reason's rule, however, is, as Wiggins reminds us, "not a despotical rule but the constitutional rule of a statesman or prince over his free subjects."[53]

Under a certain light, akrasia may be taken as evidence in favor of moral freedom, for it would be a mark against incompatibilist libertarians if a strict, deterministic relationship obtained between and among desire, belief, choice, logic, and other links in the putative linear chain that culminates in a lit cigarette. The place of eudaimonia within Wiggins's scheme (and, it may be said, Aristotle's as well) is that of a standard: at a choice- point of any consequence, we are able to consider just how each alternative measures up against the *ultimate* standard, and then we can make the choice. It is owing to the standard that we, ourselves, are subject to remorse, are willing to admit to weakness, are capable of atonement. These capacities are not the resources of entities whose choices are fixed by a rigid calculus or by truth tables.

All actions committed in ignorance are *not* involuntary, and ignorance itself is not always a passive state. Central to the mission of a moral life is an informed life, one of the moral obligations being that of knowing one's powers and potentials for bringing about morally weighty outcomes. One who has murdered one's parents is not likely to earn sympathy as an orphan, and one who has stubbornly preserved ignorance—preserved it as a possibly useful future excuse—bears the same responsibility as the drunk: the responsibility for the damage this ignorance leads to, and the responsibility for putting or keeping oneself in a state likely to have just these consequences.

There is all the difference between an ignorance expressive of natural limitations, an ignorance expressive of indifference and distraction, and an ignorance expressive of consuming self-interest. Ascriptions of blame may be, and often have been, misdirected, owing to the mistaking of one kind of ignorance for another. Having the right moral principles does not guarantee their infallible application. An illustration of this is Alfred Mele's fictitious Alice, the specialist on drug addiction who, in order to understand the nature of the problem fully, elects to become an addict. Though Alice serves a somewhat different purpose for Mele, she helps to clarify several points developed in this section. First, she was not self-deceived about the dangers. She weighed the potential risks and benefits; with eyes wide open, she entered a program of self-addiction that resulted in complete dependence. In time, however, Mele has her convinced

> that the experiment is more dangerous than she had realized and that it is time to start setting things right. However, Alice is incapable of resisting her present desire for heroin.[54]

Clearly, an autonomously established desire, in this case to further our knowledge of addictions and the means by which to rid persons of them, may result in actions that eradicate autonomy. Mele notes that had Alice really been and remained self-governing in the matter of the desire to become addicted she would have the power to rule out that desire and thus free herself of the addiction. Instead, what was an autonomously chosen course of action (to use heroin as an addict would) now is the uncontrollable desire for the same substance.

As with the drunk, who had it within his autonomous and deliberative resources to avoid the first, then the second, and even the third drink, a point is reached beyond which these resources are dulled and of no avail. It is in getting to this point that the actor is charged with full responsibility, and this is a responsibility that extends to all the consequences that were reasonably foreseeable. Self-imposed limitations, whether in the form of self-deception, ignorance, addiction, or diminished capacity, are not mitigating when the actions that bring them about were voluntary and when the actor's own rational and deliberative powers permitted such consequences to be envisaged as realistic.

The same rationale is applicable to instances of alleged "self-deception." The experimental evidence that would establish self-deception is unconvincing, as are the formal criteria typically employed in such research.[55] Less dramatic than findings from commissurotomized patients, the results of the experiments typically offer nothing beyond inconsistencies in verbal reports or physiological data in conflict with self-reports. The real world presents more compelling instances but these, too, need not be understood in terms of self-deception. What, after all, should count as an instance of deceiving oneself? Presumably, it must be on a par with deceiving others, but the analogy soon becomes doubtful. Smith is said to attempt to deceive Jones when Smith tries to get Jones to accept something that Smith does not believe. Translated as an act of self-deception, the account runs as follows: Smith attempts to deceive himself when he tries to get himself to accept something that he does not accept. The textbook example of such a process is infatuation. Jack and Jill are rapturously infatuated with each other, each refusing to see any faults in the other. Each has seen the other shoplifting often, but puts such episodes out of mind and honestly denies the fact when questioned at a later time. (The theory of repression returns!) Granting, for the moment, that there is actual amnesia, there would seem to be nothing in the case of infatuation that differs in a morally relevant way from elective insobriety or Alice's addiction. The appearance within one of powerful and sustained emotions of such magnitude as to cloud reason and perception calls for the exercise of self-restraint. To fail in this is not to have "self-deception" as an excuse, for one willfully persisted in a relationship that was conducted at the cost of autonomy itself.

For purposes of praise and blame, it is not necessary to argue against the possibility of self-deception. There is ample evidence, no less convincing for appearing regularly in the real world, that motives, desires, and beliefs may profoundly affect perception, judgment, and memory. Whether "self-deception" should be the phrase of choice is debatable, in part because the occasions creating it and the motives behind it differ significantly from those obtaining when someone is attempting to deceive another.[56] The evidence supporting the concept is various, some of it morally informing, some of it morally jejune. The latter, if it is to be taken as valid, indicates that beliefs and judgments are influenced by processes more or less built into the percipient and beyond one's power's of self-control or even awareness. If there are such processes, and they are able to establish or solidify beliefs, then the percipient or believer could not be held responsible either for the beliefs or for judgments and actions predicated on them. We would have the equivalent of some sort of insane delusion that, even if not calling for medication or commitment, surely would be legally and morally exculpatory. The morally informing evidence is different in that the actor's own participation is a necessary element in the self-deception. When this is so, the actor has precisely the same responsibility for *self*-deception as for deception. The primary difference is not in the matter of responsibility but in the matter of pardon. When Jones does something blameworthy as a result of being deceived by Smith, Jones is not held to be responsible, unless he created the conditions disposing him to be a victim of such deceptions. When Smith does something blameworthy as a result of deceiving himself, he is held responsible for both the deception and the actions arising from it.

This introduces a complication, however, where the results are *praiseworthy*; a complication, but not a contradiction. Bill lies in informing Ted that the enemy is now without firepower, but that the bunker itself must be destroyed. There is a possibility of some hand-to-hand combat, but Ted in that event is the only one with loaded weapons. Thus deceived, Ted proceeds toward the bunker, only to face a hale of enemy fire. He carries on, however, and completes a mission he would never have undertaken had he not been deceived. Though accounts such as this require a somewhat clumsy moral calculation, it is reasonable to judge Ted as having less than full courage at the outset, followed by a paroxysm of courage tied to the desire of self-preservation.

Whether or not some degree of heroism is included in the appraisal, it is nonetheless obvious that Ted is not the hero Fred is, for Fred is now marching on another bunker knowing the occupants to be fully armed. Fred, however, has courage as Aristotle defines it: he is fearful, but is not paralyzed by fear. Without fear, his actions would just be rash or even insane. How does Fred overcome his fear? He invents a little story for himself, in which he pictures his own agile and darting race toward the bunker, his loud screams confusing the enemy, his random shooting keeping their heads below ground. None of this has yet taken place, but now accepting his own narrative as complete and historically accomplished—he *really* believes what he has told himself—he then takes off and reenacts the episode. Is this self-deception? Is it blameworthy? Are there "good" deceptions? The very terminology is unfitting. Persons of character facing challenges must control their fears and doubts, replacing these with hopefulness and measured optimism. Everyone knows this long before life presents an actual and severe test, for everyone has sampled the weaker versions. Fred, one might say, is "rehearsing," not deceiving himself.

Repression, Ignorance, and Deception in Summary

The issues considered in this chapter derive their importance and urgency from morality itself; from the *reality* of moral life and the moral properties of actions and events. Why else would there be a question about "unconscious" motives, "repressed" desires, "deceptive" beliefs? The very adjectives stand in a dialectical relationship with deliberated choices based on valid and tested beliefs as to how one should act in the circumstance. Neither psychoanalytic theory nor research on deception raises telling questions against the positions defended in this chapter or previous chapters. Whether or not actions have been causally initiated or given their essential character as a result of processes and mechanisms beyond the control of the actor is, in principle, an empirical question. There may be instances that cannot be settled with any finality, others in which the evidence will be of arguable relevance, still others that hinge on how words and descriptions are to be understood. Two examples illustrate the main points. In dead of night, Robert suffers a mild stroke leaving him powerless to move his left arm. On awakening, he has no reason to believe anything has happened and, if queried, would assure us that he is able to reach for the telephone. It is in his attempt to do so that he discovers that he cannot. Would it be fair to say that he had been "deceived" into believing he had a power that in fact had been lost? And if he has been deceived, then by whom if not by himself? Here is a species of self-deception, but only in a manner of speaking.

Second: Timothy may be subject to seizures owing to a diseased brain, but this fact alone might be dismissed on the grounds that no direct connection can be made between this particular disorder and Timothy's current actions. He has had seizure-episodes all of his life, and has always been a decent, law-abiding person except on a few random occasions during one of his subclinical seizures. On these occasions, he goes into a semitrance state and may engage in destructive behavior, unrelated to anything in his immediate environment. Today, however, Timothy discovered that his neighbor vandalized the rose garden. In a fit of anger, Timothy proceeded to break all the windows of his neighbor's house. From the fact that a brain disorder has been causally linked to antisocial behavior, it cannot be established that in every case and on every occasion the presence of that disorder is exculpatory.

Moral appraisals are tailored to the situation and the particular case, but the principles that enter into the appraisal are not "situational," nor are they particularized. As indicated, there are ambiguous and hard cases. A general theory of the foundations of moral appraisal is not able to settle each of these a priori. What makes cases difficult in the real world is that they are richly colored and shaped by numerous contingencies, unique to the circumstance, highly resistant to neat classification. An incompatibilist-libertarian theory must be able to survive the widest and most credible range of deterministic challenges. Of these challenges, there are, as has been shown, successful rejoinders to those inspired by psychoanalytic theory, instances of akrasia, and putative "self-deception."

5.

PUNISHMENT AND FORGIVENESS

But I say this to you who are listening: Love your enemies,
do good to those who hate you, bless those who curse you, pray
for those who treat you badly. To the man who slaps you on one
cheek, present the other cheek, too; to the man who takes your
cloak from you, do not refuse your tunic.
—LUKE 6:27

THERE ARE GENERAL precepts that guide the administration of justice, the resolution of disputes, the award of damages in instances of injury, the setting of
penalties for serious offenses. The precepts often have identifiable scriptural
roots, even when expressed in the less righteous idiom of statutory law. The
precepts are so general and so venerable that they tend to be immune to
scrutiny. That is, questions about them seem to answer themselves, but only
when the questions, too, are general. Consider just these two fundamental
precepts:

1. Punishment should fit the crime.
2. No one should benefit from his own wrongdoing.

The first of these offers no guidance as to the nature of the "fit"; no calculus or modulus applied in the given case to determine whether, in fact, the
penalty assessed is accurately proportioned to the offense. The second precept or maxim is regularly violated under the banner of law. The state offers
to drop charges against the known criminal, in return for which the felon
gives testimony that incriminates others. For all practical purposes, a benefit
has followed a wrongdoing to the extent that the withholding of punishment
is a benefit. Indeed, until relatively recent times, courts would not deny
inheritance to a beneficiary who had murdered the testator!

The world's major religions urge toleration, understanding, compassion.
The Pope teaches that "charity is the perfection of justice." None of this is,
or is intended to be, at the expense of justice itself, which does require
punishment following the finding of guilt. It is arguable whether, in addition
to the assessment of penalties, justice calls for some degree of indignation,
some Strawsonian "reactive attitude." Aristotle defines law as reason (*nous*)
without passion (*aneu orexios*), but he also understands anger in the face of
injustice to be a natural and even required response to wrongdoing. He goes
further in noting that the praise earned by one who forcefully opposes

wrongdoing should be in proportion to the wrongdoing. Hence, more praise is earned by one who kills a tyrant than by one who kills a thief.[1]

Punishment and forgiveness create additional conceptual problems, one class of which may be dubbed the "proxy problem." In the preclassical worlds of Greece and Rome, as in contemporary tribal communities, the *lex talionis* is expressed in the form of phratric justice. One who injures the clan or phratry exposes his own community to retaliation that can be averted only by a mode of payment acceptable to the aggrieved. Moreover, the retaliatory attack is indifferent to questions of individual blame or guilt. Any member of the offending phratry will do, for it is in the nature of phratric societies that one's personal identity is just one's phratric identity. It is worth noting that the reforms of Solon and Draco in this connection gave to the Hellenic world a form of law respecting the individuated nature of moral fault. Although blame and punishment were now focused on the actual perpetrator, the ancient law continued to include among the injured and offended the widest range of family relations.[2]

With the emergence of the polis and the evolution of statutory law, a new victim-class appears, variously known as "the people" or "the state" or "society." The offender is punished to an extent that would have something repaid as a "debt to society." The offender's blame index is thus said to be reset to zero. In some jurisdictions payment is made with the offender's life, this being the law's maximum penalty. In all of these arrangements, however, there is a nest of "proxy" issues requiring clarification and justification. Bill kills Tom thus leaving Tom's three dependent children fatherless and Tom's spouse without a beloved mate. The state then convicts Bill, sentences him to death, and carries out the sentence. Having suffered the maximum penalty, Bill has, it is said, "paid his debt," the payment here made to society. It is true, of course, that Tom's wife and children are members of this society and in some sense have been "repaid" with all the other members. There is something utterly peculiar about this understanding, however, in that the loss suffered by Tom's wife and children is simply incalculably greater than that suffered by anyone else—by everyone else—as a result of this particular crime.

Besides this, it may be argued that Bill's offense ended one life and caused irreparable loss to four other lives. On what scheme of moral or judicious calculation is Bill's forfeiture of life a proportionate punishment? On what scheme is it in any way "compensatory"? Would it be fairer to allow the family to execute Bill, perhaps torturing him before delivering the lethal blow or injection? If what is called for here is the maximum penalty, there are certainly additions to death that would greatly increase the total package. Would it be more punitive to round up some number of Bill's relatives, executing them in Bill's presence, and including this in the overall calculation of just compensation? Is rape the right punishment for a rapist? If not, then how is it that death is the right punishment for a murderer?

In this final chapter these questions are engaged chiefly for the purpose of clarifying the principal arguments of the previous chapters on the nature of moral properties and the grounding of moral ascriptions. To claim that moral properties are real (though not reducible to physical entities) is to say also that they are subject to being possessed, forfeited, and, in a complex manner, even combined. This is more readily comprehended when moral properties are considered in relation to punishment and forgiveness.

Whence the Right and the Reason to Punish?

If punishment is to fit the offense, it becomes necessary to establish just what makes the offense "offensive." It is a further requirement that the magnitude or gravity of the offense be estimated. Even when it is property that is stolen or damaged, the requisite calculations are not invariably simple. The personal value of the item as a possession may greatly exceed the market value. The destruction of the sole surviving photograph of a deceased loved one may have no market value but immense personal value. One's reputation is of a similar nature in that it is not readily converted into monetary units.

On the question of just what it is that translates an action into one of "offense" and the actor as "offender," it has been argued that crimes generically are acts of *disrespect* and therefore that punishment functions as a rectification. This point is picked up below in connection with the offense as a kind of destructive or disfiguring action calling for restoration or *cleansing*. Geoffrey Cupit, for example, views injustices as modes of treating persons as less than they are and establishes a linkage between the implicit (or explicit) disrespect to a deserts scheme of punishment.[3] But there is no settled position on the matter of what persons "are" in all relevant contexts, and, as Cupit is well aware, it is often the case that treating someone in the same way in context-1 and in context-2 would constitute very different "treatments." What persons "are" is also to some extent in the eyes of the beholder. There are those who reflect on their own paintings and regard themselves as artists of great originality and depth. Others viewing the same works may regard them as rubbish. It is the rare parent whose child's sketches are subjected to objective criticism.

Punishment as a rectification for disrespect has also been discussed by Philip Pettit. Noting what he calls "the republican ideal of freedom as nondomination," he proposes that crimes be considered as a violation of this ideal. The criminal violates the ideal in at least three ways: First, the victim is placed in a position of being dominated; second, the domination restricts the range of undominated choices; third, the act itself strikes fear in those who recognize themselves as comparably vulnerable.[4] In the particular instance, however, it would be difficult to the point of practical impossibility to translate this into measured degrees of earned punishment. The fabled gigolo discovers that the wealthy widow, suffering from a terminal disease, has a domineering personality and finds most appealing only those who are submissive. Not only does he satisfy this need but in other ways provides companionship and affection, all for the purpose of being named her sole beneficiary. For the brief balance of her life, she never feels dominated; indeed, she is *not* dominated, nor are her choices restricted, nor are others in the community frightened by his conduct. Most would find in this scenario the moral wrong of defrauding another. It is possible, in the event his scheme becomes known and provable, that the courts might be receptive to claims against his inheritance. Nonetheless, there is nothing in the narrative that qualifies as domination, restraint of freedom, or public intimidation. There is also no clear measure of just what punishment is deserved by conduct of this sort. Suppose that on her deathbed the widow asks whether the apparent love and devotion showered on her by her bridegroom were sincere and that, struck by conscience, he reveals all. Suppose further that, hearing his confession, she forgives him. Has he received a just desert? What is the source of her power of forgiveness? Can he coherently and validly forgive himself?

Accepting that all offenses violate "the ideal of nondomination" may also put one at a loss when attempting to distinguish law from domination. The law, too, restricts the range of freely chosen courses of action and has a chilling effect on those similarly inclined. There is something about unlawful actions not captured by the concept of disrespect. Then, too, there is something about "domination" that fails to cover the range of offenses. What is missing from these accounts are the real moral properties abused or disregarded by the offender, the real moral properties inhering in the victim of the offense.

Punishment needs justification, for it is intended to cause loss or pain. The sources of punishment also require justification unless it is assumed that anyone has the right to punish an offender. And the actual punishments imposed call for justification if, in fact, they are to be judged as fitting. The need to justify punishment arises in part from time's arrow: the harm has been caused, the crime committed, and the past cannot be undone. The life or limb taken cannot be restored; even the property cannot be recovered. And even if the property has been recovered, there was still the temporary loss and the sadness or anger or worry occasioned by that loss. To speak, then, of punishment as a way of setting things aright is to say more than the words convey, for it is obvious that what has been done cannot be undone.

The defense or justification of punishment takes several major forms, each having the benefit of critical philosophical analysis and argument. Consider first *retributive* justifications that so punctuate the events in the Old Testament. The retributive theory of punishment classifies wrongdoing as constituting an imbalance, a net loss of value or goodness, the introduction of an evil—the evil of undeserved pain, loss, or suffering—and thus calls for a form of retribution designed to restore the balance. Reparations are in order. How much? "An eye for an eye" is the well known scriptural guide, but it scarcely captures the subtle and profound arguments that have been developed in defense of retribution.

Richard Swinburne presents an especially compelling endorsement of retributive punishment, including a specification of what is to be counted in determining what the violator owes to the victim.[5] Punishment should take into account the time and effort involved in discovering the guilty party, the emotional costs in anxiety associated with these efforts, as well as the actual losses to the victim. The ensemble of factors is then the base for reasonable judgments as to reparations. On this account, the punishment exacted now constitutes, or in some way includes, the required reparation.

Swinburne rejects the customary distinction between revenge and punishment, at least as that distinction is generally explained, arguing that the state's imposition of punishment makes sense only to the extent that the state in this is serving as proxy for the victim. As he says,

> If you suppose that the state has a right to punish which has nothing to do with its acting as an agent for the victim, it becomes impossible to provide any satisfactory retributionist justification of punishment. . . . For what else can justify the state effecting retribution? What gives *it* that right?[6]

The question itself looks toward a source of rights external to the state; that source presumably being the rational and justificatory arguments that would defend any action as right in the circumstance. But if Swinburne's conflation of punishment and revenge is sound, and if both are to be understood as retributive demands for reparation, it really should make no difference whatever just *who* exacts the punishment. That is, if it really is incumbent on the state to make out a case for it having a right to punish, *except as a proxy for the aggrieved*, there would seem to be only two plausible arguments: one drawn from contractarian political theory, which finds persons investing in the state such rights as they have in that mythic state of nature; the other developed as a principled defense of retribution for wrongs done to those for whom the state claims proxy powers. The first of these accounts is insufficient for the present purposes insofar as it fails to establish that, in the state of nature, there is something called a "right" to avenge injuries and losses in the first place. The *lex talionis* describes practices under a maxim that cannot stand as its own justification. The second account does provide a principled defense of retribution but, in light of Swinburne's rhetorical question, leads to a perplexity as well as a worrisome implication. If one actually cannot see what gives the state the right to punish, except as a proxy, then it is perplexing as to how the state acquired the right to claim proxy power. But then whatever does support the creation of proxy power should in principle be available to anyone ready to claim it. That is, if it is by stipulation necessary that *wrongs be punished*—such that the wrongdoer should expect an avenger—there is no obvious basis on which to reserve the power of punishment to the state or, for that matter, to the injured party.

Following Locke, Swinburne does give the victim pride of place in the order of avengers, citing Locke's famous lines about persons in the "state of nature" having the right to recover from the offending party "so much as may make satisfaction for the harm." Swinburne does endorse a version of contractarianism in this regard and thereby limits the right of retribution to the offended parties. It is in virtue of their having joined the civic world, with its incumbent duties and obligations, that these same parties implicitly accept the authority of the state in determining the conditions by which guilt is established and nature of the punishment prescribed.[7]

As noted in chapter 1, however, the mythical state of nature gives the theorist rather too much room for both invention and credulity. Terms such as "satisfaction" and "harm," not to mention "so much," leave utterly unanswered a number of significant questions about punishment as a "moral" (as opposed to a "psychological") mode of redress. Beings in the alleged natural state are, presumably, possessed of social and moral resources still unrefined by the rule of law and by the discipline that rule applies to civic life. What, then, supports Locke's all-too-calm conclusion that, in that state, aggrieved parties—exacting just "so much" by way of punishment as to give themselves "satisfaction"—will do anything approximating what is achieved through the rule of law? Will they fashion rules of evidence? Will they consider mitigating circumstances? Will they assign an objective value to the stolen property? Will they permit appeals and the examination of witnesses? Will they test their own sensibilities to determine whether perhaps they have felt too deeply a loss that others would regard as trivial? Moreover, just in case the state fails to match what the aggrieved would require for reparation, does the latter now have as a matter of *right* the option of breaking the contract and exacting personal revenge?[8]

Presumably, what gives the state the right is just that institutionalization of rational deliberation that is *the rule of law* and that preserves the rights of states even in the face of opposition by a majority of those living within the state's jurisdiction. The punishment of wrongdoing is a response to a set of objective conditions whose defining properties are moral properties. What makes a given rule of law "just" is not the merely evenhanded or statistically unbiased application of rewards and punishments, but the "correct" application of these. The sense in which justice may be said to "err" is precisely the sense in which it fails to identify or adequately assess the real moral content of the actions and events under review.

To punish a wrongdoer may, in fact, function as a sort of proxy-revenge but this cannot be the state's aim, except in the rare instance in which the victim would seek *only what is right*; where the victim would estimate "harm" rather than "my harm"; where the satisfaction sought is not personal but principled. What must be "satisfied" are not the feelings of those harmed, but rather the specific terms of principle by which praise and blame reach a level beyond that of mere social control. The law as *an ordinance of reason*, promulgated by those entrusted with securing the common good, is not the proxy-representative for the various human passions, ephemeral desires, often quirky enthusiasms, claims, and sensitivities of the populace. Instead, it replaces these (as they are likely to be present in any given populace at any given time) with the ideals that persons would uphold and can rationally comprehend under the most favoring conditions. It then stands as the proxy for their morally most competent selves that, in the nature of things, may not be their usual and often self-indulgent selves.

The "state" as referred to here is just that repository of just laws and powers of enforcement that comprise an ordered polity designed to promote and sustain worthy lives. What confers on this entity the "right" to punish is also what earns the fidelity to its laws on the part of those who stand to be beneficiaries, even when reluctant ones. This all connects with the arguments for moral realism previously developed. What the laws of the just state reach are those real moral properties depreciated or destroyed by unlawful actions and otherwise recognized and secured by the rule of law itself. The "satisfaction" to be enjoyed by the Lockean entity must rise to the level of *moral* satisfaction, which is different from merely *personal* varieties of contentment, pleasure, or vindication.

The inexhaustible debates between defenders of natural law theory and advocates of legal positivism may find a useful point of convergence here. Austin's "command theory," which might make a legislator of a highwayman, came to be embellished by succeeding positivistic theories, whether those of the legal "realists" or by the current school of critical legal studies. The analyses that seem to provide credible accounts of the provenance of law do not offer comparably plausible accounts of just what it is in law that attracts, as opposed to compels, us to it. The analysis that identifies the properties to which fidelity is rationally and even passionately attached sometimes depreciates the actual social and cultural forces productive of every rule of law.[9]

It is the rationality of law that addresses the requirement of the justification of actions, for every justification is minimally a *reason* that renders the act potentially right in the circumstance. But rationality alone is insufficient until it is extended to embrace the properties that render events and actions "right" or "wrong." These are finally *moral* properties (or their absence), suggested but not fully defined by such terms as "dignity," "real property," "autonomy," "integrity," "intrinsic worth," "intrinsic goodness," "virtue," "vice," and "sin." Through its rational processes and moral grounding, the rule of law is the instrument by which rational beings qua rational settle disputes, make amends, exact punishments, confer rewards, distribute resources, and regulate conduct. Rationality thus deployed and institutionalized is the ultimate and only grounding of "rights" as such, these being neither natural nor merely conventional. Nothing rises to the level of right by mere repetition or popularity or appetite. The answer to the question, "By what right does the state punish, if not as an agent of the offended party?" is, "By that very source of all 'rights,' including any the offended party might have in order to expect or deserve reparation." Offended parties, in virtue of their very victimization, as well as their possibly underdeveloped capacity for the recognition and ordering of moral properties, are less than likely to be proportionate in their assessments and scrupulous in their fact-finding. The right and power of punishment are reserved therefore to the law, not to the offended.

Readers will find in these lines Kant's influence. To be sure, something of a Kantian shadow tracks any incompatibilist-libertarian theory, for Kant's own profound and influential moral philosophy is generally regarded as the most incisive and detailed defense. The "compatibilist" Kant discussed in chapter 2 is the metaphysician. The "incompatibilist" Kant is the moralist. For Kant, freedom and morality are so mutually entailing as to render each incomplete as a concept until the other is incorporated. Owing to this, Kant's political and legislative ideals accord absolute value to freedom and are incompatible with alternative ideals in which the value of freedom is instrumental. It is the First Critique that expresses the standard with uncompromising economy:

> A constitution allowing *the greatest possible human freedom* in accordance with the laws by which *the freedom of each is made to be consistent with that of all others*—I do not speak of the greatest happiness, for this will follow of itself—is at any rate a necessary idea, which must be taken as fundamental not only in first projecting a constitution but in all its laws.[10]

This paragraph-length sentence contains four distinct elements, each illuminating vast areas of the Kantian project. It is only under conditions of freedom that choice is possible, only when free that one can be responsible in the moral sense of the term. The fullest moral life, then, presupposes the agent's free investment of his life in the ideals of morality. The first element is the conceptual and necessary relationship between freedom and the very possibility of morality. If, however, there is to be a social world at all, the preservation of freedom requires laws, some constitutive structure of society capable of securing freedom. Inevitably, laws constrain and limit freedom, thereby presenting a threat to morality itself. Those who are compelled to honor a moral maxim are merely behaving properly but cannot be said to be living a moral life.

How, therefore, should the task or aim of law be understood? This is the second element: The task or aim of law is to make the freedom of each consistent with the freedom of all. An exercise of freedom that imperils the freedom of others is one that reduces their moral standing, which is the significant respect in which unlawful conduct may be regarded generically as a form of disrespect or contempt. The law itself is contemptuous of those living under it when its aims are indifferent to freedom. Such a regime loses the right—it sacrifices the conceptual tools—by which to expect allegiance or fidelity as a moral obligation. No one can be morally obliged to support a rule of law that renders morality itself jejune.

Hence, the third element, which insists on the *necessity* of the relationship between the very concept of law and the maximization of freedom. Obedience to the law is either the outcome of fear and coercion or the expression of fidelity to principle by a rational being possessed of an autonomous will. Obedience secured by force and threats of force is compulsory, leaving its subject beyond the perimeter of moral space. It connects all conduct to one or another *hypothetical* imperative (for example, the imperative to avoid or reduce one's pain or suffering), and thus detaches the lived life from that *categorical* imperative by which one gains full citizenship in the moral world. Finally, as the fourth element, the *greatest happiness* available to a rational being is the fullest expression of that rationality in framing a form and course of life. There can be no fundamental conflict between the happiness worthy of such a being and that rule of law that has as its determinative objective securing "the freedom of each" in a manner that is "consistent with that of all others."

Those who are fit for the rule of law understand this, for it is a foundational assumption. One could not at once comprehend the concept of "forbidden," except by recognizing that there are some actions that one *can* choose but *must* not. To comprehend this much is already to know oneself to be autonomous and to know the same about kindred beings. It is to understand, therefore, that the manner in which a course of action is justified by the application of a principle, one that supplies a reason for action not confined to this or that action, but covering all actions of a certain kind; for example, destructive actions, cooperative actions, affectionate actions. The "maxim" of the action is not simply a rationale for doing something here and now, but a justification for acting in a certain way in a wide range of situations. The question then arises as to whether there is a single maxim capable of directing all actions under all conditions in every situation. If there is, then it is *categorical, a categorical imperative*: "Act as if the maxim of your action were to become through your will a universal law of nature."[11]

The customary reading of Kant that finds him taking the validity of the categorical imperative for granted has been instructively challenged by Paul Guyer. What Kant requires, if the categorical imperative is to be valid, is what Guyer identifies as "an objective and thus universally compelling end that can give rise to a universal law."[12] That is, for a rational being to be bound by a universal law it is necessary that that law is logically or conceptually required by an end so compelling as to take precedence over any other end desired by a rational being. This turns out to be "rational being" itself. In furtherance of this end, a rational being is thus able to ground the categorical imperative in that which must have "absolute value" to such a being. It is in the very logic of the matter that such a being must regard fellow rational beings as "ends in themselves."

That Kant's version of retributivism could be construed as inconsistent with such high-flown purposes has been noted often enough. Kant's arguments for punishment, however, are based chiefly neither on fear nor utility. The threat of punishment motivates the actor to understand the importance of due deliberation and also is a useful way of controlling one set of hypothetical imperatives with another. Punishment under the forms of law is also a form of embarrassment; a loss of standing and respect that reaches the moral core of the person in ways that physical pain and duress do not.[13]

Whether or not Kant is strictly retributivist or to some extent a consequentialist is an interesting question but not central to the subject at hand. There is certainly an important difference in Kant's treatments of the functions of law and the nature of morality. The difference surely permits Kant to retain his status as a deontological *moralist*, even if he qualifies as a utilitarian *jurist*.[14] More germane to the issue of punishment is whether Kant's or any other retributivist theory provides a satisfactory understanding of the justification and purposes of punishment. On this point, there is much to be said for the conclusions reached by Russ Shafer-Landau: If a single general theory should be able to establish the aptness of punishment, the actions warranting it, and the amount or degree of punishment earned by a given violation, then retributivism fails in that it settles none of this.[15] It does, however, offer partial solutions to different aspects of each of these questions.

The moral realism defended in this book finds in those acts worthy of punishment either the distortion or destruction of moral properties. The "retribution" called for is one that is as restorative as the circumstances permit. Swinburne's analysis of atonement is vital here, for it establishes guilt "as analogous to a debt," and therefore subject to some degree of repayment.[16] Sometimes what is required is an actual repayment, as in the case of stolen property, but Swinburne understands guilt itself as a species of compensation. It is, after all, a form of pain suffusing one as a result of the pain caused to others. It is also a kind of cleansing and, as has been observed, retributivist theories of punishment are not unlike more ancient conceptions of crimes as requiring a purification.[17]

Perhaps a less graphic rendering is to be preferred. In discussing the nature of moral properties in chapter 1, the concept of a "dwelling" was used to illustrate the manner in which certain properties, though real, are not reducible to sensa but require epistemic resources. Staying with this metaphor, one might say that certain actions destroy or disfigure a dwelling, even if the material components are preserved. So, too, with moral offenses: the offense of rape is incidentally physical and essentially moral in that it robs the victim not only of autonomy but of what is one of the fullest and most deeply personal expressions of autonomy. In addition to these functions, punishment secures the trust of persons in the law, thereby validating further the proxy power that just laws have by right. The trust in question is not merely the subjective feeling of confidence but an objective trust established by the predictability of retributive punishments.[18]

It is not beyond the pale of reason or, indeed, of actual cases to expect the offender, as a member of the community of rational and moral beings, not only to feel guilt and strive to atone, but also to wish for a purifying punishment. The Kantian theory requires of moral beings the desire for justice, for just deserts, and there is no bar to this desire being reflexive. If one requires that offenders be punished, then one must require the same of oneself. Gary Herbert expresses the Kantian position as follows:

> One who asserts the right of humanity in his own person acknowledges his freedom, his humanity, his rights, and coincidentally, but not unimportantly, the moral necessity of his own punishment when he violates the law.[19]

Retribution thus understood reconstructs not only what the moral offense has destroyed or disfigured in others, but in oneself. This most complex of mixtures, partaking of retribution, reformation and restoration, the just punishment would repair moral properties in the domains of action, of consequence, and of persons. In more general terms, what is involved here is an instance of rational causality as Edward Pols would have it understood:

> The rational being has, so to speak, one foot in the normative and one foot in the physical: it is an *embodied* rational primary being, and everything it does in the sphere of reason and norms it does also in the physical. Its goals, together with the reasonable steps to achieve them, are thus "real causes" . . . and so they "operate" in the infrastructure in a nontemporal way that has some resemblance to the way laws of nature are sometimes said to govern any physical process that takes place in a physical system."[20]

Rational appraisals of fault and rationally governed modes of punishment are causal in this sense, and what they causally influence, but in a nonspatio-temporal fashion, are the real moral properties inhering in character and in actions and events. This much said, it is important to distinguish this thesis from a strict Kantian argument. There is finally rather too much in Kant's own version of retributive theory that should be resisted. His inelastic application of principles of equality, leading him to a nearly peevish defense of the lex talionis, calls for the murderer not only to have deserved execution but in some sense to demand it. There have been detailed criticisms of this feature of Kantian retribution, some more accurately reaching the target than others.[21] This leads to an analysis of the fitness or proportionality of punishment. The matter is best taken up in the next section, for the utilitarians have been especially deliberate in this regard.

Punishment: When Is Enough Enough?

Jeremy Bentham's *Principles of Morals and Legislation*[22] was published in 1789 and laid the philosophical foundations of the utilitarianist movement, which engendered profound social and political reforms in the first half of the nineteenth century. "Benthamism" has been thoroughly treated in books and articles for more than a century. Its refinements, corrections, and elaborations, from the time of J. S. Mill to the present, have resulted in the by now well-known formulations of utilitarianism calling for no exegetical treatment here. The discussion of Mill's enlarged conception of "utility" (chapter 2) should make clear that the original "pleasure-pain" formulation has become rather more vestigial than animating. Nonetheless, Bentham's analysis of offenses; his distinction between private and public harm; between offenses fit for punishment and those that elude the reach of law; these and related treatments within the *Principles* continue to inform discussions of crime and punishment. Although Bentham's own rendition of the pleasures and pains constitutive of "good" and "evil" has been subjected to countless criticisms, defenses, and revisions, his analysis of the justice, forms, ends, and nature of punishment is given voice in any number of contemporary theories.

Chapter 7 of the *Principles* begins by declaring the "business of government" to be the promotion of the happiness of society, achieving this "by punishing and rewarding."[23] By its very nature, punishment is an obstacle to happiness, a source of pain, and thus always an *evil* and a mischief.[24] It must therefore be applied sparingly, withheld where unnecessary, and implemented only as a means of producing a net gain in happiness. If the law is to meet these requirements, there must be a categorical distinction between punishments that are "meet" and those that are "unmeet." The latter include all punishments that are groundless (in that there is no mischief to prevent), inefficacious, unprofitable (that is, too expensive), or needless (in that the mischief either ceases of itself or can be prevented "at a cheaper rate").[25]

Bentham's qualifications of each of the factors rendering punishment unmeet tend not only to answer the objections routinely directed against "Benthamism" but refine the-*ism* to so great a degree as to make it nearly conventional. Consider the factors that would make punishment "groundless." There can be no mischief where the putative victim has given consent to the action. Now this can only raise the gravest objections, for any number of pathological states or states of diminished capacity might be imagined such that horrific deeds are perpetrated against a "consenting" other. But Bentham requires of consent that "it be free and fairly obtained."[26] It is always possible to reconcile this aspect of Bentham's theory to traditional moral theories by requiring the conditions of "free and fairly" to be as robust as needed.

The Benthamite calculus in these matters has a superficial simplicity that quickly dissolves when the qualifications are taken seriously by those who would actually apply the rules. It is one thing to contend that punishment should be withheld when it would create a "greater evil," and that an evil is greater when it produces a net increase in pain. It is quite another task to assess "pain," to integrate its values across all sufferers, and then to compare the result with the integrated quantity of pleasure that *might* have resulted had the punishment been applied.

The same difficulties inhere in Bentham's (and in *all* utilitarian) formulations of the aims of punishment and the establishing of proportionalities. Bentham offers four objectives of punishment and thirteen rules for its application. The objectives are prevention, attenuation, motivation, and economy. Punishment is designed to prevent mischief. If it cannot be prevented, it can be lessened by inducing the perpetrator to commit the least mischievous action compatible with his own purposes. Through this same motivating power of punishment, the perpetrator becomes rather more disposed to restrain himself even in the commission of offenses. Finally, of all of the ways punishment is to be successfully deployed for these purposes, the least costly is to be preferred.

Bentham's rules of punishment have the same actuarial character as these aims, but lead to the same perplexities and wide possibilities in practice. They are instructive nonetheless. The first rule requires the effects of punishment to outweigh whatever profit is in the offense. The potential or actual offender must face a penalty that, when incorporated into the hedonic calculus, clearly establishes that crime does not pay. Recognizing that the law is not likely to have a much better than "chance" record in this regard, Bentham sets down a second rule: as the attempt is always to reach the greater of two offenses, the greater the mischief of the offence, "*the greater is the expense which it may be worth while to be at, in the way of punishment.*"[27] The remaining rules are of a kindred sort. As punishment would constrain the perpetrator to choosing the least mischief consistent with his aims, the punishment should be partitioned to reach each of the distinguishable mischiefs that might be included in the overall offense. There should be no gratuitous and wasteful punishment; just so much as is required to prevent or attenuate offenses. The same quantity of punishment is reserved for the same offenses, more or less indifferent to the identity of the offender, except insofar as specific persons differ in their sensibilities, dispositions, circumstances. The nature of the person and the nature of the overall conditions may be either mitigating or aggravating in determining the right amount of punishment.

There is even more arithmetic in the scheme, for Bentham recognizes that the law cannot be everywhere. Crimes are often unreported, criminals hard to find, evidence difficult to obtain. The deterrent power of punishment is established not only by its severity but by its predictability, and the two in combination must reach the threshold of efficacy. Thus, as the probability of punishment is the less, so its severity must be the greater. Furthermore, there is a difference between one who commits a single offense and one who offends habitually. The efficacy of a specific quantity of punishment is likely to be different in these two cases. With the habitual offender, the punish- ment must be much greater; so much so as to *"outweigh the profit not only of the individual offence, but of such other like offences as are likely to have been committed with impunity by the same offender."*[28]

The repeat offender creates a reasonable inference that the crime he is now known to have committed is but one of a number, the balance having gone unpunished. Now finally in the clutches of the punishing authority, he should receive the *total* package!

What is especially interesting in all this is the point at which Bentham sets down those rules that are "of less importance," of which there are three. Two are again actuarial, addressing the matter of how profitable punishment might be in the given circumstance. But the third rule of less importance is of importance here. It qualifies the rule that precedes it, the rule according to which one cannot achieve less than a given quantity of punishment, though that quantity is too great for the offense it would prevent. In such cases, Bentham allows the disproportion to "stretch a little," and then ex- tends the rationale to Rule Eleven: *"In particular, this may sometimes be the case, where the punishment proposed is of such a nature as to be particularly well calculated to answer the purpose of a moral lesson."*[29]

Throughout the *Principles* Bentham is at pains to differentiate the "politi- cal" sanctions from those of religion and morality. His selection of John Austin and Austin's own essays further document that differentiation that would be the veritable stamp of legal positivism. Bentham, as with his exe- getes and disciples of various orthodoxy, understood that moral and reli- gious sanctions were powerful and useful; that they could be combined with the political sanctions in such a way as to promote the ultimate ends of punishment, which are, after all, the maximization of pleasure or utility, however defined. But unlike the political sanctions, those of religion and morality "can never be reduced . . . into exact lots, nor meted out in number, quantity, and value."[30]

There is a better explanation of the failure of religious and moral sanctions to reach this level of specious exactitude. What Bentham calls the "political sanction" is just the collection of statutory laws that classify offenses and establish penalties. These laws, however, do not simply appear. They are the creation of legislators, magistrates, parliaments, monarchs, senates, tribal councils, archons, curias, and pontiffs. Each of these sources, if its legitimacy is to survive in the face of inevitable challenges both internal and external, must earn the loyalty of the ruled. It earns this by reaching something in them other than the capacity to be frightened. It reaches what are finally a set of aspirations, the most significant being moral aspirations. Law as a command does not achieve this, which is why the punishments of law may readily secure compliance without ever winning allegiance. Bentham's scheme makes better and better sense once "pleasure," "pain," and "utility" are rendered in a manner that is true to the nature of creatures fit for the rule of law. This is a nature that cannot be fully described without the ascription of moral properties and moral purposes. This is what gives the religious and moral sanctions the power they have, widely understood not only as greater and more efficacious than the political sanctions, but foundational for them.

Bentham wrote as a citizen in that Enlightenment world that would find the roots of morality in the contingent features of human nature, and the sources of all knowledge in the developing sciences. The foundations set there for the legal positivism of the next century were broad and deep enough to support scientific and logical positivisms as well. To some of the less committed, however, the entire project appeared to be a delusion. The so-called romantic rebellion against Enlightenment scientism has already been discussed. But at the extremes of critical thought even the terms of this rebellion were subjected to devastating criticism. As Nietzsche anticipated Freud's theory of unconscious motivation, so also did he and Marx serve as harbingers and authorities for an entire school of social and political criticism opposed to every rationalistic, universalistic, or even systematic theory of law and morals. What the criticism rejects is the proposition that a moral philosophy of any kind makes contact with the world as peopled.

Punishment: Citizens or Slaves of Justice?

In a letter printed in the *New York Daily Tribune* of 18 February 1853, Karl Marx sought to instruct American readers in the reality behind the myth of justice and its punishments:

> Hegel, instead of looking upon the criminal as the mere object, the slave of justice, elevates him to the position of a free and self-determined being. . . . German idealism here, as in most other instances, has

but given a transcendental sanction to the rules of existing society. Is it not a delusion to substitute for the individual with his real motives, with multifarious social circumstances pressing upon him, the abstraction of "free will." . . . Is there not a necessity for deeply reflecting upon . . . the system that breeds these crimes, instead of glorifying the hangman who executes a lot of criminals to make room only for the supply of new ones?

Jeffrie Murphy, in whose "Marxism and retribution" this letter is reprinted, has warned that moralists cannot ignore the Marxist challenge or misunderstand its supporting theory.[31] If it is the case that criminality is not a matter of character but of circumstance, and if it is further the case that punishment supports the same social arrangements of power that are productive of criminal classes, then the enterprise of moral improvement is chimerical. Murphy concludes that, just in case we are inclined to reject the Marxist account, society must be structured in a way that makes punishment intelligible; that is, that it is applied to entities understood to be rational and autonomous beings able at once to choose a better course in life and to comprehend the good reasons for doing so.

Suppose, however, that although these assumptions are plausible, they are arguable, whereas the desire for pleasure and safety is real and ubiquitous. Suppose, further, that to secure these it is practical to distribute punishments in a manner that is somewhat indifferent to questions of guilt and blameworthiness. That is, suppose the best way of maximizing utility is by punishing the innocent, and by institutionalizing this in the form of what John Rawls dubbed "telishment."[32] Rawls attempted to spare utilitarianism the embarrassment created by such a prospect, arguing that the punishment of the innocent would, by way of arbitrariness, make punishment itself useless within the "price system." If the price of actions takes on various and unpredictable values, the currency itself is devalued. It would be, Rawls says, akin to a pricing system in which one learns what something costs only after buying.[33]

But surely this is not what is *wrong* with "telishment," only what may be impractical. Actually, one might plausibly contend that the random application of punishment would achieve more and not less uniformity of conduct, relying here on the well-known effects of partial reinforcement in experimental studies of animal behavior.[34] It is in the randomization of rewards and punishments that responding becomes enduring. Anthropomorphically understood, when the animal has no basis on which to assume punishment will follow a response, the response is withheld. If, instead, there is a perfectly reliable association between environmental sources of punishment and a given form of behavior, that behavior is less likely to be withheld on occasions when the relevant environmental stimuli (for example, the police) are absent.

The point, of course, is that even if it could be shown that the liabilities of "telishment" were greatly exaggerated, there would still be something both incoherent and abhorrent in a system designed to punish the innocent. The incoherence arises from the conceptual relationship between punishment and guilt. The abhorrence arises from the wrongfulness of harming the innocent. Rather than a form of punishment, "telishment" is the sort of action that *deserves* punishment.

Are there no instances, then, in which pain might be justly suffered by the innocent for the greater good? There are many. Quarantine strips the innocent carrier of a disease of freedom of movement, of social concourse, but is justified as the only means by which to save others from contamination. Some undeserved pain and suffering are inevitable consequences of heroic deeds in which the person takes on more than his share of risk so that others might be spared. In every just war, some number of innocent casualties are unintended but inevitable, such that those waging the just war knowingly bring down death and destruction on many who are innocent. What these different instances have in common is a moral justification that, if successful, establishes that the pain and suffering were not "punishments" at all.

The rule of law does not create the "slave of justice," but rather conditions under which rational beings are able to approximate more closely that flourishing life of worthy pleasures and self-understanding. Such a life is not at the cost of feelings and sentiments. All that is forfeited is the life of one who might otherwise be the "slave of passion" or, if a Marxist, the "slave of theory."

Of the many instructive passages in Alisdair MacIntyre's *After Virtue*, readers are likely to be especially repaid by those discussing the movement from the Aristotelian to Nietzschean world view.[35] If MacIntyre is right, the bureaucratization of our moral and social problems leads to solutions based on "suppressed Nietzschean premises" indifferent to, or by now ignorant of, the radically different premises that grounded Aristotle's conception of politics and morality.[36] In the end, a political regime is either justified or is a tyranny. Justification is a matter of rationality and principle, as regimes are a matter of laws and obligations. What it is in law that would *obligate* is not the threat of punishment, not even the endorsement of majorities.[37] It is, instead, the rational contact it makes with the citizen's own rational powers and rationally framed ends and purposes. The subject of quarantine may know nothing about that physiological condition that calls for isolation, but the offender is in no such state of ignorance. The offending action is an expression of freedom, of the very moral powers that qualify one for the rule of law, which includes its punishments. The offending action is an expression of character, the development of which is at once a personal and a civic responsibility. One is responsible for oneself, for improving oneself. The state, too, has this responsibility and discharges it by way of "exemplary" justice. Offenses harm not only their victims but their perpetrators.

Punishment, properly conceived and applied, addresses both harms, compensating the victim and working toward the restoration of what the perpetrator has forfeited by way of character. John Finnis explains this aspect of punishment, referring to the offender:

> He seized the advantage of self-preference, and perhaps of psychological satisfactions . . . but all at the price of diminishing his personality, his participation in the human good: for such participation is only through the *reasonable* pursuit . . . of basic goods. The punitive sanction ought therefore to be adapted so that . . . it may work to restore reasonable personality to the offender.[38]

If the offender is guilty of pursuits that are unreasonable, such as to diminish his personality, which is to say, distort and corrupt his character, then those who would punish the offense are vulnerable to the same possibilities. The goals of justice and decency are reasonable, but can be unreasonably pursued. The reason for seeking ends that are in and of themselves desirable may be a defective reason, even an immoral reason. Thus, when the religious teacher speaks of charity as "the perfection of justice," or the obligation to love the sinner even as the sin is condemned, he completes with "forgiveness" that moral project of which punishment is but a part.

Forgiveness and Moral Responsibility

As was well understood by Aristotle, there is a difference between responsibility in the sense of "bringing something about," and responsibility as the basis of moral praise or blame.[39] The angry child who breaks a toy is certainly responsible for the destructive act, for the act is the efficient cause of the destruction. So, too, are animals responsible for outcomes achieved by way of their activities. So, too, is the actor in a hypnotically or narcotically induced trance. Likewise the mentally retarded person is unable to assess fully the likely consequences of a chosen course of action. Responsibility in such cases is a species of causality and may have no real moral properties whatever. The missing ingredient is that of rationally deliberated choice (*prohairesis*). What is called for in such cases is not so much forgiveness as understanding and mercy. It may be said that where there is responsibility without moral fault the proper response is treatment rather than reform.

Forgiveness is tied to estimations of moral fault. Where the latter is absent, the former is jejune. Mercy is different. It is something of a corrective imposed on the inevitably fallible status of moral appraisals. The merciful disposition can be expressed in the form of presumptions: when in doubt in judging others, presume the presence or absence of powers in such a way as to confer an advantage on those judged. Ancient laws that honored favorable agreements entered into by children, while nullifying those placing them at a disadvantage, exemplify the merciful disposition.

The limitations of childhood are natural and not self-imposed. As noted in earlier chapters, however, there may well be proper blame for one who has brought about his own drunken state, not to mention one whose participation in his own character-formation has resulted in diminished powers of deliberation. But nearly everyone on one or another occasion is likely to act "out of character," as the expression has it. There are times and circumstances that so weigh upon the resources of persons that they do or say things entirely foreign to their developed natures. In these instances, there is not only responsibility but, indeed, moral responsibility. Called for here is "compassion"—in the literal sense of "fellow-feeling." Specifically, it is "moral compassion," felt for fellow moral beings. It is not the only form of compassion. To have fellow-feeling is to imagine oneself in a state relevantly like the state of the other. It may be a state of pain or pleasure, gain or loss, happiness or sadness. To have compassionate grief as a chimpanzee mother holds her dead infant is to feel something akin to what the other is assumed to be feeling. Compassion of one or another sort is tied to assumptions regarding the attributes of others. Hence, there can be compassionate grief where there would not be moral compassion. What is called for on the part of those who would benefit from moral compassion is remorse or regret, but in important respects not shame. It is again Aristotle who helps to clarify the relevant differences. It was Aristotle's understanding that shame is not a state of character but a "feeling," a form of "fear" arising from disrepute. Interestingly, he reserves the state chiefly to young persons who, being guided primarily by feelings, require shame as a restraining force. For the mature person, the feeling of shame would, on Aristotle's account, be entirely out of place, since such a person should do nothing that would excite such a feeling.[40] Regret is different, for it is less a feeling than a rethinking, an after-the-fact appraisal of what one has done, should have done, could have done. To feel shame is to be in a state not unlike that of fear. It is the awareness, perhaps chiefly visceral rather than cognitive, of being the object of legitimate resentment. Shakespeare's "Oh shame, where is thy blush?" records the essentially autonomic nature of the state. Unlike embarrassment, which arises from blunders of a nonmoral sort, shame is induced in contexts featuring real moral properties. The child may have no recognition of these properties but is shamed by the manner in which others, known to have the requisite standing, have reacted. The feeling of shame here is itself not in response to the recognition of real moral properties, but in response to the reactions and appraisals of authoritative others. One might expect of the textbook "sociopath" the capacity for embarrassment, but not for shame. With regret and remorse (the latter here understood as the more grave variant of the former), there is a personal comprehension of moral fault, a personal awareness of the moral properties abused or neglected by the regretted action.

In ordinary social life and without the rigors of linguistic analysis, the dispositions of mercy and compassion tend to be withheld or exercised depending on the judged remorse of offenders. This is not surprising, just in case remorse or regret entails not only sentiments, but also, and centrally, *judgments* as to the real moral properties at issue. The judge whose harsh sentence is predicated on the assumption that the offender shows no remorse gives formal expression to the general attitude: compassion and mercy are available to those who share the very powers and attributes by which compassion and mercy come about. If it is to be moral compassion, the potential beneficiaries must establish membership in the moral community. Failing in this, they can hope only for "pity."

Compassion and forgiveness are different. Compassion carries with it a sympathetic and even empathetic attachment to the offender that may be and really is missing in forgiveness. It is useful to make these distinctions even sharper than is customary. Compassion, in its very etymology, refers to "shared" feeling; an entering into the person of the other and coming to know, no matter how imperfectly or fleetingly, the confusion, pain, distress of that person. It is an attempt to make the suffering of another one's own. Forgiveness may be driven by compassion but it is a different process entirely. Where the phenomenology of compassion has as its essential feature "sentiment," that of forgiveness has "rational deliberation." Forgiveness is extended, quantified, qualified, withdrawn, and otherwise deployed in response to moral appraisals. Forgiveness falls within the category not of a virtue but of "desert" that must be earned. This, too, is different from compassion that often extends to those, and maybe should extend primarily to those, who are otherwise *not* fit or *as* fit for the moral appraisals associated with forgiveness. The sense in which one might be blamed for excessive compassion is the sense in which one might be blamed for excessive sentimentality. But profligacy in the matter of forgiveness is a form of injustice.[41] Where compassion and forgiveness coincide, the compassion is what I have called "moral compassion," in this case a sentiment arising from a moral appraisal of the actor.

There remains beyond these considerations a phenomenological aspect of forgiveness that resists easy analysis. David Novitz writes for many when he contends that one cannot forgive another by "an act of will," though cultivating the disposition to forgive qualifies as a virtue.[42] It is, as he notes, a disposition that is also subject to excess such that one may forfeit self-respect. Less clear is the effect forgiveness has on the self-respect of those who have been forgiven, or on the manner in which being forgiven relates to the process of self-forgiveness.[43] Considered within the framework of justice, forgiveness presents additional problems. It is a canon of justice that one ought to treat equal cases equally and approach all cases with a judicious disinterest and impartiality. In the matter of forgiveness, however, it is clear at the level of fact, and at least plausible at the level of moral theory, that the offended are not and should not be "impartial" in the matter of forgiveness.[44] It is possible, surely, for a reconciliation to be effected even when the offended party has not forgiven the offender, and it is also possible for there to be complete forgiveness but without reconciliation.[45] To wit:

1. Steve and Jim are partners in a small business that requires each to devote twenty hours each week, Jim as a certified accountant and Steve as a professional draftsman. Jim and Steve take turns making disparaging remarks about each other's children, to such an extent as to create offenses each judges to be beyond forgiveness. Nonetheless, they reconcile themselves to each other for the benefit of the business and the mutual benefits it confers.

2. Mary habitually belittles Joan, owing to what Joan correctly perceives to be envy. This is because Mary is far less accomplished than Joan, though she has worked as hard and as long as Joan. Joan, aware of Mary's limitations, is prepared to forgive the insults, but expects that she will never reconcile herself to maintaining a relationship.

At law, there are conditions regarded as "exculpatory" and "exonerating." These conditions are said to remove guilt or relieve offenders of the burdens of their offense. It is unclear in such circumstances whether some species of forgiveness is even in order, for mitigation refers to responsibility and it is pointless to forgive those who are not responsible for the offense in the first instance.

Matters of this nature are not to be settled by mere terminological stipulations. Still, the richness and pliability of language is the gift of broad and enduring experiences shared by social beings. We do not mean to say the same things when employing the terms "forgive," "excuse," "pardon," "annul." To forgive is already to have judged its beneficiary as blameworthy, the judgment itself a form of punishment. Thus, to forgive is essentially to terminate the punishment, where the latter may be restricted to the verdict itself. To excuse is to withhold punishment, including that first act of punishment, which is the finding of fault. It is to discover grounds of mitigation so firm as to locate the action beyond the sphere of moral culpability. To pardon is to modify a punishment as a form of desert. To annul is to correct the initial judgment of fault and to record that no action worthy of blame or punishment has actually occurred.

Forgiveness requires atonement on the part of the offender. The latter has in some accepted sense "paid his debt" and is now reinstated. There is the assumption that the offender has been "reformed," the flawed character now less flawed. To excuse is different, for it proceeds from the judgment that a flawed character was not responsible for the event in the first place. One who is excused is not expected to atone. With pardon, we have justice correcting itself, as it were, and with annulment a correction of what had been a mistaken moral ontology. The presumed moral properties of the action were, in fact, just not there. Is there a limit to forgiveness? In certain cases, the character of the offender may have become so solidified, so resistant to reformation, as to function more in the manner of a physical cause than the source of autonomous actions. It is now a character that cannot be redeemed for the purposes of civic and social life. Needless to say, whether and when such a transformation ever takes place must always be a subject of speculation. The canons of mercy alone oblige a moral community to preserve hope even for the most refractory cases. When reality and practical concerns simply outweigh the claims of hope, the offender is now properly regarded as fit for quarantine rather than reforming punishments. There is a reciprocity required where forgiveness is sought. The offender unable truly to repent, unable faithfully to strive to improve his character, unable candidly to acknowledge fault, unable accurately to comprehend the moral properties his actions have endangered or destroyed, is not a candidate for forgiveness. Even compassion cannot be intelligibly extended or felt, for those of sufficient moral character to require compassion now confront a being lacking the very moral resources on which moral compassion depends.

It is now possible to return to that "conventional view" found to be so problematical in chapter 2 where praise is extended to those who resist temptation to wrongdoing. How odd it would be if the most praiseworthy persons were those most tempted to do wrong! The problem dissolves once it is recognized that there is in fact nothing praiseworthy about resisting wrongdoing. The law does not reward the law-abiding; it punishes the violator. What is praiseworthy is resistance to those temptations that constitute a bar to moral improvement. What is blameworthy is, of course, the desire to do wrong, even if the wrongdoing is withheld. The greater the temptation to wrongdoing, the greater the blame. What is also blameworthy is resisting activities and conditions that favor moral improvement or, to say the same, moral "health." It is easy to be misunderstood here. One of H. L. Mencken's aphorisms takes "puritanism" to be the haunting belief that someone somewhere may be happy! Moral improvement refers to an enhanced and enlarged capacity for recognizing real moral properties. It may be thought of as similar to "connoisseurship" in the realm of aesthetics. As the most significant terms of social and civic life are moral terms, indifference or hostility to moral improvement is blameworthy.

Forgiveness and the Proxy Problem

By what right does the state punish in my behalf?
By what right does the state forgive in my behalf?

These are conceptually symmetrical questions. Having addressed the first in the previous section, the second calls for less attention. The state's "rights" are a feature of statehood itself such that the difficult argument is one that would establish rights independently of the rule of law, civic organization, the polis itself. If there is ontological weight to rights as such, it is conferred not by the *powers* of those who claim or take them, but by the *vulnerabilities* of those who might be victimized by just these powers. To have a "right" in this sense is to be vulnerable in a manner that is subject to respect and protection.[46] In the enlarged sense of vulnerabilities, the offenses calling for punishment and moral disapproval are those that exploit or enlarge certain of the vulnerabilities of others in a manner that violates their rights.

As vulnerabilities are generative of rights, powers are generative of duties. The misapplication of one's powers in such a way as to infringe the rights of others is what constitutes offenses warranting punishment and moral censure. Moral censure, however—and in a manner not unlike what Bentham had in mind—is or should be a source of pain and distress. It is a punishment and therefore must be proportionate to be just. Proportionality in such cases refers not to magnitude or intensity alone but also to duration. To preserve one in a state of punishment or moral censure or blameworthiness for periods beyond what is rationally called for is to punish unjustly. A judgment as to the date of expiry is based on the gravity of the offense, the credibility and sincerity of the offender's regret, and an estimation of all factors directly relevant to the case. Judgment, having been informed by these considerations, to the effect that the offender has been punished enough, just *is* forgiveness. To put it less awkwardly, forgiveness is the expressed or implicit judgment that the price paid by the offender is proportionate within the power of reason to discern. Whatever emotion might accompany the judgment adds or subtracts from the quality of mercy or compassion by which justice refines and perfects itself. If it is the aim of justice to achieve good, to want for others what is in their best interest—as the perfect friend would want for the other—then the attainment of justice should be the occasion of joy and pleasure. Compassion and mercy are states of joy and pleasure for the good that has been restored to one who has been found worthy of forgiveness.

In its laws, punishments, and pardons, the state is the embodiment of what is best in those who form and sustain it. In its institutional projection it has little means by which to have or express sentiments. Rather, by customary attention to human frailty, by an official disposition toward clemency and away from lustful vengeance, the state is able to administer a form of justice that has the look and the spirit of friendship. As the proxy of a good and worthy people, it punishes offenders, but never loses sight of them as fellows.

If this is adequate as a defense of the state as proxy, it still is insufficient to explain and justify proxy-forgiveness extended by those who were not the victims of the offending action. The deceased has left behind a wife and infant child. The question is whether, if, and how the widow can forgive the assailant. In whose name is the forgiveness extended? Is the spouse a proxy in such matters? Can she forgive also on behalf of the now fatherless infant who will go through life with only one parent? Might it be said that she has the power to confer quasi-, but not full, forgiveness?[47]

It was Aristotle's understanding that the ideal polis is a community of friends, but with friendship itself understood in ineliminably moral terms. As he says in his ethical treatise,

> Friendship and justice seem to be concerned with the same things and to be found in the same people. For there seems to be some kind of justice in every community, and some kind of friendship as well.[48]

The perfected form of friendship (*teleia philia*) is based on neither sensual pleasure nor considerations of utility, but on virtue or moral excellence. Each friend wants for the other what is good for the other, and this for the sake of the other. It is this "friendly" (*philikon*) feature of law that attracts us to it and preserves our loyalty. As with the good friend, the law would realize in us what is best, thus preserving for us a "eudaimonic" form of life where this refers not to episodic pleasures but to the "form of life."

Praise and blame have real force and power in the world, personally, interpersonally, even internationally. They identify and illuminate the real moral properties of whatever they are justly affixed to and thus count as wrongdoing when they are unjustly meted out. As with rhetoric, rewards and punishments, and other inducements, they reveal much about their sources and targets. What a person and an entire epoch take to be worthy of praise or blame will locate both in moral space. One does not forgive by proxy, though one may have compassion for both the victim and the offender, even in equal amounts. One forgives by judgment, just as the state does; the judgment that, all relevant factors considered, the punishment of moral censure—the punishment of reduced moral standing—has run its course, the time now having arrived when the offender is to be restored, returned to the human family, better prepared now to take up the life of citizen, if not saint.

Supererogatory Acts

To speak of the saint is to acknowledge a range of actions and purposes that go beyond what we think we have any right to expect of another. "Above and beyond the call of duty" is the description of the actions of heroes. But saints and heroes generally do not regard their conduct as anything but what in fact is expected. If praise and blame are properly ascribed to persons and actions on the basis of real moral properties (rather than by way of purely local conventions and provincial taste), it is necessary to account for the gap that separates conventional standards from those embraced by exceptional persons, by saints and heroes.

At one level, there would appear to be no problem, for every talent or power expresses itself in widely varying degrees, so why not moral powers? As there are prodigious feats performed by athletes and acrobats, there are prodigious moral feats performed by saints and heroes.

Clearly, however, the analogies fail as a result of the very nature of things. The comprehension of moral properties is an epistemic achievement in that the actions and persons and events are *known* as possessing moral properties. As in chapter 1, we can say that they are thus known in just the way something is known to be a "dwelling." There is, then, a formidable intellectual challenge successfully met by those who recognize these moral contents. This is not a physical achievement based in part on constitutional factors, but rather a cognitive achievement based in large measure on creating and preserving an essentially moral *outlook*. What must be recognized in the relevant settings are not stimuli that appeal directly to the sense organs, but whole constellations of actions and purposes that must be incorporated into a coherent body of thought and judgment. Thus the achievement comes closer to what is accomplished by persons of prodigious intelligence. The achievement is part of "the genius of goodness."

It is, however, only a part; the cognitive-epistemic part by which one comes to understand the moral gravamen of the given world. To this must be added the desire to preserve all that is of moral worth, centrally life itself and all that deepens its meaning. It is not surprising that saints and heroes are known most readily through the record of their sacrifices. They forfeit all that is solely personal in the name of all that is universally good: the relief of pain and suffering, the preservation of life, the affirmation of a transcendent faith, fidelity to principle.

Saints and heroes appear to do exceedingly well what most of us do less well and less faithfully. By the same token, chess grand masters may appear to play a better game than most of us, but essentially the same game. I suspect that both of these appearances are faulty if not false. It is well-known that the great chess masters play a game quite unlike the conventional game, for they see many moves into the future, many possible board positions, whole Gestalten otherwise unseen even by very good chess players. To take a line from Thomas Aquinas, *abstrahentium non est mendacium*. The future moves, the possible board positions, these whole Gestalten are drawn from the universe of real possibilities, made possible by real properties. The Thomistic thesis according to which we are able intellectually to abstract the universal from the particular describes not some sort of delusional reconstruction of reality. *The abstraction is no lie!*

Saintly and heroic lives are lived by those who see possibilities in the given situation: possibilities that are really there and of vastly greater worth than the superficial properties readily perceived by the ordinary onlooker. Their actions are described as "supererogatory" on the assumption that saints and heroes hear the same call as the rest of us and see things more or less as we do. If that were really so, then our failure to act as they do would be nothing but rank wickedness and cowardice. To follow the arc of Newton's thought as he moves from two-body interactions to a general and universal theory of motion is not to be Newton—or somehow "like" Newton—but to have the example of a power expressed in its most sublime form. It gives one a measure of one's own powers and limitations, a reminder of the distance between one's comprehension of the physical world and what that world might really be like. To witness Mother Teresa extending unconditional love to those the world at large perceives as human flotsam is not to see the world as she does. It is rather to understand that one is failing to see whole worlds of moral properties before one's very eyes. If there is a duty to improve oneself in these respects, then it is the saint and the hero who supply examples and instruct us in just how high the bar really is.

❖ NOTES ❖

CHAPTER ONE

1. See Michael Zimmerman, "Sharing responsibility." *American Philosophical Quarterly*, 1985, vol. 22: 115–122.

2. The tendency is to explain a person's failures as arising from internal dispositions rather than external constraints. Thus, the welfare recipient is slothful and the quiz master on the TV show is judged highly intelligent. See I. Ross, and R. Nisbett, *The Person and the Situation* (New York: McGraw-Hill, 1991).

3. Bernard Williams, *Ethics and the Limits of Philosophy* (Cambridge: Harvard University Press, 1985), 135.

4. Arthur Fine, "The natural ontological attitude," in J. Leplin, ed., *Scientific Realism* (Berkeley: University of California Press, 1984), 150.

5. Stephen Stitch, *The Fragmentation of Reason* (Cambridge: MIT Press, 1990), 101.

6. A summary of Gergen's position is his "The limits of pure critique," in H. W. Simon and M. Billig eds., *After Postmodernism: Reconstructing Ideology Critique* (London: Sage Publications, 1994), 58–78.

7. Johann Wolfgang von Goethe, *Theory of Colours.* trans. C. L. Eastlake (London: John Murray, 1840). References here are taken from the paperback edition of this work published by MIT Press, 1970.

8. Ibid. p. 287.

9. Ibid. p. 284.

10. Hermann von Helmholtz, *Science and Culture: Popular and Philosophical Essays*, David Cahan, ed. (Chicago: University of Chicago Press, 1995), 80.

11. Ibid., 81.

12. Paul Feyerabend, *Against Method* (London: New Left Books, 1975).

13. Susan Haacke, *Manifesto of a Passionate Moderate* (Chicago: University of Chicago Press, 1998), 91.

14. Edward Pols, *Mind Regained* (Ithaca: Cornell University Press, 1998), 80–81.

15. See especially William Dray, *Laws and Explanation in History* (New York: Oxford University Press, 1957).

16. John M. Darley and Thomas Shultz, "Moral rules: their content and acquisition," *Annual Review of Psychology*, 1990, vol. 41: 551.

17. Charles Taylor, *Sources of the Self* (Cambridge: Harvard University Press, 1989), 27.

18. Ciaran Benson, *The Cultural Psychology of the Self* (London: Routledge, 2001), 73.

19. David Hume, *A Treatise of Human Nature*, pt. I, bk. III, sec. I, ed. L. A. Selby-Bigge (Oxford: Clarendon Press, 1973), 469.

20. Ibid., pt. III, bk. III, sec. II, 597.

21. Ibid., sec. I, 591.

22. Published in 1736, *The Analogy of Religion Natural and Revealed* was widely read and reprinted often. Used here and in later chapters is the Everyman edition (London: J. M. Dent & Sons, 1936).

23. Ralph Cudworth, *A Treatise Concerning Eternal and Immutable Morality, with A Treatise of Freewill*, ed. Sarah Hutton (New York: Cambridge University Press, 1990).

24. Ibid., 172.

25. Ibid., 173.

26. Ibid., 183.

27. Ibid., 174.

28. Shaftesbury (Anthony Ashley Cooper, Third Earl of), *Characteristics of Men, Manners, Opinion and Times* (1711; reprint, ed. Douglas Den Vyl, Indianapolis: the Liberty Fund, 2001).

29. Ibid., 20–21.

30. John Locke, *The Reasonableness of Christianity*, ed. J. C. Higgins-Biddle (Oxford: Clarendon Press, 1999); John Toland, *Christianity Not Mysterious* (New York: Garland, 1984); Matthew Tindal, *Christianity as Old as the Creation* (Newburgh, NY [1798]; Anthony Collins, *A Discourse on the Grounds and Reasons of the Christian Religion* (New York: Garland, 1976); Shaftesbury, *The Freeholder's Political Catechism* (1757); Samuel Clarke, *A Demonstration of the Being and Attributes of God* and *A Discourse Concerning the Unchangeable Obligations of Natural Religion, and the Truth and Certainty of the Christian Religion*, ed. Ezio Vailati (Cambridge: Cambridge University Press, 1998).

31. A. J. Ayer, *Language, Truth and Logic* (New York: Dover, 1952), 27.

32. Ibid., 34.

33. Passages here are taken from the reprinting of "The subjectivity of values," in J. L. Mackie, *Ethics: Inventing Right and Wrong* (London: Penguin Books, 1977). The source used and the pagination are Geoffrey Sayre-McCord ed., *Essays on Moral Realism* (Ithaca: Cornell University Press, 1988).

34. Sayre-McCord, *Essays*, 98.

35. Ibid., 111.

36. Richard Double, *The Non-Reality of Free Will* (New York: Oxford University Press, 1991), 166.

37. Gilbert Harman, *The Nature of Morality* (New York: Oxford University Press, 1977).

38. See her chapter 6 in Gilbert Harman and Judith Jarvis Thomson, *Moral Relativism and Moral Objectivity* (Oxford: Blackwell, 1996).

39. G. E. Moore, *Philosophical Studies* (London: Routledge and Kegan Paul, 1922; reprint 1965), 330ff.

40. Ibid., 333.

41. Thomas Reid, *An Inquiry into the Human Mind on the Principles of Common Sense* (1764), ed. Derek Brookes (University Park, PA: Penn State University Press, 1997); see especially chap. 4, sec. II, "Of natural language." See also Daniel N. Robinson, "Radical ontologies." in *International Studies in the Philosophy of Science*, 1995, Vol. 9: 215–223.

42. John McDowell, "Values and secondary qualities," in Sayre-McCord, *Essays*, 166–180.

43. Alexander Bird, *Philosophy of Science* (London: UCL Press, 1998), 96–97.

44. Saul Kripke, *Naming and Necessity* (Cambridge: Harvard University Press, 1980).

45. Wolfgang Köhler, "Value and fact," *The Journal of Philosophy*, 1944, vol. 41: 197–212.

46. For the developed treatment of this, see C. H. Graham and Philburn Ratoosh, "Notes on some interrelationships of sensory psychology, perception, and behavior," in Sigmund Koch, ed., *Psychology: A Study of a Science*, Vol. 4 (New York: McGraw-Hill, 1962), 483–514.

47. Thomas Reid, *Inquiry*, ch. 5, sec. VIII, 73.

48. Karl Dunker, "Ethical relativity? An enquiry into the psychology of ethics," *Mind*, 1939, vol. 48: 39–57.

49. Hume, *Treatise*, bk. III, pt. I, sec. I, 469.

50. Laurence Bonjour, *In Defense of Pure Reason* (Cambridge University Press, 1998); 151.

51. Peter Strawson, "Freedom and resentment," *Proceedings of the British Academy*, 1962, vol 48: 1–25.

52. Michael Stocker, "Desiring the bad: an essay in moral psychology," *Journal of Philosophy*, 1979, vol. 76: 738–753.

53. Michael Smith, *Moral Problems* (Oxford: Basil Blackwell, 1994), sec. 3.1.

54. Alfred Mele, *Autonomous Agents: From Self-Control to Autonomy* (New York, Oxford University Press), 6.

55. Moore, *Philosophical Studies*, 320–321.

CHAPTER TWO

1. Lloyd Fields, "Moral beliefs and blameworthiness," *Philosophy*, 1994, vol. 69 (270): 397–415.

2. Richard Swinburne, *Responsibility and Atonement* (Oxford: Oxford University Press, 1992), 49. The standard view can be found in moral treatises both ancient and modern. A version very close to Swinburne's is developed by Shaftesbury in pt. II, bk. I, sec. IV of *An Inquiry Concerning Virtue or Merit* (1699; reprinted in British Moralists, ed. K. A. Selby-Bigge [New York: Dover, 1965], 21–24). Shaftesbury recognizes a problem here, for he sees that the this might well attach virtue to a person with a strong propensity to vice. But absent all such temptation, the person may be, as Shaftesbury says, "indeed more *cheaply virtuous*." He then resolves the paradox by concluding that the arrest and loss of such propensities detracts nothing from virtue but raises it to a higher degree.

3. Swinburne, *Responsibility and Atonement*, 14.

4. Hume, *Treatise*, part III, bk. III, sect. I, 576.

5. For an informing analysis of these passages, see John M. Cooper, "Two theories of justice." Presidential Address, American Philosophical Association, Eastern Division, in *Proceedings and Addresses of the APA*, November 2000.

6. Cooper, "Two theories," 8.

7. Immanuel Kant, *Critique of Pure Reason*, trans. N. K. Smith (New York: Macmillan, 1929), B-xxix.

8. Indeed, so special that, as indicated in various places in this work, it remains unclear as to just how "compatibilist" Kant's position is.

9. Galen Strawson, "The impossibility of moral responsibility," *Philosophical Studies*, 1994, vol. 75: 5–25.

10. David Hartley, *Observations on Man, his Frame, his Duty, and his Expectations* (1749; Gainesville: Scholars' Facsimile Edition, 1966, 500. Hartley's version of compatibilism is reviewed below.

11. Pols, *Mind Regained*, 124.

12. Double, *Non-Reality*, 8–9.

13. Ibid., 163.

14. Ibid.

15. Richard Sorabji, *Necessity, Cause and Blame* (London: Duckworth, 1980), ix.

16. Aristotle, *The Complete Works*, ed. Jonathan Barnes (Princeton: Princeton University Press, 1984).

17. Sorabji, *Necessity, Cause and Blame*, 9.

18. Aristotle, *Nicomachean Ethics*, trans. Roger Crisp (Cambridge: Cambridge University Press, 2000), 1114a.

19. Sorabji, *Necessity, Cause and Blame*, 249.

20. James Boswell, *Life of Johnson*, ed. R. W. Chapman (Oxford: Oxford University Press, 1980), 411.

21. Thomas Hobbes, *Leviathan*, ed. C. B. Macpherson (1651: Harmondsworth: Penguin Books, 1974), 261–264.

22. Mark Heller, "The mad scientist meets the robot cats: compatibilism, kinds and counterexamples," *Philosophical and Phenomenalogical Research*, 1996, vol. 56: 22–26.

23. Hobbes, *Leviathan*, 262.

24. Ibid., 263.

25. Ibid., 119.

26. William James, *Psychology, Briefer Course* (New York: Henry Holt, 1892), 415.

27. Ibid.

28. Clark Hull, *Principles of Learning* (New York: Appleton Century, 1943).

29. Robert Kane, "Free will: the elusive ideal." *Philosophical Studies*, 1994, vol. 75: 25–60.

30. John Lock, An Essay Concerning Human Understanding (1690; New York: Dover, 1959).

31. Ibid., bk. II, chap. XXI, 313.

32. Ibid., 314.

33. Ibid., 317.

34. Ibid., 330.

35. Ibid., 335.

36. Gideon Yaffee, *Liberty Worth the Name: Locke on Free Agency.* (Princeton: Princeton University Press, 2000), 19.

37. Locke, *Essay*, bk. II, chap XXI, 22.

38. Ibid., 340.

39. Ibid., 345–347.

40. Ibid.

41. Hartley, *Observations on Man . . .* , 501.

42. Robert Johnson, "Internal reasons and the conditional fallacy," *Quarterly Journal of Philosophy*, 1999, vol. 49: 53–72 (Quotation from page 53).

43. Ibid.

44. Jonathan Edwards, "Remarks on Lord Kames' *Essays on the principles of Morality and Natural Religion* (1751)," in *An Inquiry into the Modern Prevailing Notions of that Freedom of the Will which is Supposed to be Essential to Moral Agency, Virtue and Vice, Reward and Punishment, Praise and Blame* (Morgan, Pa.: Soli Deo Gloria Publications, 1996), 336–337.

45. Ibid.

46. Ibid., 133.

47. Boethius, *The Consolation of Philosophy*, trans. S. J. Tester, Loeb Classical Library (Cambridge: Harvard University Press, 1997), 409. I thank Richard Sorabji for drawing my attention to this argument in Boethius.

48. Edwards, *Inquiry into Modern Prevailing Notions . . .* , 335.

49. Ibid., 1.

50. Ibid., 187.

51. Ibid., 6.

52. Ibid., 18–19.

53. Ibid., 24.

54. Ibid., 206ff.

55. Gottfried Wilhelm von Leibniz, *Discourse on Metaphysics*, trans. G. R. Montgomery (La Salle, IL: OpenCourt, 1962), 49.

56. The most economical development of the argument is chap. III of his *Groundwork of the Metaphysic of Morals*, trans. H. J. Paton (London: Routledge, 1989). For a careful study of Kant's thesis, see Hud Hudson's *Kant's Compatibilism* (Ithaca: Cornell University Press, 1994). It remains a subject of controversy as to whether Kant is a compatibilist or an incompatibilist. The position I would defend here is that his moral theory requires incompatibilist libertarianism.

57. Kant, *Groundwork* 109–111.

58. Ibid.

59. Harry Frankfurt, "Alternate possibilities and moral responsibility," *Journal of Philosophy*, 1969, vol. 66: 829–839.

60. Ibid., 829.

61. Walter Glannon, "On the revised principle of alternate possibilities," *Southern Journal of Philosophy*, 1994, vol. 32: 49–60.

62. R. M. Hare, "Prediction and moral appraisal," 1978, *Midwest Studies in Philosophy*, vol. 3: 17–27.

63. Alan V. White, "Frankfurt, Failure, and Finding Fault," *Sorites*, 1998: 51–56.

64. Joseph K. Campbell, "A compatibilist theory of alternative possibilities," *Philosophical Studies*, 1997, vol. 88: 319–330.

65. Michael McKenna, *"Does strong compatibilism survive Frankfurt counter-examples?" Philosophical Studies*, 1998, vol. 91(3): 259–264.

66. Peter van Inwagen, "Ability and responsibility," *The Philosophical Review*, vol. 87 (2): 201–224.

67. Laura Ekstrom, "Incompatibilist freedom," *American Philosophical Quarterly*, 1998, vol. 35(3): 281–291.

68. John Martin Fisher and Mark Ravizza, *Responsibility and Control: A Theory of Moral Responsibility* (New York: Cambridge University Press, 1998).

69. Ibid., 33.

70. These points are developed in Daniel Dennett, *Elbow Room: The Varieties of Free Will Worth Having* (Cambridge: Bradford Books, 1984), 137.

71. Daniel Dennett, *Kinds of Minds* (New York: Basic Books, 1996), 27.

72. Ibid., 20.

73. Thomas Reid, "Of Power." This treatise was first printed in the *Philosophical Quarterly*, vol. 51, No. 202 (January 2001). The work is introduced by John Haldane, who notes that Reid's philosophical insights on this matter are "undiminished by the passage of the years."

74. Ibid., 3.

75. Hume, *Treatise*, pt. IV, bk. I, sect. V, 247.

76. See, for example, Paul Russell, *Freedom and Moral Sentiment: Hume's Way of Naturalizing Responsibility* (New York: Oxford University Press, 1995); and his "Causation, compulsion and compatibilism," *American Philosophical Quarterly*, 1988, vol. 25: 313–321.

77. John Stuart Mill, *A System of Logic Ratiocinative and Inductive* (London: Longmans, Green & Co., 1900), 548.

78. Dugald Stewart, *Elements of the Philosophy of the Human Mind* (1792; Philadelphia: William Young, 1793), 87.

79. Roger Crisp, *Mill on Utilitarianism* (London: Routledge, 1997) 11–12. In this connection, Roger Crisp, in our personal discussions, has noted that utilitarianism has failed to develop the epistemological resources that would be needed if concepts such as "happiness" or "good on the whole" were to be rigorous enough for theoretical purposes.

80. Mill, *A System of Logic*, 550.

81. Mill, "Utilitarianism," in *The Utilitarians* (Garden City, NY: Dolphin Books, 1961), 431.

82. Wilhelm Wundt, *Ethics*, vol. 3 ("The Principles of Morality and the Departments of the Moral Life"), trans. Margaret Washburn (London: Swan Sonnenschein, 1901); 38.

83. Ibid., 52ff.

84. Ibid., 53.

85. Ibid., 57.

86. Ibid.

87. Ibid., 26.

88. Ibid., 99ff.

89. Alexander Bain, *The Emotions and the Will* (London: Parker, 1859), 138.

90. Ibid., 550.

91. Arthur Collins, *The Nature of Mental Things* (Notre Dame: University of Notre Dame Press, 1987), 149.

92. Ibid., 150.

93. *Treatise,* pt. III, bk. II, sec. III, 414–415.

94. Hume, *The Dialogues of Plato*, 2 vols., trans. Benjamin Jowett (New York: Random House, 1937), 239ff.

95. Stanley Rosen, *Plato's Sophist* (New Haven: Yale University Press, 1983), 14.

96. Aristotle, *Rhetoric*, 1355a, in: *The Complete Works of Aristotle*, vol. 2, ed. Jonathan Barnes (Princeton: Princeton University Press, 1984).

97. Ibid., 1358a.

98. Ibid.

99. Ibid., 1354a 20–27.

100. Ibid., 1357a 2–3.

101. Ibid., 1360b 4–17.

102. Ibid., 1366a 13–15.

103. Ibid., 1365a 37.

104. Socrates, *Menexenus*, 235d, in *The Dialogues of Plato*, vol. 2, ed. Benjamin Jowett (New York: Random House 1937).

105. Aristotle, *Rhetoric*, 1374b 24–25, in Barnes, *Works of Aristotle*.

106. Ibid., 1369a 5–6.

107. Ibid., 1374b 15–17.

108. Ibid., 1386b 12.

109. Eugene Garver, *Aristotle's Rhetoric: An Art of Character* (Chicago: University of Chicago Press, 1994), 194.

110. Joseph Butler, *The Analogy of Religion*, pt. I, chap. 6, 87.

111. Ibid., 89.

112. C. D. Broad, *Five Types of Ethical Theory* (London: Kegan Paul, 1934), 55.

113. Michael McKenna, "Moral theory and modified compatibilism," *Journal of Philosophical Research*, 441–458.

114. Kane, "Free Will: the elusive ideal."

115. Kane, "Free Will," p. 35.

116. I discuss this at some length in "Radical Ontologies," *International Studies in the Philosophy of Science*, vol. 9 (3): 215–223.

117. The best English language study of Maine de Biran's philosophy remains Philip Hallie, *Maine de Biran: Reformer of Empiricism 1766–1824* (Cambridge: Harvard University Press, 1959). This section is heavily indebted to Hallie's treatise.

118. Ibid., 115.

119. Peter Strawson, "Freedom and resentment," *Proceedings of the British Academy*, 1962, vol. 48: 1–25.

120. Aristotle, *Nicomachean Ethics*, bk. III, chap. v, 17–19.

121. Thomas Aquinas, *Summa Theologiae* (2 vols.), ed. Anton C. Pegis (New York: Random House, 1945), vol. 225–238.

122. Ibid., 234.

123. William Wallace, *The Modeling of Nature* (Washington: Catholic University Press, 1996), 20.

124. Ibid., 23.

125. The full title of the lectures is instructive: *A Demonstration of the Being and Attributes of God, More Particularly in Answer to Mr. Hobbs, Spinoza, And their Followers, Wherein the Notion of LIBERTY is Stated, and the Possibility and Certainty of it Proved, in Opposition to Necessity and Fate.* All references here are to the eighth edition (London: Printed by W. Botham, for James and John Knapton, 1732); Samuel Clarke, *A Demonstration of the Being and Attributes of God*, 87–100.

126. Ibid.

127. Ibid., 100–103.

128. Samuel Clarke, *G. W. Leibniz and Samuel Clarke Correspondence*, ed. Roger Ariew (Cambridge: Hackett Publishing, 2000), 29.

129. Isaac Newton, *Opticks or A Treatise of the Reflections, Refractions, Inflections & Colours of Light* (4th edition, London, 1730; reprint, New York: Dover Publications, 1952). The quoted passage is from Newton's "Query 31."

130. Clarke, *Demonstration*, "Fifth Reply," 83.

CHAPTER THREE

1. Robert Kane, "Responsibility, luck, and chance: reflections on free will and indeterminism," *Journal of Philosophy*, 1999, Vol 96: 217.

2. Geoffrey Chaucer, "The Knights Tale," in *The Canterbury Tales*, pt. 2, lines 1663–1669.

3. *The Works of Ralph Waldo Emerson*, vol. VI, "The Conduct of Life" (Philadelphia: The Nottingham Society, n.d.), 27.

4. Thomas Nagel, *Mortal Questions* (New York: Cambridge University Press, 1979).

5. James Brady, "Recklessness," *Law and Philosophy*, 1996, vol. 15(2): 183–200.

6. Susan LaBine and Gary LaBine, "Determinations of negligence and the hindsight bias," *Law and Human Behavior*, 1996, vol. 20: 501–516.

7. Kenneth Simons, "Negligence," in, *Responsibility*, ed. E. Paul, F. Miller, and J. Paul (Cambridge: Cambridge University Press, 1999), 52.

8. Brian Rosebury, "Moral responsibility and 'moral luck,'" *Philosophical Review*, 1995, vol. 104: 499–524.

9. Andrew Latus, "Moral and epistemic luck," *Journal of Philosophical Research*, 2000, vol. 25: 149–172.

10. Susan Suave Meyer, "Fate, fatalism and agency in Stoicism," in *Responsibility*, ed. E. Paul, F. Miller, and J. Paul, 252.

11. Ibid., 258.

12. As Richard Sorabji pointed out to me in a discussion of this matter, Aristotle's is a *philosopher's god* engaged in the contemplation of things sublime, not mundane.

13. J. L. Austin, "A Plea for Excuses," in his *Philosophical Papers* (Oxford: Oxford University Press, 1961).

14. Steven Suerdlik, "Crime and Moral Luck," *American Philosophical Quarterly*, vol. 25 (1988): 79–86.

15. See, for example, Justin Oakley, "Consequentialism, moral responsibility, and the intention/foresight distinction, *Utilitas*, 1994, vol. 6(2): 201–216.

16. For an informing discussion, see Jonathan Dancy, *Moral Reasons* (Oxford: Blackwell, 1993).

17. Roger Crisp, "Utilitarianism and accomplishment," *Analysis*, 2000, vol. 60: 264–268.

18. Ibid., 265.

19. Ibid., 266.

20. Ibid., 266–267.

21. Susan Wolf, "Sanity and the metaphysics of responsibility," in *The Inner Citadel*, ed. John Christman (New York: Oxford University Press, 1989), 137–151.

22. Edward Sankowski, "Blame and autonomy," *American Philosophical Quarterly*, 1992, vol. 29: 295.

23. Gregory Mellema, *Collective Responsibility* (Amsterdam: Rodopi, 1997).

24. Williams, *Moral Luck*, 20–39.

25. For a good example, see Richard Parker, "Blame, punishment and the role of result," *American Philosophical Quarterly*, 1984, vol 21: 269–276.

26. Wolf, "Sanity," 143.

27. Robert Young, "Compatibilism and conditioning," *Nous*, 1979, vol. 13: 361–378.

28. Ibid., 367.

29. See Daniel N. Robinson, *Wild Beasts and Idle Humours*, especially the final chapter.

30. William C. Mathes and Edward J. Devitt, *Federal Jury Practice and Instructions* (Sr. Paul: West Publishing, 1965), 308.

31. For an interesting study of the rationale adopted by jurors, see Norman Finkel, *Common Sense Justice* (Cambridge: Harvard University Press, 1995).

32. The authoritative analysis is H.L.A. Hart and Tony Honore, *Causation in the Law*, 2nd edition (Oxford: Oxford University Press, 1985).

33. Susan Hurley, "Justice without constitutive luck," in *Ethics*, ed. A. P. Griffiths, Royal Institute of Philosophy Supplement 35 (New York: Cambridge University Press, 1993).

34. See, for example, John Austin, "If and cans," *Philosophical Papers* (Oxford: Oxford University Press, 1961).

35. Alfred Mele, *Journal of Philosophy*, 1998, vol. 95: 581–584.

36. Harry Frankfurt, "Freedom of the will and the concept of a person," *Journal of Philosophy*, 1971, vol. 68: 5–20.

37. Herbert Fingarette, "Feeling guilty," *American Philosophical Quarterly*, 1979, vol. 16: 161.

38. At 1132b32, Aristotle reports that "there are double penalties for a drunken offender; the first principle lies in him, in that he had the power not to get drunk"; *Nichomachean Ethics*, 46.

39. Robert Noggle, "The nature of motivation (and why it matters less to ethics than anyone might think)," *Philosophical Studies*, 1997, vol. 87: 89.

40. Ibid., 91.

41. Richard Swinburne, *Responsibility and Atonement* (Oxford: Clarendon Press, 1989), 63.

42. J. M. Darley and M. P. Zanna, "Making moral judgments," *American Scientist*, 1982, vol. 70: 515–521.

43. Michael S. Moore, "Causation and responsibility," in *Responsibility*, ed. E. F. Paul, F. D. Miller, and J. Paul, 36.

44. For an excellent treatment of the subject, see James Hawthorne and Luc Bovens, "The preface, the lottery, and the logic of belief," *Mind*, 1999, vol. 108: 241–264.

45. Thomas Nagel, *The Possibility of Altruism* (New York: Oxford University Press, 1970).

46. The main lines of his position are drawn clearly in Gilbert Harman and Judith Jarvis Thomson, *Moral Relativism and Moral Objectivity* (Oxford: Blackwell, 1996).

47. Ibid., 17.

48. Ibid., 18.

49. William Alston, *Epistemic Justification* (Ithaca: Cornell University Press, 1989), 122.

50. William James, "The Will to Believe," in *The Writings of William James*, ed. John J. McDermott (Chicago: University of Chicago Press, 1977), 717–735.

51. Ibid., 718.

52. Gottfried Wilhelm von Leibniz, *Theodicy*, trans. E. M. Huggard, ed. Austin Farrer (La Salle, IL: Open Court, 1985), 128–129. Candide was published in 1759, five years after the *Poem* and the Lisbon earthquake. This natural disaster brought into focus the abiding tension between "optimists" and those who found the world to be a place of conflict and suffering. An excellent study of the works spawned by the disaster is Victor Gourevitch, "Rousseau on providence," *Review of Metaphysics*, 2000, Vol. 53: 565–611.

53. Katherine F. Drew, *The Lombard Laws* (Philadelphia: University of Pennsylvania Press, 1973), 84–85.

54. Scott A. Davison, "Moral luck and the flicker of freedom," *American Philosophical Quarterly*, 1999, vol. 36: 248.

55. Ibid.

CHAPTER FOUR

1. Clarke, *A Demonstration of the Being and Attributes of God*.

2. The reader may refer to the text and notes on Hobbes in chapter 2 for citations from *Leviathan*. Clarke's excerpts from Hobbes are from both *Leviathan* and *De Cive*. As to whether or not Hobbes regarded the state of nature to be historical, his own words are clear: "I believe it was never generally so, over all the world; but there are many places where they live so now" (Hobbes, *Leviathan*, 187).

3. Clarke, *Demonstration*, 227.

4. Ibid., 229.

5. Ibid.

6. Hobbes, *Leviathan*, 225.

7. Bernard Mandeville published an early version anonymously in April of 1705. The first full version, which included *An Enquiry into the Origin of Moral Virtue*, appeared under the author's name in 1714. Cited here is the two-volume Oxford edition of 1924 republished as a facsimile by the Liberty Fund, Indianapolis, 1998.

8. Mandeville, vol. 2, *Enquiry*, 39.

9. Ibid., 208.

10. Mandeville cites Aristotle, Epicurus, Horace, and other classical figures, not to mention Hobbes, who paid close attention to the role of passion in human affairs. A half-century earlier, Pierre Gassendi had done much to revive Epicureanism and the materialistic atomism with which it was compatible. These important trends were all in the direction of secularizing the subject of morals and attaching it to the larger world of natural science.

11. Mandeville, *Enquiry*, vol. 1, 369.

12. For a biographical summary, see editor A. A. Brill's "Introduction" in *The Basic Writings of Sigmund Freud* (New York: Random House, 1938). The most complete account of the psychoanalytic search for explanations is Henri Ellenberger, *The Discovery of the Unconscious*. (New York: Basic Books, 1977).

13. Freud, "History of the psychoanalytic movement," *Basic Writings*, 939.

14. Arthur Schopenhauer, *The World as Will and Representation*, vol. 1., trans. E.F.J. Payne (New York: Dover, 1969). Schopenhauer was thirty when the first edition appeared in 1818. A revised second edition was published in 1844, then the third in 1859, the year before he died. The German "Vorstellung" in the title translates typically as "representation," though even Schopenhauer was inclined to render it as "Idea;" hence, Freud's citing the work as *The World as Will and Idea*.

15. Ibid.

16. Charles Darwin, *The Descent of Man, and Selection in Relation to Sex*, 2nd edition. (London: Murray, 1882); *The Expression of the Emotions in Man and Animals*, 2nd edition (London: Murray, 1890).

17. Darwin's discussions of unconscious processes are scattered in the major works. Referring to them, Howard Gruber and Paul Barrett note that they "fall short of Freudian theory." Darwin's references to unconscious processes could not have been lost on Freud, however. Howard Gruber and Paul Barrett, *Darwin on Man* (New York: Dutton, 1974), 233.

18. In, for example, such works as those of George Romanes, *Animal Intelligence* (1883) and Wilhelm Wundt, *Lectures on Human and Animal Psychology* (1894). James Mark Baldwin's 1909 presidential address to the American Psychological Association was titled "The influence of Darwin on theory of knowledge and philosophy." These three works are included in the 28-volume *Significant Contributions to the History of Psychology*, ed. Daniel N. Robinson (Westport, CT: Greenwood, 1978).

19. "History of the psychoanalytic movement," in *Basic Writings*, 939.

20. Freud, *The Interpretation of Dreams*, in *Basic Writings*, 482.

21. See, for example, *Graham v. Darnell* 538 S.W. 2d 690, where the Church of Billy Graham failed to receive funds bequeathed by Tom Pruett, the court satisfied that Pruett had been "deluded" as to the "true feelings" his lifelong estranged daughters had for him.

22. Ernest Nagel, *The Structure of Science* (London: Routledge, 1961), 352.

23. Freud was of two minds on the prospect of a neuroscience of psychoanalysis. For a review and appraisal of his proposed, and then withdrawn, scheme, see K. H. Pribram and Merton Gill, *Freud's "Project" Reassessed* (New York: Basic Books, 1976). For a detailed inquiry into the biological foundations of Freud's theories, consult Frank Sulloway, *Freud, Biologist of the Mind* (New York: Basic Books, 1979). That the project was miscast in ways overlooked by Freud is illustrated by Daniel N. Robinson, "Psychobiology and the unconscious," in *The Unconscious Reconsidered*, ed. K. S. Bowers and D. Meichenbaum (New York: Wiley, 1984).

24. Ariela Lazar, "Deceiving oneself or self-deceived? On the formation of beliefs 'under the influence,' " *Mind*, 1999, vol. 108: 265–287.

25. See, for example, chapter 6 of John Sabini and Mark Silver, *Emotion, Character and Responsibility* (New York: Oxford University Press, 1998).

26. For his development and defense of the argument, see Rene Descartes, "Second meditation" in his *Meditations on the First Philosophy*, in *The Philosophical Writings of Descartes*, vol. 1, ed. and trans. J. Cottingham (Cambridge: Cambridge University Press, 1984), 16–19.

27. Locke, *Essay Concerning Human Understanding*, vol. 1, especially 448–480.

28. Ibid., 460.

29. See Mary Douglas, "The person in an enterprise culture," in *Understanding the Enterprise Culture: Themes in the Work of Mary Douglas*, ed. S. Heap and A. Ross (Edinburgh: University of Edinburgh Press, 1992), 41–62.

30. An informing account of the group and of the special problems Locke's philosophy addressed and created is provided by Christopher Fox, *Locke and the Scriblerians* (Berkeley: University of California Press, 1988).

31. George Berkeley, *Alciphron*, in *Alciphron in Focus*, ed. David Berman (London: Routledge, 1993). For Reid's "brave officer" critique of Locke, see chapter 6 of his *Essays on the Intellectual Powers of Man: The Works of Thomas Reid*, ed. William Hamilton, 6th edition (Edinburgh: Maclachlan & Stewart, 1863). For Reid's critique of Hume on this same issue, see Daniel N. Robinson and Tom L. Beauchamp, "Personal Identity: Reid's answer to Hume," *The Monist*, 1978, vol. 61: 326–339.

32. This is discussed at greater length in Daniel N. Robinson, "Cerebral plurality and the unity of self," *American Psychologist*, 1982, vol. 37: 904–909.

33. Ian Hacking, *Rewriting the Soul: Multiple Personality and the Sciences of Memory* (Princeton: Princeton University Press, 1995), 146–148.

34. Daniel Dennett, *Consciousness Explained* (Boston: Little Brown, 1991).

35. The classic case is Morton Prince's Miss Beauchamp; Morton Prince, *The Dissociation of a Personality: A Biographical Study in Abnormal Psychology* (New York: Longmans, Green, 1905).

36. Hacking, *Rewriting*, 233.

37. The first book-length presentation of postoperative evaluations following therapeutic commissurotomies was Michael Gazzaniga, *The Bisected Brain* (New York: Appleton Century, 1970). Subsequent research had a rather quieting effect on the generalizations arising from the initial findings.

38. Derek Parfit, *Reasons and Persons* (Oxford: Clarendon Press, 1984, 249.

39. W. Griesinger, *Mental Pathology and Therapeutics*, trans. C. L. Robertson and J. Rutherford (New York: Wood, 1882), 18–19.

40. Parfit developed the thesis in a graduate seminar, "Selves," organized by Galen Strawson and myself in Oxford, Trinity Term 2000.

41. Reprinted in E.D.H. Johnson, ed., *The World of the Victorians* (New York: Charles Scribner, 1964); 45–46. Pierre Cabanis was the physician in whose arms Mirabeau died. A disciple of the French Enlightenment, he wrote influentially on the relationship between physiology and mental life. His major treatise is *On the Relations between the Physical and Moral Aspects of Man*, 2 vols., ed. George Mora trans. M. D. Daidi (Baltimore: Johns Hopkins University Press, 1981). It is in his Eighth Memoir that he discusses the relationship of diet (asceticism, fasts, abstinence) and religious and moral feelings; vol. 2, 393–396.

42. I discuss this at some length in chapter 3 of *Wild Beasts and Idle Humours*.

43. Ibid., 141–152. For the actual trial proceedings, see *Rex v Hadfield*. 40 George III 1800, in Howell's *State Trials*, vol. XXVII, 1820, 1281–1356.

44. Julien Offroy de La Mettrie, *Man: A Machine*, trans. Mary W. Calkins (La Salle, IL.: Open Court, 1912), 105. For authoritative essays see G. S. Rousseau, ed. *The Languages of Psyche: Mind and Body in Enlightenment Thought* (Berkeley: University of California Press, 1990).

45. For fuller discussion of these developments, as well as selections from major works, see Daniel N. Robinson, *The Mind: An Oxford Reader* (Oxford: Oxford University Press, 1998); and idem, *An Intellectual History of Psychology*, 3rd edition. (Madison, WI: University of Wisconsin Press, 1995), especially chapters 9 and 10.

46. Illustrative is Henry Maudsley, *Responsibility in Mental Disease* (New York: Appleton, 1876). It is in such works that one sees the strength of conviction on the part of those leading the movement.

47. Thomas Nagel, *The View from Nowhere* (Oxford: Oxford University Press, 1986), 199.

48. Examples abound. Consider only A. Damasio, *Descartes' Error: Emotion, Reason and the Human Brain* (New York: Putnam, 1994) Paul Churchland, "Folk psychology and the explanation of human behavior," in *The Future of Folk Psychology: Intentionality and Cognitive Science* (Cambridge: Cambridge University Press, 1991), especially chapter 2; and Daniel Dennett, *Brainchildren: Essays on Designing Minds* (Cambridge: MIT Press, 1998).

49. Donald Davidson, "How is weakness of the will possible?," in *Moral Concepts*, ed. Joel Feinberg (New York: Oxford University Press, 1970).

50. All references are from the previously cited translation by Roger Crisp.

51. David Wiggins, "Weakness of the will, commensurability, and the objects of deliberation and desire," in *Essays on Aristotle's Ethics*, ed. Amelie Oksenberg Rorty (Berkeley: University of California Press, 1980), 241.

52. Wiggins, "Weakness," 257.

53. Ibid.

54. Alfred Mele, *Autonomous Agents: From Self-Control to Autonomy* (New York: Oxford University Press, 1995), 138.

55. The typical "paradigm" is one in which a baseline measure is obtained from experimental subjects. They are then given an instruction that would motivate them in such a way as to alter the baseline levels. New measures then indicate the predicted alteration, but with the subjects denying that they did, in fact, alter their standard. A typical study is G. Quattrone and A. Tversky, "Causal versus diagnostic contingencies: on self-deception and on the voter's illusion," *Journal of Personality and Social Psychology*, 1984, vol. 46: 237–248.

56. A most interesting target article, with criticisms and replies from the author, is Alfred Mele, "Real self-deception," *Behavioral and Brain Sciences*, 1997, vol. 20: 91–136.

CHAPTER FIVE

1. Aristotle, *Politics*, 1267a15, in Barnes, *The Complete Works of Aristotle*.

2. See chapter 1 of *Wild Beasts and Idle Humours*; and Douglas MacDowell, *The Law in Classical Athens* (Ithaca: Cornell University Press, 1978), especially 109–118.

3. Geoffrey Cupit, *Justice as Fittingness* (Oxford: Clarendon Press, 1996).

4. Philip Pettit, "Republican theory and criminal punishment," *Utilitas*, 1997, vol. 9(1): 59–79.

5. Richard Swinburne, *Responsibility and Atonement* (Oxford: Clarendon Press, 1989), especially chapter 6.

6. Ibid., 94.

7. Swinburne, *Responsibility and Atonement*, 96n.; Locke, *The Second Treatise on Civil Government* (Buffalo: Prometheus Books, 1986), sec. 10. I am indebted to Richard Swinburne for this clarification of his position.

8. On this question Swinburne, in a personal communication, would say that the exercise of that option would render the aggrieved quite literally an "outlaw," the rule of law now rejected.

9. For the influential foundational arguments of legal positivism, see John Austin, *The Province of Jurisprudence Determined* (1832; reprint edition New York: Library of Ideas, 1954). Their refinement was authoritatively developed by H.L.A. Hart in *The Concept of Law* (Oxford: Oxford University Press, 1961). An influential statement of the theory of legal realism is John Chipman Gray, *The Nature and Sources of Law* (New York: Macmillan, 1921). The classic statement of "fidelity to law" is, of course, Lon L. Fuller, "Positivism and fidelity to law—a reply to Professor Hart," *Harvard Law Review*, 1958, vol. 71: 630 ff.

10. Immanuel Kant, *Critique of Pure Reason*, trans. Norman Kemp Smith (New York: St. Martin's Press, 1965), 312 [B373].

11. Immanuel Kant, *Groundwork of the Metaphysic of Morals*, trans. H. J. Paton (New York: Harper & Row, 1956), 89.

12. Paul Guyer, *Kant on Freedom, Law and Happiness* (Cambridge: Cambridge University Press, 2000), 145.

13. An excellent discussion of this aspect of Kantian theory is Thomas E. Hill, Jr., "Punishment, conscience, and moral worth," *Southern Journal of Philosophy*, 1997, vol. 36 (Supp.): 51–71.

14. For an interesting exploration of this, see Mark Tunick, "Is Kant a retributivist?," *History of Political Thought*, 1996, vol. 17: pp. 60–78.

15. Russ Shafer-Landau, "The failure of retributivism," *Philosophical Studies*, 1996, vol. 82(3): 289–316.

16. Swinburne, *Responsibility and Atonement*, 81.

17. Johann Klaasen argues for this in an article published in the *Journal of Social Philosophy*, 1996, vol. 27(2): 51–64.

18. This function of punishment has been discussed insightfully by Susan Dimock, "Retributivism and trust," *Law and Philosophy*, 1997, vol. 16(1): 37–62. I do not accept her claim, however, that the "purpose" of law is to maintain basic trust of this kind.

19. Gary Herbert, "Immanuel Kant: Punishment and the political preconditions of moral excellence," *Interpretation*, 1995, vol. 23(1): 61–75.

20. Edward Pols, *Mind Regained*, 136.

21. Particularly apt is Douglas Lind, " Kant on capital punishment," *Journal of Philosophical Research*, 1994, vol. 18: 61–74.

22. All references are to the edition of 1821 reprinted in *The Utilitarians* (New York: Dolphin Books [Doubleday], 1961).

23. Ibid., 73.

24. Ibid., 164.

25. Ibid.

26. Ibid., 165.

27. Ibid., 171.

28. Ibid., 174.

29. Ibid.

30. Ibid., 175.

31. Jeffrie Murphy, "Marxism and retribution," *Philosophy and Public Affairs*, 1973, vol. 2: 218–243.

32. John Rawls, "Two concepts of rules," *The Philosophical Review*, 1955, vol. 64: 3–13.

33. Ibid.

34. The authoritative work here is B. F. Skinner and Charles Ferster, *Schedules of Reinforcement* (New York: Appleton Century, 1957).

35. Alisdair MacIntyre, *After Virtue* (South Bend, IN: Notre Dame University Press, 1981); see especially chapter 9, "Nietzsche or Aristotle?"

36. Ibid., 114.

37. The limited authority enjoyed by majorities *as majorities* is wisely assessed by Robert George, *Making Men Moral* (Oxford: Oxford University Press, 1994), especially 71–82. George considers Lord Devlin's famous contention that, as the function of law is to preserve social cohesion, the law may be fashioned to endorse or forbid whatever threatens that cohesion and needs no justification beyond that.

38. John Finnis, *Natural Law and Natural Rights* (Oxford: Clarendon Press, 1980), 264.

39. For an excellent discussion, see Richard Sorabji, *Emotion and Peace of Mind*, (Oxford: Oxford University Press, 2000), 325–340.

40. Aristotle, *Nicomachean Ethics*, bk. IV, chap. 9, 1128b.

41. Tara Smith gives compelling reasons for eliminating tolerance and forgiveness from the class of virtues and vices, insisting that they both must be authorized by principles of justice, in her "Tolerance and forgiveness: virtues or vices?," *Journal of Applied Philosophy*, 1997, vol. 14(1): 31–41.

42. David Novitz, "Forgiveness and self-respect," *Philosophical and Phenomenological Research*, 1998, vol. 63(2): 299–315.

43. Some argue that self-forgiveness is always right, whatever the nature of the offense, though it calls for authentic moral self-appraisals; see Margaret Holmgren, "Self-forgiveness and responsible moral agency," *Journal of Value Inquiry*, 1998, vol. 32(1): 75–91.

44. William Young analyzes this feature of forgiveness in "Resentment and impartiality," *Southern Journal of Philosophy*, 1998, vol. 36(1): 103–130.

45. A particularly interesting analysis of the grounds of forgiveness and its relation to reconciliation is Uma Narayan, "Forgiveness, moral reassessment, and reconciliation," in *Explorations of Value*, ed. Thomas Magnell (Amsterdam: Rodopi, 1997).

46. For the fuller discussion, see Rom Harre and Daniel N. Robinson, "On the primacy of duties," *Philosophy*, 1995, vol. 70: 513–532.

47. Piers Benn reaches just this conclusion in "Forgiveness and loyalty," *Philosophy*, 1996, vol. 71(277): 369–383.

48. Aristotle, *Nicomachean Ethics*, bk. VIII, chap. VIII, 1159b.

Voltaire, 51, 56, 141
voluntarism, 53, 72, 104, 138–41

Wallace, William, 103
White, Alan, 72
Wiggins, David, 172–73
Williams, Bernard, 7, 109, 118–19, 129–30,
    133, 136, 144

witch trials, 168–69
witnesses. *See* bystanders and witnesses
Wolf, Susan, 117, 120–21
Wren, Christopher, 169
Wundt, Wilhelm, 81–82, 85, 99

Yaffee, Gideon, 62
Young, Robert, 120–21

NEW FORUM BOOKS

New Forum Books makes available to general readers outstanding original in-
terdisciplinary scholarship with a special focus on the juncture of culture, law,
and politics. New Forum Books is guided by the conviction that law and politics not only reflect culture but help to shape it. Authors include leading political scientists, sociologists, legal scholars, philosophers, theologians, historians,
and economists writing for nonspecialist readers and scholars across a range
of fields. Looking at questions such as political equality, the concept of rights,
the problem of virtue in liberal politics, crime and punishment, population,
poverty, economic development, and the international legal and political order,
New Forum Books seeks to explain—not explain away—the difficult issues we
face today.

PAUL EDWARD GOTTFRIED, *After Liberalism:*
Mass Democracy in the Managerial State

PETER BERKOWITZ, *Virtue and the Making of*
Modern Liberalism

JOHN E. COONS AND PATRICK M. BRENNAN, *By Nature Equal:*
The Anatomy of a Western Insight

DAVID NOVAK, *Covenantal Rights: A Study in Jewish*
Political Theory

CHARLES L. GLENN, *The Ambiguous Embrace: Government*
and Faith-Based Schools and Social Agencies

PETER BAUER, *From Subsistence to Exchange and Other Essays*

ROBERT P. GEORGE, ED., *Great Cases in Constitutional Law*

AMITAI ETZIONI, *The Monochrome Society*

DANIEL N. ROBINSON, *Praise and Blame:*
Moral Realism and Its Applications